When The Korean World in Hawaii
was Young 1903 – 1940

하와이의 초창기 한인사회: 1903 – 1940

When the Korean World
in Hawaii was Young 1903-1940

First Published 20 June 2012

Author   ROBERTA CHANG, SEONJU LEE
Publisher Lee Chan-kyu

Published by Bookorea Publishing Co.
Registered 1 February 1998 (No.105-90-11628)
Address   A-1007, Woolimlions Balley,
          146-8 Sangdaewon-dong, Jungwon-gu,
          Seongnam-si, Gyeonggi-do, 462-807,
          Korea
Tel   +82 2 704-7840
Fax   +82 2 704-7848
E-mail   sunhaksa@korea.com
Website   www.bookorea.co.kr

ISBN 978-89-6324-185-2 (93300)
$ 17.00

This work was supported by the National Research Foundation of Korea(NRF) Grant
funded by the Korean Government (NRF-2007-361-AL0015)

When the Korean World in Hawaii was Young 1903 – 1940

하와이의 초창기 한인사회: 1903 – 1940

ROBERTA CHANG
with **SEONJU LEE**

북코리아

CONTENTS

FOREWORD

The Ewha Institute for the Humanities at the Ewha Womans University in Seoul, Korea with the support of the Korea Research Foundation began in 2007, collecting and preserving materials related to Korea's historic living past, its government, people, and culture.

In 2008 Roberta Chang, a Korean American born in Hawaii, was invited to speak at Ewha Womans University about Koreans in Hawaii. Ms Chang presented a video documentary, *The Legacy of the Korean National Association*. At that time Ms. Chang donated 35 copies of interviews with the second generation of the first Koreans who immigrated to Hawaii between 1903 to 1924. The interviews had been taken over a span of nearly 20 years in Hawaii starting from 1993. After studying the documentaries, I obtained Ms Chang's consent to transcribe nineteen of the valuable interviews. It took me three years to select, study, transcribe and document the findings. The result is the publication of this book by the Ewha Institute for the Humanities.

These Korean Americans who were interviewed were descendants of the first Korean immigrants to Hawaii who came in large numbers, officially sanctioned by the Korean Government in 1903. Actually, their parents were the first in such a large number to officially arrive and settle in the United States. Witnessing the situation in which many of the second generation of Korean immigrants were passing away, Ms Chang felt the desperate need to record them before they all died. Most of these second generation Koreans were born in the 1910s and 1920s. They told stories of their parents and themselves. There have been other researches on the first Korean migrants to Hawaii and their picture brides through several photographs and written records; however, this is a rare book based on verbatim interviews speaking in English taken from videos in which we can feel the nuances of their personal experiences and deep thoughts. Ms Chang also furnished relevant photographs among her 1,000 collection on the subjects discussed by the interviewees.

Oral interviews of personal life are records of one's personal experiences as it is without any glamorization od abstraction with certain historical significance. Through oral interviews captured on videos, people can describe a specific point of their lives affected by the tenor of their time which becomes part of history. The 19 oral histories in this book show how in a foreign land similar people gather together and depend on each other; how fear in people evokes religious faith; how they firmly unite to help their homeland in need; and how they turn against each other according to opposing leaders. These oral interviews of the early migrants to Hawaii are, thus, private experiences and yet, also vivid records of Korean history in the making.

The Korean migration to America started at the end of the Chosun dynasty when several men, suffering from the fall of their nation and poverty, answered the call of recruiting laborers to the Hawaiian sugarcane plantations. The men who came to Hawaii without spouses settled after they started families with the picture brides who began to arrive in 1910. The precarious homeland, eventually, became a Japanese colony and lost all freedom and economic power. The liberation of the homeland seemed to rest more on the efforts of the people living abroad than from within. The Hawaiian-Koreans supported the March First Independence Movement in 1919. The Korean Military in Manchuria was first supported by funds gathered in the form of tithe coming from the Korean churches or the Korean National Association and subsequent newly formed Korean organizations. The leaders of the Korean society in Hawaii appealed for political help directly to Washington. After the liberation from Japan, what had enabled Dr. Syngman Rhee to become the first President of the Republic of Korea was receiving the American government's recognition. His political and economical foundation were first established in Hawaii. All of the 19 interviewees introduced in this book were involved in someway with President Rhee, either supporting or against him, revealing again that their private histories are a part of Korean contemporary political history.

The lives of the Hawaiian-Koreans show the archetype of diaspora. As their homeland became the colony of the Japanese, they agonized that there was no longer a free homeland to which they can return. They all united under the patriotism of liberating their homeland. As diaspora is closely related to religion, the Hawaiian-Koreans made a Korean community first centered around the Methodist Church and later around the church Dr. Rhee established.

The interviews of the 19 people are not all lamentations. Although the historical circumstances were somewhat sorrowful, the Koreans in Hawaii enjoyed freedom and self-realization, a contrast from the life in the homeland. They believed that they can do anything or become anything according to their efforts and will power.

For instance, Maria Whang left her patriarchal husband in Korea who had several concubines there. She brought her two children to America. She taught the plantation children and organized the Korean Women's Association. Dorothy Kim Rudie's father, Kyungpok Kim, came to Hawaii in 1901 as a sailor on the ship called Mongolia in 1901 before other Koreans started to arrive in droves to work in the plantations. When the Koreans arrived, he helped many of them with his know-how of surviving, and it is said that his funeral was full of the Koreans who had received help from him. Nora Pahk who followed her parents to Hawaii became the first Korean to become a teacher at an American school. But when it was discovered she was an alien, she was dismissed. Aliens were not allowed to teach in American schools. She then, went to nursing school and became the first supervisor of nurses. Manuel Kwon who was born from a Korean father and a Spanish mother became the principal of the Wahiawa High School and the chairman of a Korean association. Reverend Chan Ho Min and his wife Mollie Min who dedicated themselves to the Korean church and educational work, underwent the creative work of turning a wasteland into a community.

When the Korean World in Hawaii was Young is an important source of the emigration stories that tell of human acculturation, assimilation and international interactions through tragedies or abundant success. For example, we can learn from the interviews what the American immigration laws were like and how Koreans could receive citizenship. To keep the increasing number of the Chinese and Japanese in check in Hawaii, the Koreans' migration was allowed in 1903. Testimonies through the interviews are actual stories of circumstances in which the first generation immigrants as alien-born residents were restricted in receiving permanent-residence status until 40 years later.

Koreans could only re-enter Hawaii with a Japanese passport after visiting Korea during Japan's occupation of Korea. An example is the story of the American-born citizen Hazel Pahk Chung, who had to forfeit her American citizenship when she married Euicho Chung who went to Korea for a visit and was termed "ineligible alien" when he returned to Hawaii. The Koreans were without a Korean Consul to plead their causes.

There is a saying that when an elderly person passes away, it is equivalent to a library disappearing. Mary Hong Park born in 1908 and still living, even at the age of 1023und her. Encountering the interviews of Mary Hong Park, who has an unaffected, innocent laughter at her elderly age, I began to think that with her interviews, what will not disappear is not just libtary but history of her times. It is a blessing that the many meaningful interviews taken by Ms Chang throughout the years are here with us forever.

I want to thank Roberta Chang who devoted her life to recording the lives of the Hawaiian-Koreans. I also thank the Korea Research Foundation for providing the financial support so that this book which will serve as an valuable book of Korean history can come into being. I want to express my appreciation also to Director Miyoung Jang of The Ewha Institute for the Humanities at Ewha Womans University, Prof. Youngmi Kim, and Prof. Byoungjoon Jung, of the Ewha History Department, who showed much encouragement and introduced Ms Chang to our faculty. Finally, I thank Soyoung Lee and Junghae Sung for helping with the transcribing of the interviews and Prof. Tae-Hyeon Song and President Chan-kyu Lee and Eun-kyung Jung of BooKorea for publishing such a wonderful book.

June, 2012
Seonju Lee

머리말

이화여자대학교 이화인문과학원은 한국연구재단의 지원을 받아 2007년부터 한국역사와 한국문화와 이주에 관한 살아있는 역사를 수집하는 아카이브 작업을 진행해왔다.

2008년 이화여자대학교는 하와이에서 태어난 한국계 미국인인 로버타 장 선생님을 초청하여 하와이의 한인들에 대한 강연을 부탁하였다. 장 선생님은 자신이 제작한 〈국민회의 유산〉이라는 비디오 다큐멘터리를 상연하였다. 당시 장 선생님은 1903년에서 1924년 사이에 하와이로 이민 간 첫 한국인들의 자녀들인 한인 2세대들에게 한 인터뷰 35점을 이화인문과학원에 기증하였다. 인터뷰는 1993년부터 시작해서 거의 20여 년 동안 진행한 작업이었다. 이화인문과학원의 연구교수인 나는 그 기증 자료를 점검하면서 로버타 장 선생님의 동의를 얻어 그 소중한 인터뷰 자료 중 19점을 선별하여 책으로 발행하기로 하였다. 그 자료를 선별하고 녹취하고 편집하며 책으로 출판하기까지 3년이 걸렸다. 그 결과물이 이화인문과학원에 의해 출간된 바로 이 책이다.

인터뷰에 응해준 이들 한국계 미국인들은 1903년 한국정부의 공식적인 허가를 받아 대규모로 하와이로 온 첫 한국인 이민자들의 자녀들이다. 실제로 미국에 많은 사람이 공식적으로 도착하여 정착한 것은 이들의 부모가 처음이었다. 한국인 이민자의 2세대들 중 많은 이들이 세상을 떠나는 상황을 지켜보면서 장 선생님은 그들이 모두 하직하기 전에 그들의 삶과 역사를 기록으로 남겨야 된다는 절박한 필요성을 느꼈다. 여기 2세대 한인들 대부분은 1910년대와 1920년대에 출생했다. 이들은 자신의 부모님과 자기에 대한 이야기를 해주었다. 하와이의 한국인 첫 이주자나 사진신부에 대한 이야기는 그간 여러 사진이나 기록을 통해 연구가 되어 왔다. 하지만 이 책은 이들이 영어로 말하는 이야기를 비디오로 촬영한 구술 인터뷰를 전부 녹취한 뒤 책에 적합하게 편집하여 만든 매우 진귀한 책으로, 이 속에서 우리는 그들의 개인적 경험과 깊은 사고의 뉘앙스를 생생히 느낄 수가 있다. 로버타 장 선생님은 또한 자신이 소장하고 있는 1,000여 점의 사진에서 구술자들이 얘기하는 주제와 관련된 사진들을 추려내어 책에 실을 수 있게 했다.

　　구술생애사는 어떤 역사적 의미로 포장되거나 추상화되지 않고 자신들의 개인적 경험을 있는 그대로 이야기한 기록이다. 자기 생애를 구술함으로써 사람들은 시대의 색조에 의해 영향을 받은 자신들의 삶을 한 특정 시각에서 묘사하게 되며 그렇게 제시된 구술 자체가 역사의 한 단면을 보여주게 된다. 하와이의 첫 이주자들의 구술은 그 나라의 언어를 전혀 모르고 아주 다른 인종과 풍토를 가진 나라로 이주했을 때 사람들이 어떻게 생존해 가는가를 보여준다. 이 책에 실린 19개의 구술자료는 이국땅에서 사람들은 어떻게 서로 비슷한 사람들과 모여 의지하며 사는가, 삶에 대한 두려움이 어떻게 사람들에게 신에 대한 믿음을 불러일으키는가, 고국이 어려울 때 어떻게 그들이 군건히 뭉쳐 고국을 돕는 역할을 하는가, 동시에 지도세력에 따라 사람들이 어떻게 서로 반목하게도 되는가를 보여준다. 하와이의 초창기 이주자들의 구술은 그러므로, 사적인 경험이면서 동시에 한국 역사가 만들어가는 과정에 대한 생생한 기록이 되고 있다.

　　한국인의 미국이주는 고국의 쇠락과 가난에 허덕이던 조선 말기의 몇몇 남성들이 국가가 모집한 하와이 사탕수수농장의 노무자에 지원하면서 시작되었다. 대부분 홀로 하와이에 온 남성들은 1910년 경부터 오기 시작한 '사진신부'들과 가정을 이루면서 터전을 잡기 시작하였다. 위태롭던 고국은 결국 일본의 식민지가 되어 자유도 경제력도 잃은 상태가 되어 버렸다. 고국이 해방하느냐 못하느냐는 국내에 있는 사람보다는 오히려 해외에 나와 있는 이들의 노력 여하에 더 달려 있었다. 하와이의 한인들은 한국감리교회나 국민회를 중심으로 조국의 독립자금을 십일조의 형태로 모아 1919년 3.1 운동과 만주의 한국 군인을 지원했다. 한인사회의 지도자들은 세계의 강국으로 부상한 미국의 워싱턴에 고국의 독립을 위한 호소를 하였다. 해방 직후 이승만 박사가 미국의 인정하에 초대 대통령으로 선출된 데에는 하와이에서 다진 그의 정치적·경제적 기반이 크게 작용했다. 여기 실린 19명의 구술자는 그들 자신이나 그들이 부모들이 이승만 박사를 지지하든가, 혹은 반대하든가 하여 실제 생활 속에서 이승만 박사와 연관을 맺게 된다. 이 또한 그들의 개인사가 한국의 현대사의 한 부분임을 증거한다.

　　하와이의 한인들의 삶은 디아스포라의 원형을 보여준다. 이들은 고국이 일제 식민지가 되어 돈을 벌더라도 되돌아갈 자유로운 고국이 사라졌다는 슬픔에 괴로워했다. 이들은 고국을 해방시키겠다는 충정으로 모두 하나가 되었다. 디아스포라가 본디 인간의 원초적 경외감인 종교와 밀접히 연결되어 있듯이, 하와이의 한국인들은 한국감리교회를 중심으로 한인 공동체 사회를 이루어갔고, 나중에는 이승만박사가 설립한 한국기독교회를 중심으로 공동체를 이어갔다. 농장과 일터에서 열심히 일한 다음 이들은 교회에 모여 타향살이의 설움을 달랬고 돈을 모아 독립자금을 고국에 송금했다. 고국의 독립이라는 집단적 꿈은 아주 오랜 세월이 지나서야 이루어졌다.

19명이 들려주는 구술은 고난을 많이 담고 있지만 전혀 슬픈 한탄이 아니다. 역사적 상황은 이토록 기구하나 하와이의 한인들은 고국의 삶과는 다른 자유와 자아실현을 누렸다. 이들은 자신이 하기에 따라 무엇이든 할 수 있고 어떤 사람이든 될 수 있다고 믿었다. 예를 들어 첩을 여럿 둔 가부장제 남편을 떠나 자녀를 데리고 미국으로 온 마리아 황은 농장의 어린이들을 가르치고 한국여성단체를 조직하였다. 한국인이 오기도 전인 1901년에 몽골리아호 선원으로 하와이에 내린 로디 김의 아버지 김경복은 유일한 한국인으로 하와이에서 살다가 몇 년 후 한국인이 오기 시작하자 한국인들에게 자신의 생존 노하우를 알려주며 도왔고 그의 장례식에는 그의 도움을 받았던 한국인들로 가득했다 한다. 아기 때 부모를 따라 이민 온 노라 박은 한국인 최초로 미국학교의 교사가 되었고 동양인에 대한 편견에 교사를 계속하기가 힘들게 되자 간호학교에 들어가서 최초의 수간호사가 된다. 한국인 1세 아버지와 스페인 여성 사이에서 태어난 혼혈아 마뉴엘 권은 와이아와 고등학교 교장선생님이 되고 한인단체의 회장으로 한인공동체의 핵심이 된다. 한인 교회와 교육 사업에 헌신한 민찬호 목사와 부인 몰리 민은 아무런 기반이 없는 황무지에 문화를 심어 공동체를 만드는 창조적인 작업을 하였다.

본서 *When the Korean World in Hawaii was Young 1903-1940*는 사람들의 사회적 적응과 동화, 국가에 대한 충성과 국제관계의 복합적 작용을 슬픈 비극적 개인사나 칭송받을 성공적 개인사를 통해 전해주는 이민사의 중요한 자료이다. 우리는 미국의 이민법과 한인들의 시민권이 어떠했으며 어떤 경로를 거쳐 변화하는가를 이들의 구술을 통해 유추할 수 있다. 점증하는 중국인과 일본인을 견제하기 위하여 1903년부터 한국인들의 이주가 허용되었고 1924년에는 하와이에 아시아인들의 입국이 원칙적으로 금지된다. 1세대 한국인인 외국태생 거주자(Alien-born Resident)들이 영주권을 받기까지는 40여 년을 기다려야만 했고 하와이의 한인들이 식민지인 고국을 방문하고 돌아올 때에는 일본 시민권과 여권으로만 들어올 수 있었던 상황이 여기서 구술되고 있다. 미국태생 시민권자인 헤이즐 정이 한국에서 태어난 남편과 결혼하자 "부적격한 외국인"과 결혼한 것이 되어 미국 시민권을 잃게 되는 상황, 일본이 진주만을 공격하자 일본의 식민지였던 한국인이 일본과 같은 적국 외국인으로 오해받고 곤경에 처하는 상황, 그러한 상황에 대처하기 위해 한국영사도 없는 한국인들이 한인단체의 이름으로 한인임을 증명했었던 실화 등이 이들의 구술 속에서 증언된다.

노인 한 사람이 세상을 떠나면 도서관 하나가 사라지는 것과 같다고 한다. 1908년에 태어나 현재 생존하고 있는 메어리 홍 박은 103세임에도 당시의 사람들과 사건들을 생생히 기억하며 상세한 구술을 해주었다. 주름진 얼굴에 생기있는 순진한 웃음을 띠며 전하는 메어리 홍 박의 구술을 접하며, 그녀의 구술로 인해 우리가 잃어버리지 않게 된 것은 단지 도서관이 아니라 그녀의 시대의 역사임을 실감한다. 로버타 장 선생님이 오랜 세월에 걸쳐 수행한 귀중한 인터뷰 자료가 여기 우리와 함께 영원히 남게 된 것은 참으로 축복이다.

나는 먼저 자신의 생애를 바쳐 하와이의 한인들의 삶을 기록한 로버타 장 선생님에게 감사드리고 싶다. 귀중한 한국의 역사서가 될 이 책이 나오도록 경제적 지원을 해준 한국연구재단에도 깊이 감사드린다. 책이 출판되기까지 많은 관심과 격려를 보내주신 이화여자대학교 이화인문과학원 장미영 원장님, 로버타 장 선생님을 연구단에 소개해주신 사학과의 김영미 교수님과 정병준 교수님께 감사드린다. 녹취를 도와준 이소영, 성정혜 선생님과 책을 훌륭히 만들어주신 송태현 선생님과 북코리아의 이찬규 사장님, 정은경 씨에게 감사드린다.

2012년 6월
이선주

PROLOGUE

Professor Dr. Seonju Lee of the Ewha Institute for the Humanities selected for publication and presented in this book nineteen interviews which I conducted since 1993 with Korean Americans in Hawaii. They are among nearly a hundred interviews with second generation Koreans.

All but one of the interviewees were sixty years old or older at the time of the interviews. The interviews were centered on the lives of their parents who were part of the first large organized immigration to Hawaii, U.S.A. starting from 1903. The interviewees were second generation Korean Americans. Only two of them were born in Korea and had come to Hawaii at ages 2 (1921) and 3 (1912).

We must be aware that the second generation of the first wave of Korean immigrants in Hawaii covers several decades: four decades from 1900s to 1930s. The life experiences of each decade differed by the tenor of the Korean community political struggles of their time. Like the first immigrant generation, the older second generation Koreans were personally, engrossed with matters related to the Korean Independence Movement. As the decades moved on, the younger set of the second generation descendants could only speak distantly of their parents' dedication to Korea's liberation. Most of the interviewees in this book were born during the second decade (1910s and early 1920s). Two of them were born in California. However, these two had parents who had come first to Hawaii.

Questions regarding their families, childhood schooling, and religious affiliations, invariably resulted in discussions regarding Dr. Syngman Rhee's role in Hawaii. Of the nineteen interviewees, ten had direct contacts with Dr. Rhee or their parents were intimate friends with him. Since the formation of political Korean groups became enmeshed with religious and education organizations, Rhee played a large part in the lives of many of the older second generation children. Some portion of the interviewees' remembrances of their involvement in the Korean Independence movement were discussed in these interviews.

Anyone who wishes to have a better understanding of the history of Koreans in Hawaii needs to be aware of the major organizations established during the first four decades of Koreans in Hawaii. The first eight organizations which are listed below were established by the first generation, shrouded by the political divide among the Koreans. The last three organizations were established by the younger set of the second generation. These interviews may offer some understanding of the effects of these organizations on the early settlement of Koreans in Hawaii, but the references and discussions are not intended to be an in depth presentation of these organizations. An in depth discussion must be left to another publication.

The major Korean organizations or churches to which they or their parents belonged are the following:

1 The Korean Methodist Church, established in 1903

Korean Methodist Church, Honolulu, 1905.

Honolulu Methodist Church School, circa 1908.

Korean Methodist Episcopal Church, Honolulu, 1915.

Korean Methodist Church, Honolulu, 1933.

Korean Methodist Church, Wahiawa, 1936.

2   The Korean Episcopal Church Congregation, 1906

St. Luke's Episcopal Church

St. Luke's Episcopal Church later, called St. Luke

3 The Korean National Association, in 1909

Korean National Association First Officer in 1909 In front of the Ahana Building near Miller Street.
First president middle sitting: Won Myung Chung.

The Korean National Association This headquarter was built in 1915 when the property of the earlier KNA building was bought by the Territory of Hawaii. It was on Miller Street also. Next to the Governor's Mansion.

Korean National Association Membership Certificate, 2,000 members at peak in the 1910s.

19

Korean National Association, April 14th, 1913

The Korean National Association
Kook Min Hur headquarter at Millier
Street on Miller Street. Honolulu.

Whole View of KNA

4 The Korean Military Brigade, in 1914

Korean Military Brigade, Honolulu, 1915.

5 The Korean Christian Church, in 1918

Korean Christian Church, Honolulu, circa 1930.

Korean Christian Church, Wahiawa, circa 1935.

WAHIAWA KOREAN CHRISTIAN CHURCH
DECEMBER 21, 1986

6 The Korean Christian Institute, in 1918

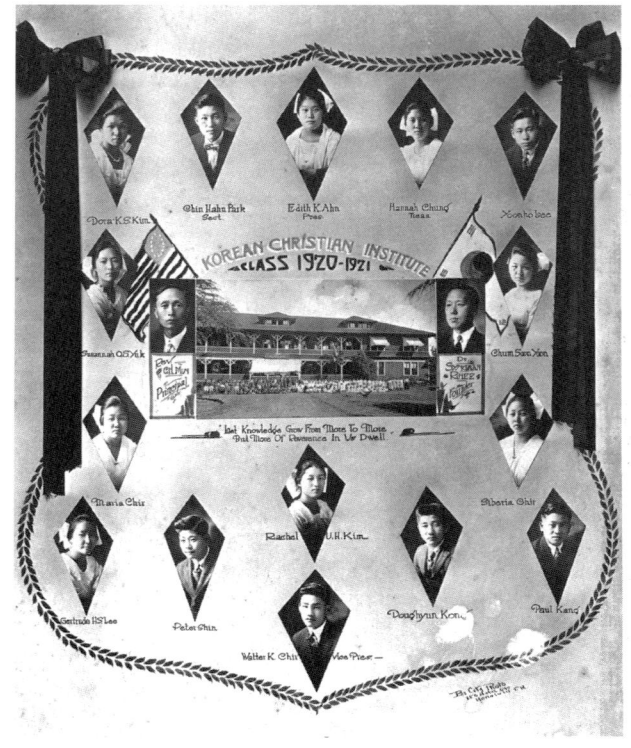

7 The Dongji Hoi, began in 1918 (incorporated in 1920)

Dongji Hoi Rally at the Korean Christian Institute, 1930. Young Ok Kang Collection

8 The Korean American Club, in 1923

Korean American Club members, 1926.

Korean American Club members, 1935.

Cloud Owen, president
and founder of the Korean
American Club, circa 1930.

9 The Korean University Club, in 1926

Korean University Club members, 1926.

10 The Taeguk Club, sometime in the mid 1930s

11 The Delta Fraternity and Sorority, sometime in the mid 1930s.

Even though most of these organizations deeply, affected the Korean community of their times, I have not found any meaningful research done on all of these organizations. Undoubtably, these organizations all pertained to or were affected by the turbulent years of the Korean Independence Movement. Further discussion and research are needed to fully understand the place of these organizations in the Korean American history.

The interviews recorded in this book may contribute to further interest in these organizations and the lives of Koreans, *When the Korean World in Hawaii was Young.*

Roberta W.S. Chang

프롤로그

나는 1993년부터 2세대 한국인들을 인터뷰하기 시작하여 거의 100여 건을 수행해왔다. 이화인문과학원의 이선주 교수가 내가 한 인터뷰 중 19개를 선정하여 출판을 준비하였다.

구술자 중 1명을 제외하고는 구술 당시에 이미 60세가 넘었다. 인터뷰는 1903년부터 처음으로 미국 하와이로의 이주가 큰 규모로 구성되었을 때 왔던 그들의 부모들의 삶에 중점을 두고 이루어졌다. 구술자들은 모두 2세대 한국계미국인들이며 두명을 제외하고는 미국에서 태어났다. 한국에서 태어난 두 사람은 2살(1921년)과 3살(1912년) 때 하와이로 왔다.

우리는 하와이로의 한국인 이민의 첫 물결이 탄생시킨 2세대들의 삶은 1900년대에서부터 1930년대까지 무려 40여년에 걸쳐 있음을 유념할 필요가 있다. 1900년대에 태어난 사람과 1910년대, 1920년대, 1930년대에 태어난 사람들의 각각의 생애 경험은 자신의 시대에 해당되는 당시의 한인공동체의 정치적 투쟁의 색조에 따라 달라졌다. 나이가 더 많은 2세대 한국인들은 첫 이민세대들과 마찬가지로, 한국독립운동과 관련된 일들에 개인적으로 깊이 몰입하였다. 미국에서 보다 늦게 태어난 2세대일수록 그들은 한국의 해방을 위한 자신의 부모들의 헌신만을 또렷이 말할 수 있게 된다. 이 책에 실린 구술자들은 대부분 1910년대와 1920년대 초반에 태어난 사람들이다. 이 가운데 두 사람은 캘리포니아에서 출생했고 그렇지만 두 사람 다 그들의 부모들은 하와이의 첫 이주물결 때 이주한 사람들이다.

그들의 가족이나 어린 시절과 학창시절과 소속 종교에 대한 이야기들은 예외 없이 하와이에서 이승만 박사의 역할에 대한 이야기로 연결되어진다. 19명의 구술자중 특히 10명은 이승만 박사와 직접적인 관계가 있거나 그들의 부모들이 이박사와 친밀한 관계에 있었다. 한국인의 정치단체의 형성은 종교단체나 교육단체와 깊이 연관되어 있었기 때문에, 이승만 박사는 1920년대 이전에 태어난 나이든 2세대들의 성장기 삶에 커다란 역할을 하게 된다. 한국독립운동에 2세대들이 개입한 데 대한 기억들이 이 인터뷰 속에 들어있다.

하와이 한인의 역사를 보다 깊이 알기를 원하는 분들은 하와이 한인들이 1903년에서

1940년 동안에 설립한 중요한 조직들을 알아둘 필요가 있다. 아래 목록 중 1에서 8까지의 조직은 한인 1세대들이 만든 조직들로, 여기에는 한인들 간에 정치적인 분열의 그림자가 드리워져 있다. 마지막 세 개의 조직은 보다 젊은 2세대에 의해 만들어졌다. 여기 실린 인터뷰들은 하와이에 한국인들이 초기에 정착하면서 세운 이러한 조직들의 활동과 영향을 어느 정도 이해하는 데는 도움을 주겠지만, 인터뷰 속에서의 조직에 대한 언급과 이야기는 이 조직에 대한 어떤 깊이 있는 설명을 위해 의도된 것이 아니다. 한인 공동체의 조직들에 대한 보다 깊이 있는 논의는 또 하나의 출간의 몫으로 남겨두겠다.

2세대 한인들이나 그들의 부모들이 속했었던 주요한 한국인 조직이나 한인교회들은 다음과 같다.

1. 한국감리교회 (1903년 설립)
2. 한국감독교회 (1906년 설립). 후에 성 누가교회로 개명
3. 국민회 (1909년 설립)
4. 한국군사여단 (1914년 설립)
5. 한국기독교회 (1918년 설립)
6. 한국기독교협회 (1918년 설립)
7. 동지회 (1918년에 시작하여 1920년에 조직형성)
8. 한국계미국인 클럽 (1923년 설립)
9. 한인 대학생 클럽 (1926년 설립)
10. 태극클럽 (1930년대 중반 설립)
11. 델타 남녀대학생 클럽 (1930년대 중반 설립)

이러한 조직들은 대부분 당시의 한인사회에서 큰 역할을 하며 영향을 미쳤지만, 나는 이 조직들에 관한 어떤 의미 있는 선행연구들을 아직 발견하지 못했다. 의심할 나위 없이 이들 조직들은 모두 한국독립운동을 향한 혼란과 열정의 세월에 녹아들어서 독립에 중대한 영향을 주었다. 한국계 미국인의 역사에서 이들 조직들의 위치와 위상을 충분히 이해하기 위해서는 보다 깊이 있는 논의와 연구가 요구된다.

이 책에 실린 인터뷰들은 하와이의 초창기 한인 세계에서 한국인들의 삶과 공동체에 대한 보다 심도 있는 관심을 불러일으키는데 기여할 것이다.

Roberta W.S. Chang

Interviewee

My name is Mary Hong Park. I was born in Seoul, Korea on May 3, 1909 on a Sunday morning. My brother, Tae Hee Hong, was, also, born in Seoul, in the Myungdong area; he was two years older than I. My father, Rev. Han Sik Hong, was assigned by the Methodist Mission at Myungdong in Seoul, to go to the Korean Methodist Mission in Hawaii alone. The rest of the family followed him a year later.

Myong Dong 1911; Rev. Hong, Han Sik with Son, Tae Hee before he left for Hawaii. Korean Methodist Church in Seoul, Myung dong.

Rev. Han Sik Hong and his family in front of the Maui Korean Methodist Episcopal Church, circa 1912

I was three years old and my brother was five years old, when we arrived in Honolulu. We were in quarantine a few days because both my brother and I had come down with measles on the ship. Dr. William Wadman, who was the Superintendent of the Methodist Mission in Honolulu, got us out the quarantine station, and we were taken to the Methodist Church Compound in the Punchbowl area in Honolulu. I don't know how long we stayed there. Maybe a week or two later, our whole family was sent to the Honakaa, Papaloa area on the the Big Island (another name for the Island of Hawaii),

Family Photo; Left to right: Mary, Rev. Tae Hee Hong, William, Hong, Hannah Chung, Hei Ja Chung, John Hong, circa 1922.

where my father started his first preaching mission for about a couple of years before we came back to the Punchbowl Compound area in Honolulu.

As I recall, we first lived on Liliha Street because by that time, I was about 5 years old and I remember having attended a kindergarten on Liliha Street. We may have not lived there too long, but I remember my first Christmas gift from my father. He had us hang up stockings up on the porch and I found a doll the next morning and my brother found a pistol. I always cherished the idea of gift giving because that was our first Christmas gift. Then, we moved back to the main Compound near Punchbowl, where we stayed until maybe 1915 or 1916. That is where my brother, Bill, was born. He was named after Dr. William Henry Fry, who was the new Superintendent of the Methodist Mission.

Then, we were sent to Maui and we lived there for about four years and at that time, I attended Maui Spreckelsville Public School from 2nd grade to the mid 5th grade. My brother was already in the 7th or 8th grade. But because Spreckelsville School had classes only up to 5th grade, he had to go to Wailuku by train daily to attend school, but, I was able to stay in Spreckelsville to continue my grade school education.

Then, my father's mission assignment was changed again, so we had to go to Kauai, another island north of all the islands. Later on, I graduated from Lihue Intermediate School and went on to Kauai High School. I was in the second semester of my sophomore year there, when my parents were transferred again back to Honolulu. By that time, the Methodist Church had been moved from Punchbowl Street to Fort Street because the old property was bought by the Hawaii Territorial Government to establish Public Offices of Honolulu.

So, we lived on Fort Street on the Methodist Mission grounds for about 4 years. By that time, I had graduated from McKinley High School and had entered the University of Hawaii. Just before my graduation, my father gave up the pulpit because of a transition between the first immigrants and the young Korean Americans in the Methodist Church's congregation. The Methodist Mission realized that the growing new congregation was increasingly, the young members who needed an English speaking minister. So, they had Reverend Fritz Pyun to be the minister. We still continued to live on Fort Street and Rev. Fritz Pyun lived in the back of our quarters, which was the dormitory for boys who were attending the University of Hawaii. These boys were from the other island or from the rural areas of Oahu. I think it was after I graduated from the University of Hawaii, when we moved out of the Fort Street Mission house, and we went into a rented house. The Mission demolished the old parsonage quarters because it was too old.

Rev. Fritz Pyun did not stay at the Hawaii Methodist Church Mission long. The young people could not accept him because he was, too, fanatically, religious. He was too strict. He returned to Korea. A new minister, Rev. Doo Wha Lim was sent to us. He and his family, also, lived in the new dormitory which was converted into a two story building. The upstairs was for their lodging and the lower floor for parishioners who visited the Pastor or who lingered on the compound after services or social gatherings.

In the meantime, we lived in a rented house, until my father bought a property in Kaimuki. We moved to Pahoa Avenue in Kaimuki. We owned that house, until it was passed on to my oldest brother. I stayed there, until I got married in 1934 to Ernest K. H. Park.

I can remember the days on the island of Maui when we were very young. We were happy, there. It was a plantation home, a three bedroom house. Of course, we were given a better home than the average Oriental immigrants because my father was a Reverend and the Methodist Church supported our family. We had a kitchen with a wooden stove with a iron cast range. They delivered logs once a week and my father had to use the axe to chop up the wood to use in the iron range. We did not have a sewer system. We had a pipe in the kitchen. We had an "outhouse" (toilet was outside of the house and run by flowing underground water). The water used to fall from the sink down to a cement trough on the ground and when the trough got really moldy, once a week a plantation worker would clean up the trough for all the residents in the camp, which was a Portuguese camp. The Portuguese camp was on a higher level than the ordinary Oriental plantation workers. The ordinary plantation worker had a kitchen outside of the living area, and it was on dirt floor. The chickens would come in and out of the kitchen area, and we would just throw old rice on the ground. The chickens would just help themselves. We did not have refrigerator or iceboxes in those days, so we kept our food all in the "safe" which was made out of wood and a screen.

In those days to preserve the food, we made "jang-jorim" which is meat cooked in soy sauce, which could be kept for about a week or so. The butter would stay a little more firm in the safe because the air would pass through the cabinet. In the Portuguese camp between every few houses, they had a cement cast outdoor oven because the Portuguese ate a lot of bread. They use to bake their bread once every week or two weeks in the same outdoor oven. My mother got to learn to make bread from them and they let her use their oven. But since we didn't need that much bread, she would wait for the Portuguese to bake their bread first, and she would put one or two loaves in their oven for our family. Now, I will tell you how they prepared the oven. It was a round dome like thing, height of your standing height. It came up to a little higher than your hip. They would burn all their wood inside the door and close the door which was made out of iron. And they would burn the wood for maybe a couple of hours until it became charcoal. They would wait with a long handle. They would mop the floor of the oven and, then, put the bread in and after maybe a couple of hours, the bread would be all done. We all would look forward to those days because my mother kept some dough aside and we would have a feast with raised donuts.

Q **You mentioned something about your mother preparing rice for you to take to school?**

A Once a week, the meat truck would come. So, she would make "jang-jorim"; she would buy the cheap cuts like the shin of the cow and make a dip after she cleaned the shin. Then, she would skin the meat, toes and all. Then, she would make a great pot of soup which, maybe, would last about a week or so. It was very nutritious.

Now, when we went to school, there was no cafeteria at that time, so we had to take our own lunch. A lot of times, the lunch can had two compartments, one for the rice and one for the "banchan", that is, the side dishes which you eat with the rice. So, a lot of times we had daegu or jangjorim, with something salty that would help not to spoil the banchan. Since we had no place to hang our lunch bag, we used to hang it on tree branches in the schoolyard. And sometimes, when it was ant season, we would find ants in our rice. So, what we did was just pour water in the rice and when the ants floated up, we would just drain the water and enjoyed our lunch. We thought nothing of bacteria or think that it was kind of odd to be eating those things, but the Korean food kept us healthy. We did not have dessert, we never thought of buying fruits because the only time we really did enjoy fruit was on Christmas Day, when we were given apples and oranges at church.

There was quite a number of Korean members in Camp One which was in Spreckelsfield, but later, many of them moved to Honolulu to find better livelihood. So, there were very few Korean families left, gradually, but enough for us to have church service every Sunday. On special days, like Christmas, New Years, and Thanksgiving, Korean people from Paia Camp #3 and Kihei area made a point to come to church services. Other than that, I remember that we learned to sing all of the church hymns in Korean. So, to this day, I can remember some of the songs in Korean words. We did not speak in English at that time. In the same yard of the church there was another building which was used for the Korean Language School. We attended that language school just before we were old enough to attend the English school. When we were old enough to go to the English School, we went to the Korea Language School after the English School finished for the day...say about 3 o'clock and then, we'd stay at the Korean school, until around 5 o'clock in the afternoon. Then, we'd all return home, and it was time for dinner, for our bath, and back to sleep for the next day.

Spreckelsfield was a sugar plantation. Last year, when I visited Maui, I wanted to go to see the place where we lived. There was nothing, there's no Spreckelsville now. There used to be a post office, railroad station, church, plantation medical dispensary, a park and a mansion for managers of the plantation who was important on the plantation. These and other important persons had their homes there. The Spreckelsville Beach was nearby, so that we were able to go and spend some days and learn to swim there. Now, there's no Spreckelsville. Now, it's covered with wild sugar cane fields which are still owned by the Baldwin family.

(The Baldwin family were descendants of the first Methodist missionaries in Hawaii. They were originally from the East Coast of

America. The Baldwins supported the Methodist Churches for many years, but for some reason, the Baldwins who ran the Maui plantations supported Dr. Syngman Rhee's Korean Christian Church on Maui years later.)

Q **Could you tell us what years this would be? Your memory about Spreckelsville seems to be so vivid. That town had a fantastic history because of Mr. Claus Spreckels… about how old you were and what years were you there?**

A This was in 1916. I remember it was during World War I. We were in school. We had to buy war savings stamps. We thought it was a such a great thing when we fill 25 cent war stamp books. It would amount to $5. I was in the second grade so I must have been about 7 years old.

Q **Tell us once more your full name and also, your Korean name, and what year you were born.**

A I was born in 1909 and my name was Suk Hee at birth. My English name "Mary" was added later. In my generation, the family name ended in "Hee". I was told the custom was that for the first two generations, the beginning is the same and after that, the ending's the same. So, my father's ending was Sik and his name was Han Sik and his brother's name was Jang Sik. Then, when it came to our generation we were all Hee. So, my first cousins were all named Hee, that is, the name ending was Hee. Now my nephews, their beginnings are the same. My nephew and their first cousins are all starting with Ki, and I found out that their children would start with Suh. My paternal grandfather was Sung Tae and the ending was the same for my father's first syllable. This was explained to me by relatives and they said that the tribe was the "Hong tribe". They meet at least every ten years, and at that time, they all would select a chairman.

Q **Okay, let's go on with your personal life.**

A While on Maui, during the World War II, we learned a lot about demand and supply. My brother and I went around picking coffee beans because the horses and cattle needed feeding. Now, we did sell some of the beans. I think they were 20 cents a bag. We held back several bags about 15, 20 bags hoping that the price would go up. Then, the war ended. We got stuck with the beans. That was our first lesson in demand and supply.

Q **Tell us about life on Fort Street in Honolulu.**

A We were in high school and my brother was attending the University of Hawaii. We were pretty active because all our friends about our age used to come to our church. The church was the social center and we had social parties at the dorm because the dorm had a big area where they always had parties for the church. Now, that was when social dancing was quite popular and we wanted to have social dancing during our parties. We had music from phonograms and we enjoyed ourselves. The Methodist Mission objected to that so, they used to send someone to watch what ever we did, and we rebelled.

Finally, I guess the elders gave in, so we did enjoy every weekend. Teenagers and college age kids came and enjoyed themselves in our Mission grounds. Another gathering that we enjoyed was our choir which met once a week and Donald Youngak Kang, who had a good ear for music was our music director. He never played any instrument for us, but he was very good with tones. His wife Fannie Nam, was our church organist and we enjoyed him for many years. And we used to compete with Rhee's Christian Church choir. We always were better singers.

I got married in 1934 to Ernest K.H. Park who was at that time working for Pearl Harbor. He had gone to the University of Hawaii, but did not finish because his brother, Edward, who was also his twin brother, was also attending college, and financially, their parents couldn't afford two of them going to college. So, since my husband had an opportunity to work at Pearl Harbor, he quit his school and went to work. At that time, very few people owned their homes so, we lived in a rented house on Powell Street, which rent was only $21 a month. From there we moved to Nuuanu and then, to Puunui. Later on, when my father built a home at Kam Heights, we moved to that home and shared the house with my brother, Bill, who was, also, married.

(This indicated that nationwide Depression in America hit the families of Hawaii very hard, also.)

Q **Could you tell us a little bit about your husbands' family? I understand that they were very prominent among the Koreans in Hawaii.**

A Well, Ernest, my husband, had a twin brother, Edward Park. There were three other siblings who were born in Korea and came to Hawaii with their parents when these other children were very young. Kwan Mo, Kwan Doo, and Esther Park arrived from Korea so, they were aliens. Kwan Mo was sent to a theological college in Kentucky and when he finished, he returned to Korea where he got married and had one daughter named Soon Yang. I was informed, Kwan Moo was involved in the 1919 Independence Movement rebellion. He was immediately, arrested because the Japanese was arresting all the Korean young men who had Western education. Kwan Mo was one of them. I was told that during his imprisonment he contracted tuberculosis, and later years, I don't know how long later, he died of tuberculosis, so he died in Korea. Then, Kwan Doo graduated from the University of Hawaii with a degree in architecture, and he was the first structure engineer in Hawaii.

Esther graduated from the university and was teaching in Hawaii, until she had to give up her teaching job because she was told that because she was an alien, she would not be able to hold a government job. So, she was given a job as a, more or less, matron at private boarding schools in Hawaii. Then, she was offered a scholarship by the YWCA to get further training and join the staff of the YWCA on Richard Street. Eventually, she became the Director of the YWCA in Korea after World War II.

Eddie, the twin brother of my husband finished university as a civil engineer. So, he worked for the City and County. By that time, Ernest, also, worked for the City and County of Honolulu. The twin brothers, Ernest and Edward, decided to form a company, which they called "Park and Park". And, they worked together for several years until they split in 1959. Then, Ernest had his own office, and Eddy had a corporation of his own.

Ernest and I adopted three children: Erna, Susan, and Michael Park. They were all three years apart. Erna and Susan were adopted in Honolulu. Michael came from Korea. Ernest did well at work, but he was a compulsive gambler, which I didn't know. So, when I found out that we were losing our home in Kahala in 1964, I got a divorce. Now, I had to take care of the three children alone because Ernest couldn't afford to take care of them. I was fortunate that I found work at the Palama Settlement and later, I was working at Leahi Hospital as a social worker.

I started off my employment life during the depression years, when there weren't many jobs, working as a clerk at the Palama Settlement. The Director of the Settlement thought I had more ability than just a clerk and so, he gave me permission to attend classes at the University of Hawaii in the afternoon. After I graduated with a degree, Palama Settlement gave me a job as a social worker. I worked there for several years.

At Palama Settlement, I helped Dr. Rhee's wife, Francesca Rhee, get medical help for the children who were at the Korean Christian Institute, the orphanage that Dr. Rhee established. So, the Rhees and I knew each other well. Dr. Rhee, himself, knew me well, also, because of my father. There was a time my father, although a Methodist Church Minister, was a very close friend of Rhee, when Rhee was the Principal of the Methodist Mission Boys' School in 1913 to 1915. They were greatly involved in the Korean Independence Movement, but with different views. Rhee and my father broke close relationship in 1916, but they were distant friends.

Then, I was offered a job at Leahi Hospital. To prove myself that I could handle it, I accepted the job, although I was needed at home to take care of my children. A couple of years later, I resigned and stayed at home to take care of the children, until I was was asked to come back again in 1954, which I did and stayed, until I retired in 1975. So now, I'm finally comfortable because I have earned Social Security and Government Pension.

Q **Were there things happening to you such as joining Korean organizations?**

A During the war years, lot of our friends were members of the Korean Delta Fraternity and Sorority. They wanted Ernest and me to join. Our initiation fee was $150. Most of the members were Korean Christian Church members from Rhee's Church. But we joined, and that's how we became very good friends with persons like Harry Choi and his wife Kwon Haemi, all Rhee's church members. Robert Choi, I knew him, when he was still in high school. He always took me as an older sister. He used to invite us to go up mountain-apple picking. When he graduated from high school, he was offered a job by Ewa Plantation. As we grew up older, he used to invite Mrs. Yang (Peggy Tai Yang, Dr. You Chan Yang's wife) and myself to his home for chicken dinner. He wasn't married at that time. He was a good cook, so he was a very good friend of mine, until he past away.

  This is how we – the Methodist Church members and the Korean Christian Church members – still could be good friends.

Q **Tell us more about the differences between you as a Korean Methodist church member and the Korean Christian church members. What happened there? How come you were friends with the other church members, such as the Delta Fraternity being a Korean Christian Church base organization?**

A Well, I didn't know very many Korean Christian Church (Rhee's church) people. There were a few that used to come to the Fort Street Methodist Church grounds just to join our social functions or just to meet some of the girls or boys.

Q **But tell us the history between the Methodist Church and the Korean Christian Church having an effect on the second generation.**

A I don't know, I was too engrossed in our own activities.

Q **But you do know the beginnings of the Korean Christian Church.**

A   Not too well, because we were living on Maui at that time…when the church separated, actually separated…

Q   **What church separated?**
A   The Methodist Church and the Korean Christian Church that Dr. Rhee started.

Q   **Only the Methodist Church first exited, right? Then, from the Methodist Church, there was a split. Dr. Rhee had left the Methodist Church…and began his own church, splitting the congregation of Koreans.**
A   That's right.

Q   **So, making friends with the Korean Christian church members was kind of different.**
A   For me, it was. Because all the time, until I graduated from high school, I mean, just before graduating high school, we were living on a different island, so we had no contact with the Korean Christian Church people.

Q   **But you were one of those who broke the ice between the two congregations, so to speak, right?**
A   I guess it was because the other side came around to our Fort Street Methodist area. We had more modern activities in the Honolulu Methodist Church for the youngsters.

Q   **So, you became friends, by accident.**
A   Yes, by accident. There'd be girls coming to our church, not to attend church, but to come around our parsonage where we had socials and we became friends. When I was attending the University of Hawaii, I think the majority were Methodist students. There were one or two that were Christian Church people, like Yo Imi Kim, O'Neil Hwang…They were strong Christian Church members. Other than that, I think the rest were all Methodist.

Q **So, there was a friction between the two churches?**

A Yes. Because they got that feeling from their parents. They themselves, I don't think felt it too much. Like the Delta Frat was started, of course, by Donald Kang, who was a Methodist, but those Christian Church people belonged to it, too, as well as members of the YMCA. The YMCA was where the Methodist and Korean Christian Church young people met, and I guess, that's how Donald Kang could start the basketball team with both kinds of youngsters at that one place, meeting, informally.

Q **What about Wilbert Choi (his family were strong Rhee's supporters)? What do you know about his circumstances?**

A As I told you, he was the first FAJ representative to go to the mainland. And because some were not in the financial situation where they could go to college, he was one of those who had to work after he graduated from high school. Luckily, for him being a FAJ Representative without a college degree was prestigious.

So, Ewa Plantation hired him because he was the FAJ representative. At first, they thought he was Chinese. Because Ewa Plantation Managers had a very difficult time with Koreans, they had vowed that they would never hire a Korean. They did not know Wilbert was Korean when they hired him. Later, they found out that he was Korean, but because Wilbert did well for them, they kept him, until he was offered a job by Doris Duke, the multi-millionaire heiress. He became her Head Landscaper at her beautiful home along the Diamond Head sea shore, called the Black Lagoon. And then, from there, he became very wealthy.

Q **At that time, Wilbert became the unofficial leader in the Korean Community, didn't he? He was famous in the Korean Community, wasn't he?**

A Yes, somehow, because Wilbert worked for USCD, he had contacts with the Korean prisoners who were in the Japanese Army as laborers. The Korean prisoners were caught in Okinawa and brought to Hawaii for imprisonment along with the Japanese soldiers. But they were not placed in the same prison camp. Wilbert Choi had a soft heart. He made contacts with the Korean prisoners. Wilbert took them on as one of the big projects for Delta Frat to take over. They gave the Korean prisoners Christmas gifts, special food and other things. So, we at Delta Frat made packages of cigarettes, candy, etc. We cooked dinner for them on special occasions. Wilbert had the facilities to do these things because he was living in one of Doris Duke's quarters... at the beautiful "Black Lagoon" near Waikiki. He could use the

Wilbert Choi, circa 1930s.

yard space there, and Delta Frat had all the cooking things to be able to handle a big project like that there. We enjoyed doing that.

Q **So, Wilbert became sort of like a role model. His family from Wahiawa was exceedingly, strong Rhee supporters, weren't they?**

A Yes, and his family always worshiped Dr. Syngman Rhee. Their relationship was so close that Wilbert got to know a lot of Korean Generals that used to come by to Hawaii, who were, likely, sent by Dr. Rhee after he became President.

Q **Because of Wilbert's stature in the community?**

A Yes. And Wilbert became the idol of many young people. Many years later, Wilbert rescued Dr. Syngman Rhee from the riots when Rhee was deposed in 1960.

Q **What other activities were going on among the Korean societies, so to speak? You were in the thick of the Korean**

societies after the war, so you must know a lot.

A After the war, I was only engrossed in the University of Hawaii activities not only Korean activities. While I was at the University, Ms. Ha Soo Whang was on the staff of the International YWCA. At that time, they had all different ethnic groups, separately. She got the high school and university girls to form a club called the Hyung Jay Club. And I think Sarah Lee Yang was the first member. Later on, Rose Shon and myself became members. I was the first delegate from the Hyung Jay Club to go to Asilomar Conference in California. That was in 1932. Sarah Lee and Rose Shon qualified to be delegates, but Sarah Lee was already on the Mainland, and Rose was on her way to the Mainland. So, I happened to be the next qualified person.

Q **Tell us about this seminar in Asilomar. I believe that that was an important event and broaden your experiences.**

A Asilomar Conference. It was a YWCA's Conference for young professionally, working women. It was all in the California area. It was about a one week conference. I forget now what the goal was or what the theme was at that time. It's been so long ago. That was in 1932. Asilomar is near Monterey and Carmel.

Q **And who were there?**

A From Honolulu, we had one from the Chinese club, Gladys Chung Tan, and one Portuguese, Roseline Corea. Including me, there were three of us.

Q **It seems that, that experience broaden your life experience for persons as young as you to travel in those days. Was that an annual thing?**

A I guess so. That was my first trip to the Mainland — the Continental United States of America. Hawaii was American, but it was a Territory of America.

There was no plane to go to the Mainland at that time and I was an alien. So, because I was an alien, I had to get a Japanese passport. Remember that when I arrived in Honolulu for the first time from

Korea, Korea was occupied by the Japanese. All Koreans at that time were considered as Japanese citizen. So, because I had a Japanese passport, when I went to the Asilomar Conference, I was the last one to get off the ship in California because I was considered a foreigner.

Years later, I had another problem with my citizenship and that was in 1952, when we went to California. We were going to the Rose Bowl game. Then, after that we were going to Mexico, but, I couldn't get a visa to go to Mexico. There were four of us, Eddie, his wife Bettie, Ernest and myself. I told them you folks go ahead and while you folks go to Mexico, I shall go to Washington D.C. and visit Polly, Mrs. Yang, wife of Ambassador You Chan Yang. Polly was my closest friend. So, I was fortunate in going at that time, when it was the inaugural year for the President of America. Since the Yangs (Ambassador You Chan Yang) were invited to the inaugural, I was able to go to the Georgetown Inaugural Ball with them. Also, I went to the inaugural ceremony because I was asked to accompany Mrs. Yang. I had a wonderful time and experience.

Q **Polly Yang. Would you explain your friendship with her and her husband?**

A She was the Ambassador's wife so she was recognized for her high position in the Korean Society everywhere. Dr. You Chan Yang was at one time a physician in Honolulu. He was quite famous because he is the one who introduced insulin for diabetes and he treated some of the well-known Hawaiians. He was a popular doctor for the wealthy, royal Hawaiians. He was always someone my family knew because he was a Methodist, when he was a child up to college days.

The Methodist people felt Dr. Yang betrayed the Methodist Church because he and Dr. Dae Bong Kim were the two that were given scholarship to a Methodist University in Boston to get their Medical Doctor's Degree. Dr. Kim remained loyal to his faith in the Methodist Church, but Dr. Yang changed to follow Dr. Rhee.

Q **What happened?**

A Y.C. Yang was always loyal to Syngman Rhee since 1914 when they both were members at the Methodist Church years ago. They kept their relationship even when Dr. Rhee broke away from the Methodist Church. Years later, Dr. Rhee appointed Y.C. Yang to become the Ambassador from Korea to United States in 1950. Dr. Y.C. Yang had never become an American citizen. The Walter Mccarran Immigration Bill to allow aliens to become USA naturalized citizens hadn't been passed until 1952. Since Y.C. Yang remained a Korean citizen, Yang could be appointed as the Korean Ambassador to America, by Dr. Rhee.

Q **Let's get back to the point where you said that Yang was a traitor to the Methodist Church because he was educated with support from the Methodist congregation, and after he was educated, he broke away and followed Rhee to his church ...**

A By the time Yang broke away, it was after he graduated from College that the Christian Church had a stronghold on the community.

Q **Then, he decided to follow Dr. Rhee. Tell us a little bit more about the Ambassador. This is very interesting, you are saying things I've never heard before.**

A Well, Dr. Yang knew of me and I became a very good friend with him, when he married Pauline Tai. Pauline Tai and I were chums at the University, although she was one class below me. That was her first marriage to Y.C. Yang, and this was his second marriage. He had married a Caucasian woman that he knew at Boston University. They had one daughter named Peggie. Peggie just recently died... about a year ago.

Q **What happened to the first wife?**

A You Chan was a widower, quite early. His wife was active in the Hawaii local society. She was quite active in the Korean community, also. At one time, I think she was the President of the Board of the YWCA on Richard Street. When their daughter, Peggie, was still very young, she wanted to give Peggie, some oriental culture experience, so, she took Peggie to Korea. I don't know how long they lived in Korea, whether it was one or two years. That's where and when Mrs. Yang contracted trichinosis...pork disease. When she came back to Hawaii, she was hospitalized. She was very seriously ill and she died of that disease. Then, You Chan married Pauline Tai, my close friend.

Q **Was Pauline a Korean Christian Church member?**

A No, her family were Methodists, not exactly strong church members, but strong Kookminhoe members...very strong members. Pauline's father was a very good looking, physically well-built man, unusually tall, more than the average Korean man. And, he always had a good position on the plantation staff. Before he retired, he was "Head Luna" (head boss) at the Aiea Plantation.

You Chan and Pauline had two children, Sheila and Channie. The children resided in Washington D.C. when they were growing up. They were seldom seen in Hawaii. Peggie, Dr. Yang's first daughter by his first wife, sort of disappeared and so did Channie.

Q **Let's get back to your personal life. I'm very impressed about some of the meetings and conferences you attended, especially, Asilomar in California. Were there other similar conferences that you went to?**

A That was the only major conference....that was the only organization outside of the Korean organization we able to go to in those days.

Q **You belonged to Delta Frat. Tell us a little bit more about Delta Frat. (It was a Korean association, mainly made up with young Korean Christian Church members. Although Delta Frat seems to indicate that members were college students or graduates, most of the members were not affiliated with the colleges nor were college students.)**

A When I joined the Delta Frat, it was mostly a social club. In 1959, because Robert Choi was very interested in Korea and in President Rhee, he suggested that Delta Frat members make a trip to Korea. He would make all the arrangements. Since Delta Frat had quite a bit of money in the treasury, they divided it evenly, among all the members. There were several members, most of the members, in fact, made the trip in 1959. We took the Pan Am, and Pan Am had that airplane with a big belly. It took us, I think, over 30 hours to get to Korea because we stopped in Midway and in Japan, and then, Korea. The welcoming group arranged by Rhee's direction gave us a wonderful reception.

Q **Last week, you were telling us about your relationship with Dr. Rhee. When you got there, you stayed at the Blue House.**

A Well, out of respect for my father (who was against Rhee and could not go to Korea because of Rhee), I went to Korea, perhaps, unknown to Rhee. I stayed in the background among the group who met with Rhee. This was my second trip to Korea. I had already been to Chung Wha Dae when the Vice-President had been Lee, Ki Bum. His wife, Mrs. Lee took us and gave us a tour of Chung Wha Dae at that time. So, I wasn't too interested in meeting President Rhee, but I went for the gatherings with my friends in the Delta Frat group. I kept a low profile because I really didn't really want to have pictures taken with Rhee, out of respect for my father. My father and President Rhee, socially they got together, but politically they never did agree.

Ironically, a strange phenomenon happened years later, when they were dying, however, that put Rhee and Rev. Hong together: both of them died on the same day. My father died in the morning at Kuakina Hospital and President Rhee died about four hours later at Maunaloa Hospital.

Q **What did they agree on, and politically, what did they disagree about?**

A Because of the opportunity that the Methodist Mission gave to the Korean community to become Christians and settle in Hawaii, my father was always very loyal to the Methodist Church. My father felt that Dr. Rhee should have been loyal, too. My father didn't feel that there was anything wrong for the Korean Methodist Church in Hawaii to be attached to the Methodist Mission on the Mainland. President Rhee's excuse to pull away was that he said that the Mission wanted to keep all the money. Rhee said that the Koreans should handle the money here, among the Koreans, although the Koreans didn't collect that much where they could have been self-independent.

Q   **Tell us a little bit more about how you remember Dr. Syngman Rhee.**

A   Well, I was a youngster, oh maybe about 5 or 6 years old. I don't believe I remember seeing him when I was that young, but I do recall when I was a bit older that he used to ask me to pull his white hair. He used to wear his hair short. When he started the Liliha School, he had Mrs. Choo, who was Salome Han's mother to take care of him... like being a matron, and also, be a cook for the girl's school which Rhee started.

Because Mrs. Choo and my mother were very good friends, one weekend Mrs. Choo said that she'd let me stay over at the girls school for the weekend. I stayed and I got the "nits"... lice in my hair. After that, my mother said no more of going to the girls dormitory.

Then, our family was sent to Maui, where my father became the Pastor of that Methodist Mission there. (It was a time when there was a friction between Rhee and the Kook Min Hur. Rev. Hong was the President of Kook Min Hur.) I guess the separation (between Rhee and Rev. Hong) wasn't clear cut because I remember Dr. Rhee and maybe, two or three of his "haole" – Caucasian – teachers had accompanied him and came to visit Spreckesville, where our family lived at that time. He visited our family. Maybe, he came to look around and see whether he could start a Korean Christian Church there, which later on became a very strong area at Paia for Koreans. I remember having to pull his white hair again, there, and we also had a gathering at the camp on the beach. That's all I can remember as a child of having seen him.

When Dr. Rhee and his wife, Francesca, came back to Hawaii (1935) after having lived on the Mainland for several years (they were in Austria, where they met and married; then, they stayed in California for a short while before coming back to Hawaii), they lived in Kalihi at the girls' dorm and Mrs. Rhee took care of him. I guess, she was just like a matron of the Rhee's girls' school because once a year, Mrs. Rhee brought the children to us for their general physical exam (at Palama Settlement, where Mary was the social worker). Or, if something was really, wrong with them medically, they also, used to come to Palama Settlement. As a social worker there, in that way, I helped Rhee's school very much.

Q **Were these children orphans at their school?**

A Most were, I guess, orphans, but I didn't know any of the children's background well. I knew them when they used to come to Palama Settlement, knowing that they were Koreans and were from Rhee's school. Mrs. Rhee brought some of them. Also, I did see Dr. Rhee visiting Dr. Yang at his office, which was nearby.

During one of Dr. Rhee's visits to our house, he invited my father to go to a movie with him. Whether my father did or not, I don't remember. But I know there was an invitation. So, my father always said they were friends and that he had nothing against President Rhee, except that politically, he didn't agree with Rhee.

Profile of
Mary Hong Park

Mary Hong Park is the most extraordinary
interviewee among the nineteen persons
presented in this book. Born in 1909 in Korea,
she arrived in Hawaii at age 3. I have been
interviewing her intensely, for the past fifteen
years. This author and Mary have been friends
for more than 45 years. Since I first formally
interviewed Mrs. Park in 1993, I continued to
see her almost weekly, or called her for detailed
information about certain events in the past.

Mary Hong Park is the daughter of
Rev. Han Sik Hong, a Minster of the Korean
Methodist Church, who had significant
relationships with the major figures in the
Korean Independence Movement. Rev. Hong
had a close relationship with Dr. Syngman Rhee
at the crucial time when the Korean community
began to become dysfunctional as a united
community.

Mary Hong Park's own life story in Hawaii
is very important because she has in depth
knowledge of the various Korean organizations
in Hawaii. She was privy to the nuances of the
interpersonal relationships among the first and
second generations either immigrants or local
born because she had numerous friends from
both sides of the Korean political divide. Her
detailed accounts expand nine decades.

Moreover, Mary Hong Park is married
into another iconic family of the past: she was
married to Ernest Park, the son of Chong Su
Park, the Second Commander of the Korean
Military Brigade in Hawaii under Commander
Young Man Pak. In addition to her own parental
heritage, her husband's family history adds to this
recollection of the past. The story of Chong Su
Park, Mary's father-in-law, deserves a full review
at another time.

My name is Mary Lee Moon Han, and I was born in November, 1918 in Waialua, Hawaii. My father, Man Kee Lee, came as a plantation sugar worker in 1903 from Korea. He left my mom, Si On Lee, and my older sister and brother in Korea. He came alone because my mother refused to come with him. She refused to leave with him because at that time in Korea, my father was a spoiled child. He drank and gambled, and so, she didn't want to come to Hawaii and suffer. She stayed with her mom, and I understand from the story that she told me, that during the harsh winter, their son passed away when he was an infant. So, we never had a brother. Many years later, I re-

Man Kee Lee (back, standing left) and Seon Joo Lee (Back, standing right) families. Front, left to right: Mary Lee (Moon Han), Si On (Man Kee Lee's wife), Ruth Lee (Mack), Harry Choi, Wan Soon Lee Choi, Smith Choi.

member my mother telling me that my father used to send friends whoever was going back to Korea...he would tell them...please go and tell his wife that he had changed and to please come to Hawaii with their daughter, but she never believed that he would change and so she did not go to Hawaii. Finally, in 1918 he, personally, went to get them, and that's why I call myself the "love child" because I was conceived in Korea, when he came to get my mother and sister.

My mother always told me the story that she was very sick coming to Hawaii on the ship because she was pregnant with me. She was sick with me, plus, being seasick. My older sister was already 17 and half years old, almost 18 years old. She came along to Hawaii. The sad thing was that when they landed, my sister couldn't de-board because she had "pink eye" and it was infectious. She had to be sent back to Japan, where all Korean immigrants had to go first for a physical examination. Can you imagine my mom letting her to go back to Japan alone? But she had to, that was the law. So, after a few months my sister came back all healed.

We then, settled in Waialua, and this is where I was born. My father worked at the Waialua plantation mill. I remember that she frequently told me she was so afraid of everything because she couldn't speak English. She would dress me in a bright Korean dress so that she can spot me when looking out the kitchen window to see wherever I was. So, I was really so precious to her, as she always used to say. She was so afraid of everything in Hawaii that she told my father to stay home during the day and to work on the night shift. During the night she used to have a young boy come to spend the nights at the house. By telling me all these stories, I realized how precious I was to her.

Finally, my father found Mr. Seon Joo Choi to marry my older sister. The young man was very likable because he didn't drink, he didn't smoke, and he didn't gamble. So, my father introduced them. At first sight of my sister, Choi fell in love with her. He used to work at Schofield Military Barracks. He walked all the way to Waialua every weekend to visit her...imagine, from Schofield to Waialua Plantation to visit her. Then, they got married.

My father resigned from his plantation job, and we all moved to Honolulu and he became a barber for a while. Then, later my father joined my brother-in-law in his laundry business; we all moved back to the Schofield Military Barracks area. At that time they called it "Leilehua Village." He used to pack

Father Man Kee Lee with Ruth, daughter. Background is Onyong Camp area in Wahiawa, near Wahiawa Elementary School.

Mary Lee (Moon) and Ruth Lee (Mack) at young ages in front of the Onyong Camp which was originally a Chinese camp in Wahiawa.

the laundry on his shoulders and deliver them. We really never suffered financially. We didn't know what "depression" meant in 1929 and thereafter, because the Schofield Military soldiers got paid regularly, so they were good customers. The soldiers paid their bills regularly. The laundry and tailor business in that area became very popular among Koreans. Many new families moved there, also. Most of them had some kind of laundry business there, too.

Wahiawa, which was very close to Schofield, was called the "Korean Town" of Hawaii. Most of them worked at the tailor or laundry shops in the same area. Then later, I remember we finally moved to the town of Wahiawa, where Top-Hat Club is now; my brother-in-law bought a house near there, and we all lived together, and that is where we grew up. We went to Wahiawa Elementary School, and graduated from Wahiawa High School.

After graduation, I went to Honolulu everyday with our brother-in-law, where he had another type of business. By that time, he owned a radio store. I went to Honolulu with him to study at a Secretary Commercial School. After school I waited for my brother-in-law, and then, came home with him to a good dinner: mom did all the cooking. It was a long ride from Honolulu

Duke Duk Man Moon, circa 1934.   Chong Hurn Moon, widower, and children Thomas, Daniel,
Duke Duk Man, and Beatrice, circa 1935.

to Wahiawa. All I did was eat and study, and then, I graduated in 1939 from the Commercial School. In the meantime, I met my husband, Duk Moon. Right after business school graduation, we got married in 1939. Our oldest son, Ronald, was born a year later, 1940.

Grandfather, Chong Hurn Moon carrying Ronald, infant.
   Insert: Hawaii State Chief Justice Ronald Moon, grandson of Bok Dok Ahn Moon, a picture bride, circa 2000.

Registration form for alien status issued by the United Korean Committee and certificate of alien registration issued for Man Kee Lee in 1942.

Then, World War II began.

The military wanted all of us to help in the war effort so we all had to work for the USA Army. I worked for about 8 months as a secretary to the Chief Engineer. Then, after eight months my second child, Eric was born. After working in the army for a while, my husband worked at Ford Island as a time keeper. Then, he worked for his father for while in Wahiawa at a shop he started. Then, Duk decided to open his own store. After his father retired,

Chong Hurn Moon's son Duke Duk Man Moon took over his father's shop in 1940 and opened Duke's Clothing, circa 1940. Insert: Chong Hurn Moon tailor shop in Wahiawa, circa 1930s.

we bought the building his father had rented and we opened a trading store. In the beginning, we thought of having a toy store, but we found out it was seasonal, so, we decided to open a trading store. We added children, men and women goods, trading at a small country store. We lived upstairs until 1958, when my oldest son, Ronald, graduated from Mid Pacific High School and College. We finally, could afford to buy a home on Glenn Avenue, a specially, very nice area in Wahiawa. We've been here ever since.

As we were growing up, we always had to go to church; it was always the Korean Christian Church. We also went to the Korean language school after the English school. People even now ask me, "Where did you learn how to speak Korean?" or "When did you come from Korea?" I said, "No, I was born here." Those days, as soon as we were at home, we always spoke Korean. I'm very, very grateful that we had that opportunity to learn Korean, and to speak Korean at home. The Korean language just comes naturally to me even now.

Duk, my husband, joined the Christian Endeavor (a study group at the Korean Christian Church), but he did not have a lot of time; yet, when any elderly person who needed to have letters translated written in English by their children who lived on the Mainland (the USA Continent), he would make time to help them. My children were brought up, knowing that helping other people was the thing to do.

Q   **Could you explain what "Christian Endeavor" means?**

A   In those days, the Church was not only on Sunday service, but it was a place where people met. Christian Endeavor is young people's group that met in the evenings. My husband, Duk was always in charge of that. That was when we went to Christian Endeavor. My children grew up knowing that Sunday was always a family time. We would go riding or do some activity, but all had to be back by six o'clock. Duke who also took care of the children's choir, was a Sunday school teacher and president of the church congregation. He was very, very active in other Korean community affairs; plus, he was the President of the Wahiawa Community Association. He was very active in the general community, not only for Koreans. So, he was a very, very busy man. People admired him for that. Finally, in 1970 he passed away with lung cancer which is very ironic because he did not smoked,

Mary Moon Han at her remodeled store, circa 1980.

never drank, and was a very good church man. I always used to tell people that, yes, he was only 55. I guess he finished his work down here, and God needed him more up there.

As soon as he passed away, I could have sold the business and not have to worry too much. But, I remodeled the store and worked at it until I retired about 1980. All of my children all went to college because they knew that they all had to go to college. And this is how the children were brought up, knowing that they had to go to college. All four of them have college degrees. I give my husband a lot of credit because no matter how busy he was, he spent time with the children. Today, I'm really proud of all of them.

Of course, everyone knows that my oldest son, Ronald, is the Chief Justice of the Supreme Court of Hawaii. My second son is an attorney on the island of Kauai, and my daughter is a speech therapist, married to an optometrist. She works for him. And my youngest son works for the City and County, as a manager of the open market. So, they're all doing fine. Now, I can retire, but still I try to keep the Korean culture, the Korean background and teach them at home. We still attend the same church. Our church just celebrated its 80th anniversary a couple of months ago.

We had a club called the Taeguk Club. It was formed in the 1930s as an athletic club in Wahiawa. It was all male, and gradually, they

invited women to join. We became a cultural club. At one time, it was a huge Club, but since then, it's been cut down to like two, three families. We tried to keep it going because we feel that we don't want to lose it. Our husbands started this Club in the 1930s, and we still wanted to be here to help, culturally. But over the years, the Club did not meet monthly. Now, we do meet whenever we feel it's necessary, at least every three, four times a year. Lately, we've just elected a young man originally from Korea. His name is Peter Choi. He settled down in our town because he has a business in Wahiawa.
So we feel that the Club may carry on into the future.

Q **What did you say was the goal of the Taeguk Club way back in the beginning?**

A Way back in the beginning, it was started as an athletic club. The members were all men. They used to participate in baseball, basketball and volley ball competitions. Very active. And then, gradually, when the young men got married, heir wives were invited to join. We changed the Constitution to become a little more cultural and humanitarian for Korea. Whenever there were floods in Korea, we sent money to the orphanages in Korea. We sent food, clothing whenever it flooded. Every year, it seems Korea has floods. Duk was active in other local American clubs or organizations, but his heart was always in Korean activities for Korea, too. We always had clothing drives; we always sent whatever money we could to Korean orphanages; we adopted an orphanage.

Q **What were the years for these activities?**

A In the 1930s, 1940s. We started the Taeguk Club when some of us were in high school. Our parents were so strict, they wouldn't let us out. The only time we could go out was when we attended the church services or the Korean youth club or the choir. Those days we had lots of members.

Q **Were these members, mainly, members who lived in Wahiawa?**

A Yes, it was. But, there was a very talented member, Donald Yong Gak

Kang, who was more like a leader of youth groups in Honolulu. He was a Methodist. It did not matter to him, if we were Rhee's followers. He helped us form our group, too. He is well known for the formation of young Korean leaderships everywhere. So, he would come by to help us establish the club. The membership of the Taeguk Club was mostly from Wahiawa. However, as time pasted by, we had members from Honolulu because they were, originally, from Wahiawa who then, moved away. They still felt attached to us. The highways from Honolulu improved and we all have cars, so they can come to Wahiawa, easily.

Q **How different is Taeguk Club from the Korean American Club? And is the Korean American Club, also, based in Wahiawa?**

A The Korean American Club is more businesslike because it owned a building. Our parents belonged to it. The forefathers had the foresight to buy property to put up a community building. The founder was Mr. Cloud Owen, Philo Owen's father, one of the most well-known families in Wahiawa. But, they were not Korean Christian Church members. Mr. Owen ran a grocery store for a long time. He had many sons, and he was very active in everything. We were very young when the Korean American Club began in 1923. Mr. Owen started a membership for the Club, and one of the activities was to handle burial sites maintenance. The Club owned a truck, and he would take all of us to visit all the members' graves and put flowers on them. He would cook whenever we had a meeting. He would do the cooking when we had parties at the Clubhouse. The Korean American Club members were from all over, even from Waialua and Honolulu. In the beginning the Club initial membership fee was minimal. Now, to join the club, there is a $100 initiation fee. The Korean American Club was more businesslike, but they tried to keep the Korean culture alive by teaching us Korean things and getting us together to play. We played volleyball. I remember being very athletic because of that Club.

As far as the Taeguk Club is concerned, it's more cultural and fellowship. We had parades, wearing Korean clothes. The members were very active in the established local community, whenever they needed help with Korean things.

Q **Were there other differences, like age group that joined the clubs?**

A Yes. The Korean American Club got started by our parents, and then, we took it over as they passed away. But the Korean Taeguk Club was started by our husbands. Age and interest were different between the two Clubs. Those people in the Korean American Club were more businessmen. They had money, but the Taeguk Club was for cultural reasons and fellowship, like I said, it was an athletic club for the younger set.

Q **So, would you say that the Korean American Club members were more on the wealthy side?**

A I think so, because most of them had businesses or they had a good job. And to me, they were older, they were more settled, whereas the Taeguk Club had younger people, just graduated from high school, just getting started in business, and so now, our children joined as members.

Q **What was the year did you say Taeguk Club began?**

A I think Taeguk Club started in the 1930s.

Q **Do you think the Korean American Club and the Taeguk Club had any connections with the Korean Liberation Movement?**

A The Taeguk Club was not interested in the Liberation Movement and the Korean American Club, too. I think the churches were more involved. The church that I went to – the Wahiawa Korean Christian Church members – were the follower of Syngman Rhee, the first president of Korea. He was the founder. So, naturally, whenever he needed money, we raised money to help him, whenever he came to Wahiawa. We always had him over for a gathering. As far as the Taeguk Club is concerned, we were not interested in the Liberation

Movement. Individually, they may have been, but not as a Club. Neither was the Korean American Club. I think in those days the churches were more deeply, involved in the Korean Independence Movement.

Q **You said that the Korean Christian Church in Wahiawa just recently celebrated its eightieth anniversary. So, it's a little bit younger, by just a few months younger, than the Korean Christian Church in Honolulu.**

A Yes, I think so, because Dr. Syngman Rhee founded Liliha Church first, and then, the country churches came after. We just recently changed our church's name to the Wahiawa United Church of Christ because we have so many intermarriages. Now, a non-Korean person can join the Church no matter what nationality. So, we felt we should change the name in the late 1980s.

Q **What's the membership now?**

A We have about 40–30 very active members. It's not large. But it's like a family church. We have different nationalities. We have some Filipinos and in fact, there are Japanese. So, that's what we wanted; we wanted people from the community to come and feel that they could worship with us and so, this is now our makeup of the people, all different and a lot of intermarriages.

Q **Tell us about the development of the Korean Christian Church in the younger days, like say, I understand that it was flourishing a whole lot in the 1930s, maybe?**

A Oh, yes. That is when we were growing up. When you think about it, it was the only meeting place for our parents, and so, it was like political, plus, worshipping. If they wanted to get together, it was the church. At that time, most of them didn't have automobiles and some were far away in Honolulu. This was our meeting place and we grew up socially and politically at the same place of worship. I remember they use to have meetings during the week; and on Sundays, for worship; so, the church was used for many purposes.

Q **What was the relationship with the Koreans from the Korean Methodist Church, which was located toward the middle of the Wahiawa shopping area. You all called it "down church" and yours "up church"?**

A Yes, we all went to either "up or down" church. It's so funny. Even now, we just refer to the churches as "down church and up church". When you say "down church", it's the Methodist Church. In school, we are all good friends and we got together, but then, when Sunday came, the Methodists went to their church and we came to our church. Sometimes, because we didn't have that many members, as time went on, we tried to join together. We even talked about maybe we should join together, but it was funny, it just stayed that way. Maybe our next generation will just forget all about that "down church and up church," but somehow, even at our age, it still is "down church" and "up church." Socially, we're friends, we're all good friends. It's just that we just don't go to each other's church. I guess it is because one group was anti-Syngman Rhee and one group was for Syngman Rhee. I think that was the basic reason; religiously, it's the same thing, we worship the same God and same everything. But to me...well, I guess maybe it's like the pilgrims in the olden days, when maybe they used the church politically. I think the same thing was just carried on.

Q **Tell us about Syngman Rhee: What do you know about him and what was his relationship with Wahiawa? How did he get himself involved in the church activities?**

A Well, as a young child, I always knew about Dr. Syngman Rhee. I remember my parents, even Duk, used to talk about him. They said we always have to help collect money for Rhee for the Independence Movement. This is how we grew up in our home, that whenever we had extra money and if Rhee needed to have it to go to Washington D.C. to fight for our Independence, we all donated no matter how poor we were. I remember, it was Duk who said to his dad when he was young: "How come we give money to Dr. Rhee? We can't even have butter on the table except only once a week and yet, you give money to him." The thing that was really funny to me was that he questioned his father, but, Duk grew up helping Dr. Rhee all his life, even to adulthood.

Duk was American, but his heart was for Korea. And so, as we grew up and whenever "March First" came around, we'd all be dressed in Korean clothes and our parents would celebrate. I remember in those days we had to go to Honolulu because they would have a big meeting and everybody dressed in Korean dress. That is how we celebrated "March First 1919." That was supposedly the Independence Day.

At our Church, Rev. Park, Dong Whan, one of our first ministers, said he was involved in the Independence Movement in Korea. We could see his burns that he suffered on that day. They had put him in jail because he was active in the Korean Movement on March First. When he was put in jail, he was burned on his hands.

Yes, I remember Dr. Syngman Rhee always. Whenever he came to Hawaii, he would visit us in Wahiawa, too. We would invite him, and sometimes we had big huge spontaneous parties. Rhee was always blowing on his fingers. I used to ask my dad why he's doing that? My father said that Rhee was tortured by the Japanese. They would put sticks or something under his finger nails and burn the sticks. Because of that, he blows his fingers still to this day. And he always had twitches on his face – all this from all his suffering, and so, we, ...the Korean Christian Church, which he founded, ...naturally, we back him up whenever he needed money. We supported the poor Korean people, too. Everybody was poor those days. Even many poor Koreans would save their money and helped Rhee's Independence Movement...even after the war in 1945 ended and Rhee became our First President.

Another thing I remember in 1959, President Rhee invited many of his backers, anyone who wanted to go to Korea. Eighty-one persons went from here. There were Methodist people, too. Yes, because it was opened to anyone, but naturally most of the ones who went were the Korean Christian Church people, but I remember the Methodist Reverend's family and his wife were there; they went with us, and that's the time they adopted a little daughter because he had two sons only. So, they adopted a daughter in Korea.

I think people who really know about Dr. Syngman Rhee's history, whether Methodist or Christian Church members, they know he did something for our country.

As we grew up, we knew Dr. Rhee lived on Wilhelmina Rise. We used to visit him there, when we could. My brother-in-law, Seon Joo Choi, was a very active supporter. He was very active politically, and he was one of the founders of the Korean Christian Church in Wahiawa. So, as we grew up, that's all we knew about Dr. Syngman Rhee. And so, we knew his background from what we heard from our parents; that's how much we knew.

Q **Tell us more about your brother-in-law, Mr. Seon Joo Choi.**

A Seon Joo Choi had so much foresight. He was married to my older sister. He bought properties; he was the first who opened a bowling ally in Wahiawa. He was very active at Church, plus at the Dongji Hoi, which was the Club that was formed to help Dr. Syngman Rhee. Seon Joo had only up to eighth grade education, but he was the only one among my parents and my older sister who could read and write English. He knew how to sew, how to run a business, and he bought a huge property, business property, in the middle of Wahiawa Shopping Center, which up to today, his sons are managing. From this property bought, it contains everything they have businesswise: the "Speed World Burger," "Dot's Drive In," and other shops that they own. Smithy Choi is his son and Anthony Choi is his grand son who handle the properties. Smithy was a successful, well-known business man, very active in many of the Korean clubs, the Taeguk Club, the Dongji Hoi, and the Korean American Club.

Q **Where did Mr. Seon Joo Choi come from and when?**

A From Pyongyang Do. He must have come in 1903 or maybe little after, because I remember my father saying that after he came here, he saw this young man who never drank, never gambled. Choi knew my dad had a daughter in Korea and he wanted to meet her. As far as just exactly what date my mother and my sister came, I have no idea.

Q **Let's talk about Dongji Hoi, what do you know about Dongji**

Hoi?

A All I know of Dongji Hoi when my parents and my brother-in-law were active in it, is that, the main purpose was to help Dr. Syngman Rhee get independence for Korea. So, no matter how poor we were, they always paid dues or when Rhee needed extra help. I remember my parents, helping. I was very young at that time, so, all I can remember as a child, is that Dongji Hoi, is Dr. Syngman Rhee's organization. My parents became members of Dongji Hoi, early, after it was established.

Right now, the purpose of Dongji Hoi is mostly scholarship for the Korean children who are going to Korea. The interesting part of it is that most of the ones who are getting the university scholarships are the new immigrants' children (coming to Hawaii in the 1990's). They are so bright. But lately, we began giving to local Korean kids and our main purpose is helping them, culturally, too. Most recently, there are not that much cultural activities. I think right now our activities are mostly to help the children get scholarships. We still have Dongji Hoi.

One interesting thing that I remember about Dr. Syngman Rhee is that he established the Korean Christian Institute, and when they sold the property, half of the money had gone to the Inha College in Incheon, Korea. That's why it's name is: "In" for Incheon and "Ha" for Hawaii; they joined it to make it "Inha".

Q **Were there many interchanges between the Wahiawa Korean Christian Church and Honolulu Christian Church? Did the Korean Christian Church in Wahiawa and Honolulu Church have very strong ties?**

A Yes, I remember whenever it was always "March First" or some event, the Honolulu Korean Christian Church would be the one to initiate things because they were a larger group. We would attend, and even now, whenever they have something, we would try to help them. I remember at one time their church in Honolulu didn't have a minister, and Rev. Richard Kim, who was our minister, felt that they needed him, so they asked our permission, if they could ask to him to be their minister. Naturally, we felt we're sister churches, and if they needed our help, we could go along, so, he went over there. We had a lot of ministers, and because we were such a small church, we let him go to the Honolulu Korean Christian Church.

In the beginning, the ministers came directly, from Korea, so, our church was like a training place. They would come here, learn the culture, learn maybe better English, and then, as soon as they want to better themselves and get more salary, they would move on to a bigger church in the city. If you come to our church, you would see all the ministers' photos that we had over the years. We felt that it was sort of our duty to help the new Korean ministers. We felt good that at least they got their training over here. Once they knew the ropes they moved on, after all, they all have to make a living. We are such a small church; we can't pay them too much.

After a while, we began to realize we were losing our younger people to attend church—even our own children—because they couldn't understand the Korean language; whereas, we older persons sat through the Korean sermons and the services, but the younger children, they won't. Once the youngsters went to college and came back, they won't come back to our church.

This is why we thought, we'd change to the name to the United Church of Christ and have services for other mix blood parishioners. But it still was hard to get a minister. We tried to get them, especially, when the immigrant Koreans started coming to our church, but somehow, the cultural difference is like a foreigner, so different, we just couldn't get along, you know. We Korean Americans had to have our own services.

The other nationalities had their own services, too, at the same building, but at different times. We rented the church building to them for minimal a monthly amount so that they can have their own church service after our church service. It's like doing missionary work. We feel that if they needed our help, we would give them some help. So, that's the difference now. We don't have the word "Korean" in our church name, but basically, we are Korean. We have the Korean flag on the podium beside the American flag and the Hawaiian flag to show that it's for everyone.

Q **What about the Korean Christian Institute (KCI)? Do you know anything about that or students who attended the school?**

A Yes, I didn't go to the KCI, but I remember Duk telling me that he was there for while because they were from Big Island (another name for the Island of Hawaii), and they had no way to go to high school on that Island. Dr. Syngman Rhee would go around to the country side and whoever wanted to go to school he would bring them to Honolulu. Because Duk's mother died when he was very young, I remember he said he had to go to the Korean Christian Institute (KCI) at one point for a short while. He remembered how poor they were at the Korean Christian Institute and how bad and negligible the food was there, but then, he was grateful at least that he had a place to stay for little while, while his father was getting settled in the city of Honolulu.

Q **What year do you think it was?**

A Oh, gee. I have really no idea how long ago that was, because he said he was very young when that had happened. And I remember Gertrude Lee, saying she had gone there to KCI, and so many others had gone to KCI, and some went to the Susannah Wesley Home. I think the Wesley Home was a Methodist Church Mission. Quite a few other Korean children, also, went to the Korean Christian Institute.

Q **Tell me, what you know about Duk's family.**

A Well, I know he was in some place in Hilo and Honokaa (towns on the Big Island – the Island of Hawaii). He was born in Honokaa, and he said he remembers his mother who died very young...she was only 26 years old.

Q **Could you give me Duk's father and mother's whole name?**

A His father's name was Chong Hurn Moon and his mother's last name was Park. In those days, they kept their maiden name, so, as far as first name, I'm not too sure.

Q **How did they come?**
A She was a picture bride.

Q **What year?**
A I don't know what year.

Q **Was Duk the oldest?**
A Duk was the oldest and Dan Moon was two years younger.

Q **Duk was born in 1915, so his mother must have come in 1914 or 1915, same as my mother.**
A Later, Beatrice was born. When she got married, she became a Kim. She died when she was only about 46 years old.

Q **Did Duk's father came to Hawaii alone?**
A Yes, he must have been here as a bachelor like most of them.

Q **Before 1905?**
A Before 1905. So, he was in the sugar plantation, I suppose, on the Big Island, Hawaii. And his wife came as a picture bride. She died so very young. She was only 26 years old, and Duk told me that she always went to church. He remembers going with her even those days, and sometimes in the evenings, too. He would be holding her dress and walking everywhere with her; then, one day, he said she wasn't there and he asks his dad, where his mom was; he said in the hospital. Duk never saw her after that.

Q **So, how many children were there in that family?**
A Four. All two years apart. Duk, Dan, and then, came Beatrice, and then, came the younger son, Thomas, whom they called, Dike. All two years apart. Two birthdays were in April and two birthdays were in May, so, strictly every two years. They had a very sad life because of losing their mother so young. They had a grandmother on the Pyo side, the maternal side. Duk and Jacob Pyo were first cousins. Jacob Pyo's mother and Duk Moon's mother were sisters, so, their grand-

mother, were on both sides. Duke and Jacob, Mable, and Helen were first cousins. The oldest in the Pyo family was Helen Pyo Park. We all lived in Wahiawa and belonged to the same church.

Jacob's mother used to come and help take care of the Moon children once in a while, but mostly, Duk's father raised them, himself, especially, when they were in Wahiawa and he opened a tailor shop in Schofield.

Q **I guess in your generation you all married Koreans so that's why everybody is related.**

A That's right. Especially, in Wahiawa, the saying goes, better be careful because you can be speaking badly about their relatives.

Q **In Honolulu, the younger set of your generation married Koreans.**

A No, all of my four children married outsiders...non-Koreans. That's why it's so ironic because Duk was such a patriotic Korean, a true Korean-Korean, but then, all his children married different nationalities.

Q **That generation is slightly older than you, right? Weren't some of them born in Korea? When they came over to America, they were called "1.5" just like your sister who was born in Korea. They were all within the "second generation," but very different in their life time.**

A Yes. During my time, I think, we were marrying only Koreans so much that all the Koreans became related. But later, the younger set of the second generation who were born here after 1920's began to intermarry. That's why when my sister, Ruth married Mack, a Caucasian, my father wouldn't give her away (walk the bride down the aisle). So, Duk had to give her away at the marriage ceremony. After they got married, our father began liking Mack so much that he couldn't do enough for his son-in-law...because Mack was so nice, so very nice. Sadly, Mack died very young. Mack was only 41 years old when he died. So, Ruth had a rough time...widowed so young in her late 30s. She had a rough life.

Q   **Let's talk more about the 2nd generation who lived up to adulthood...your generation.**

A   Yes, I remember going to Leilehua High School and we mostly, hung around with Korean people because in those days we'd go to church, Korean language school, and somehow, we just got directed to Korean friends, only, and married Koreans. But, Bessie Lee, who moved away from Wahiawa after high school graduation and whom I haven't seen for years and years, married a Caucasian because she worked among them at the University of Hawaii. She was one of my best friends, when we were seniors in high school.

It was because of the Korean Students' Alliance, too, which gave us the opportunity to hang around with Koreans our age, no matter what church we attended. Donald Yong Gak Kang formed the Korean Student Alliance. We always had meetings during school time, lunch time, or after school. All the Korean girls would sit around together, having our lunch or just chitchatting in those days. Yet, on the side, I did have some Japanese friends, too, but most of our friends, either in church, club work, we always hung around with Korean guys and gals. When the general non-Korean community wanted Korean entertainment, even though a few of us don't know how to dance Korean dancing or anything Korean, we'd dance because we had Korean dresses.

Q   **So, none of the political things such as the Korean Independence Movement seeped into your relationships?**

A   No, not in school – no politics – that to me that was great. But, once in a while, on Sundays some speaker would say something at our own Church, but after that, it didn't mean anything. Maybe for somebody older than us, but I didn't think so for our age group.

Q   **Who married whom between the Churches? Didn't it make a difference?**

A   No, it didn't. It really didn't. Whether we were from "down church or up church" nothing like that affected us. When you think back, that was good to have friends from either side. Even though whatever our parents instilled in us, we still could be friends.

Q **What about the war? How did it effect Wahiawa and your generation?**

A Well, when the Second World War came – I never forgot that it was a Sunday – and my husband, Duk got up early with Ronald (their first son). Ronald was few months old and Duk woke me up and said, "Mary, look at that. They're really having real maneuvers. They're practicing for real because I even see a plane with red paint on it, just like a Japanese plane." We really thought it was a maneuver because in those days, they were rumors that there would be a war. Then, one of my neighbors living on Olive Avenue and one of my friends came running up and said, "This is a real war. Somebody got shot across the street on Kamehameha Highway." It was one of my Japanese friends that I knew that got shot because he went out at the corner of Olive Avenue and Kamehameha Highway. It was a shoe store called Bailey Shoe Store. He was out there on the street and he happened to just lean forward to look up and a bullet got him.

Profile of
Mary Lee Moon Han

Mary Lee Moon Han was born 1918 in Waialua, Oahu in a family of ardent followers of Dr. Syngman Rhee and were Founding Members of Rhee's church in Wahiawa, the Wahiawa Korean Christian Church.

Mary married into a family, the Moon family, of Wahiawa who were with equal intensity of dedication to Dr. Rhee. Both set of parents, the Moon and the Lee families, were outstanding leaders in the Korean community in Wahiawa. (Mary married Joseph Han late in life after her husband, Duke Moon, died.)

The Moon family is highly esteemed in Hawaii because Mary's son, Ronald Moon, became the Chief Justice of the Supreme Court of Hawaii, the first Korean to achieve a high position Statewide. This achievement is a reflection of the Moon family's dedication to community life.

Without a planned agenda, Mary's informal discussion of the Lee and Moon families' history in Wahiawa lead to the discussion of the unique place of the legacy of Rhee's affect on the second generation Koreans in Wahiawa, during the most vulnerable time of the Independence Movement. Wahiawa remained Rhee's stronghold for his advancement in the political struggle to retain power throughout his entire life in Hawaii and Washington, D. C. Wahiawa had the strongest component of the Rhee's organization: the Dongji Hoi.

Mary Moon Han's casual description of the past greatly, elucidated the many tiers of political development among the second generation. We can consider Mary as a member of the second decade of the second generation. This differentiation of the decades among the second generation Koreans is important to understand their perception of the Korean settlement in Hawaii. Other than Mary herself, that particular set of the second generation began to withdraw from deep participation in the Independence

Movement, even before Korea was liberated. They were unlike the older second generation who were ten years or more older. Within the second generation, there were so many drastic changes, politically, within one decade that we cannot evaluate the entire second generation as one entity and its affect on our major interest: the Korean Independence Movement in Hawaii.

From Mary Moon Han's discussion we can come to understand part of the reasons for the attachment between the Wahiawa second generation children of the 1910s with Dr. Rhee. Many of the Wahiawa second generation youngsters were the first in large numbers to have benefited from Rhee's establishment of the Korean Christian Institute (KCI). The KCI allowed them or a sibling or a relative to stay in Honolulu for their education. During those early days the travel to Honolulu was long and tedious which made it more feasible to stay at the KCI dormitory.

The idolizing of Rhee among the young Koreans began in 1914 when the first girls' dormitory began under Rhee's efforts. Thus, most of these Wahiawa youngsters remained grateful and loyal to Rhee for many years, thereafter. One of the life long lasting dedicated youngster starting from her KCI attendance was Gertrude Lee of Wahiawa, who became a wealthy business woman. She was the major Korean figure even years later in Hawaii in support of InHa University in Incheon, Korea. This discussion of the second generation begs further examination at another time. Suffice to say that Gertrude Lee was always among the strong supporters of Rhee.

Mary Moon Han's interview is filled with valuable pertinent historic profiles of the second generation Koreans in the transition from being involved in their parents' emersion in the Korean Independence Movement and the youngsters' thoughts of breaking away from their parents' preoccupation. We must keep in mind the tiers of the second generation when trying to understand Mary Moon Han's references to the "second generation."

Mollie Hong Min   Dr. Thomas S. Min

I'm Dr Thomas S. Min and I'm happy to narrate my mother's personal history. My mother, Mollie Hong Min, began writing her autobiography when she was in her eighties. She finally, had time to sit down and write about herself. We found her handwritten story in a loose leaf notebook after her death.

Mollie Hong Min, circa 1909.

My mother, Mollie Hong Min, was born in Pyongyang, Korea on October 18, 1887. She described Pyongyang as a beautiful city that was completely, surrounded by a large wall. There were two large rivers which ran on either side of the city, one on the East side, called Tuman Gang, which flowed towards Seoul, and the other, Bok Dan Gang, which ran toward Manchuria. The city was protected by very high stone walls and there were four large gates which were opened in the morning and closed in the evening by the government guards. Her parents lived in a large and beautiful house in the city, while Grandfather and Father lived in the

Mollie Hong Min's parents: In Taik Hong, father; Marjorie Hong, mother and brother, Chi Pom Hong.

country during the summer months to look after the farms on his land.

While growing up in the city, she lived with her mother and grandparents in a very large and beautiful house and she described the home as having many servants. Her brother, Chi Pom Hong, was three years older. Her father and grandfather were gone throughout most of the year, during the farm season, because her grandfather owned a very large farmland, many miles off from the city. The work was done by tenant farmers there, and they grew many products which were brought into the city to be sold. When the late fall weather began, her grandfather and her father came back and lived in the city with the rest of the family.

My mother— this was not mentioned in her autobiography — told me later about some humorous but, sad period of that stage in her life.

During the winter months when her grandfather and her father were back living with them in the city, every evening after dinner they would leave the house and go to a nearby tea house where all the wealthy Korean males gathered, no females there, supposedly, or theoretically, but Kyesangs (female entertainers) came to sing songs and create verses and poems and so on. In actuality, the men did considerable drinking. My mother told me that every night, her grandfather and her father drank so much at the tea house that they were brought home on two wheelbarrows and dumped on the front lawn. Then, a servant had to come out and carry them into their bedrooms and put them to bed.

Mollie's mother and grandmother, finally, got sick and tired of this, so they packed up the two children and they took them way up on the hills to a Buddhist Ladies' Priest temple in Hwanghae Do, as I said, because of her father and grandfather's excess drinking. Her mother and grandmother left word behind that they would not return, until the men stopped drinking. Well, they stayed there for several weeks, and then, a messenger arrived at the temple with a letter from her grandfather, saying that they will reduced their amount of drinking. Grandmother sent back a letter, saying that they will not return, until they stop their drinking, completely. They waited there for a whole year, and finally, a messenger arrived with the message that they had stopped drinking and would never drink again. So, grandmother and mother, all happily, packed up their things and went back home with the children, and thereafter, they had a good life and everyone was happy.

During the early period in Pyongyang, I would say in the late 1880s, two missionary families came to the city to start churches, schools and hospitals. They were Dr. William Noble with his wife, and Dr. Hall with his wife. They set up religious groups to teach Christianity. They set up a Girls' School and a doctor's office and worked very hard for the Korean people. Dr. Noble was a physician. He set up a medical clinic where they gave free medical care to anyone that was willing to not be treated by herbal doctors. They worked very hard for the Korean people. Years later, Dr. Hall was killed by a very bad man. So, Mrs. Hall went back to America and returned soon afterwards as a doctor with her two little children, a daughter and a son. There was a tragedy again, when her daughter died of an illness. Then, her son went to America and, also, came back as a doctor

My mother's brother Chi Pom became a Christian and took her to Sunday School every Sunday. Chi Pom became very involved with the missionaries early on. Mollie, also, attended a Girls' School that was teaching U.S. history, geography, arithmetic, and so on. Then, Mrs. Hall found out that Mollie could read and write English well. She had been tutored in the English language by a private tutor at home. So, at the age of 13, Mollie became an English teacher at this missionary school.

Chi Pom Hong continued with his Christian faith. He became very,

Rev. Chi Pom Hong and wife Agyon Kim Hong, circa 1910.

very strongly, caring for his Christian faith, and in July of 1903, Dr. Noble induced Chi Pom to go to Hawaii as a Christian missionary for the Korean immigrants who had arrived in Hawaii during the past year. Dr. Noble, also strongly, suggested that Mollie go with him and attend English schools in Hawaii. Since the rest of the family did not want to remain behind without the children, their parents sold their large home in the city and went with them. The farmlands were given to the poor tenant farmers that had worked on those lands. The family got on a small boat that rowed down to the first southern port, which was Nampo. Sailing on a small boat was the only way to row down to Nampo. That took three days and three nights. Then, they got on a larger boat and, again, slowly rowed down to Incheon. Finally, it reached Busan, and there, they got on a larger boat that crossed over to Japan. There in Japan, they, finally, got on a large ship, named the S.S. Coptic. It took several weeks to reach Hawaii. They finally, reached Honolulu on October 15, 1903, where they started a new life.

In Hawaii, Chi Pom Hong was placed in charge of the Korean Methodist community as a lay minister, and Mollie went to join the Kawaiahao Seminary for Girls, which was made up of a student body of white (Caucasian) and elite Hawaiian girls. Because of her Christian faith, they took her in without charging tuition.

Then, Bishop Edmund Hughes, who was the Head of the Methodist Church throughout the West Coast of the USA Mainland and Hawaii, who came to Hawaii on several occasions for conferences, met Mollie. When she graduated at Kawaiahao School, the Bishop appointed her to go to San Francisco to attend the Methodist Deacon. Theological College. The Methodist Women's English Board paid Mollie Hong's tuition until she graduated. She was the only Oriental and most likely the only Korean student at the Deacon School. During the years at college, many churches and organizations in San Francisco and California asked her to speak about the Christian Movement in Korea. She became well known and respected. Mollie graduated from the Deacon School in 1913.

After her graduation, Bishop Hughes suggested that Mollie marry a Korean and made an arrangement for Mollie to meet Rev. Chan Ho Min. Chan Ho Min liked the arrangement. They were married on June 4, 1913 at Bishop Hughes' home, where numerous guests were invited.

Chan Ho Min had been sent to Hawaii as a young man to help the ministry for the Korean immigrants in 1905. He was ordained before going to Hawaii and became the first official Pastor of the Korean Methodist Mission Church in Honolulu in 1905. At that time Bishop Hughes had gotten to know Chan Ho, quite well, in Hawaii. The Bishop, also, met with Chan Ho when Chan Ho was in Los Angeles to further his education at the University of Southern California in 1911 to further study Divinity to become an Elder. Although Rev. Chan Ho Min lived in Hawaii at the same time when Mollie was there, they were not formally, introduced. He was very much older than

Mollie. (He had been previously, married in Korea. This part of his background is not clear, whether his wife died or they were divorced.)

After they married, they both went back to Los Angeles where Chan Ho Min continued his schooling at the USC for three years. My father finally received three degrees: Bachelor of Arts, Bachelor of Divinity, and Master of Arts.

About my father's background: Rev. Chan Ho Min was born in Pyongsan, Hwang Hae Province on October 21, 1878, the son of Hyung Chan Min and Matilda Sur Min – I don't know why a lot of these Korean

Rev. Chan Ho Min, circa 1909.

immigrant people – even that far back in the 1800s had American names like "Matilda" and "Mollie". I don't know from where she got that name, "Mollie". Maybe, it was because they were Christians. That could be it. My father had graduated from the Methodist Mission College Pae Jae in Seoul at the same time with Dr. Syngman Rhee. They became life long friends from that time onward. My father was ordained a minister prior to coming to Honolulu, Hawaii. He had arrived in Hawaii on August 8, 1905. Mollie left Hawaii in 1909. In 1911, Chan Ho left Hawaii and went to Los Angeles to attend the University of Southern California.

After my parents married, they lived in a tiny upstairs apartment in Los Angeles. Mollie took up nursing courses at the Methodist Hospital and took special courses at the University of Southern California. She received a USC Resident Teacher's appointment. When World War I started, Mollie joined the Red Cross in Los Angeles as a volunteer despite the fact that her first child, Paul, was born on June 10, 1914.

When Chan Ho continued his studies at the USC even after they were married, they needed some livelihood to care for the growing family.

So, Mollie bought a larger house in which was near Santa Monica, a farm outside of the busy City of Los Angeles. Mollie began raising produce, chickens, turkeys, rabbits which were sold to restaurants, and she was able to

Min Family grows: Mollie, Rev. Min; standing, Thomas; lower child, Paul; infant, Philip. circa 1919.

continue sending Chan Ho to USC until he received his Degree in Divinity, and, finally, his Master's Degree in Divinity, also. At that time, two more children were born in California, Thomas, on January 4, 1917, and Philip, on September 7, 1919. Her parents and Chi Pom and his family from Hawaii, came to live with the the Min side of the family at the farm. The extended family lived there for several years.

When my father completed his studies and received his degree in Divinity, Dr. Syngman Rhee asked Chan Ho to return to Hawaii with his family to become Minister of the first Korean Christian Church, which Syngman Rhee had formally begun in 1918. So, the Min family left California and arrived back in Hawaii in December, 1919. There my father became the Pastor of Rhee's, Korean Christian Church. My father was, also, the Principal of the Korean Christian Institute (KCI) established by Rhee, which was where some Korean children of the immigrants went to live, while their parents worked in sugar fields throughout Hawaii. My father, also, worked there to teach these Korean children. Because money was quite short, my mother, Mollie began to take in sewing which she continued for many years.

The first home that the family lived in Hawaii was in Kaimuki on Third Avenue. This house was rented and paid for by the Korean Christian Church. One reason for the subsidy was that my father's salary was only, about thirty dollars a month. He did not have enough money to pay the rent. A few years later, Mollie bought a house in Kaimuki on Sierra Drive, which was a good large house with many rooms. We lived there very comfortably. Since there was a large area of backyard of this house, my mother built another large two-story, four-bedroom, two-bathroom house at the cost of only, $5,000 dollars at the time. Somehow, she was able to borrow money from the mortgage department from the Bank of Hawaii because she knew the Head of the Bank of Hawaii Mortgage Department. He was willing to lend her money quite often. Actually, she was able to continue the mortgage payments as long as she was alive. Subsequently, she bought an even larger house in the front of Diamond Head that was called Crater Road, and it was quite a large house. We lived there for another few years. Then, she bought a house in Makiki on Anapuni Street, which property contained another house in the front of our house. There was a cottage in the back that was rented to tenants. Then, she bought another house up in Makiki Heights, a large, beautiful house, which again, she also, rented after we moved out, and she moved us back to Anapuni Street. There, she built a twelve-bedroom apartment, which was always filled with tenants.

All of this took considerable work and effort on her part. This made her quite tired, I'm sure. But, still she looked after the children's well-being. For example, when I went away to medical school in 1939 in Philadelphia, Jefferson Medical College in the State of Pennsylvia, she wrote to me and said that she would come out and look after me during my second year to make sure that I was studying well and not working too hard. She had heard that during my first year, I was working in a boarding house as a waiter to get free room and board and that made her unhappy. She brought my youngest brother, Andrew, along with her to visit me. They got on a bus in LA, I believe, and rode all the way across the country to New York City, where I met them. We stayed in the City for a few days. The New York World Fair was going on at that time, so we saw that, among other things, in the City. Then, we went back to Philadelphia just before school started. She found us a very nice apartment in West Philadelphia, and I was again, able to eat good Korean food with kimchi.

Within a few weeks after she arrived in Philadelphia, she went around the West Philadelphia area and found this little factory that was making ladies' hairpins of some sort. She went in to talk to the owner. At that moment they were having their daily afternoon prayer meeting, so she joined in and gave a long prayer. The owner was so impressed that he hired her right away and she worked there for the rest of the summer and led the prayer meetings every day during the weekdays.

At the end of the school year, my brother Paul had ordered a Plymouth car from a car dealer. We were supposed to pick it up in Detroit. So, we took a bus to Detroit and got the Plymouth and drove toward the West Coast, stopping at many places, including South Dakota to view the statues of the early Presidents at Mount Rushmore. We, also, drove down to Yellowstone Park and saw Old Faithful, and we continued on to Reno. Then, crossing the Sierra Nevada mountains with the snow on top, we got out of the car to make snowballs. Andrew and I threw balls at each other. And finally, we ended up in Los Angeles, where the car was shipped out. I saw both of them, Mother and Paul, get on a ship before I had to return to Philadelphia to continue my studies. I believe the ship was either the Lurline or the Matsonia.

I graduated from the Jefferson Medical College in 1942 and entered an internship for a year; then, I was drafted into the US Army as a Medical Officer. My first post was down in Charleston, South Carolina, in a large army hospital, and I was surprised to see my mother come to South Carolina to see me without advanced notice, again. This was in early 1943, when she came there. I wondered how she was able to get to the USA Continent from Hawaii. There were no airplanes for common citizens and no passenger ships, crossing the Pacific Ocean at that time because of the on-going World War II. Only military ships crossed the Pacific. However, my mother, Mollie was able to come to the United States Mainland because she was very focused on getting her goals, and for some reason, she wanted to look after me, again. So, she tried to join the WAC Army, (the Women's Army Corps). The WAC Administration Board in Hawaii interviewed her, and they said she was too old (she was 55 years old at that time). She created such a fuss when she was rejected that they, actually, reported her complain to authorities in Washington, D. C. The authorities sent for her and paid her way to Washington D.C. She traveled first by naval vessel, and then, cross the country by USA Air Force airplane, all paid by the military, I guess.

Mollie met the General of the WAC Army in Washington, D.C., and again, the General said she was too old. The WAC Army General – female, of course – had a long talk with her and personally, said again that she was too old. The General said that she wished that Mollie was younger, because she would have made a very good soldier, but that she really, is, too, old.

At that time after she was rejected, I received a telephone call at the hospital from my mother. I didn't know that she was in Washington, D.C. She said that she was on her way to Charleston by train to see me. So, I immediately, looked for a hotel room and met her when she came in. A day and a half later – she said she was there for a week. She came to the hospital and met all the other doctors there and the nurses. They all made her happy by saying how well I took care of the ill soldiers and so on, so then, she was happy to go on home. She was able to take a train to Los Angeles to see some friends of hers. After she was there for a week, I got a call from her good friend in Los Angeles, saying that my mother was in the hospital. I immediately, ask for a leave and I was able to catch a military flight to the West Coast. I found her in

Left to right, Mollie, Francesca, Syngman Rhee.

a small hospital there.

Apparently, as soon as she had reached LA, she developed urinary infection, and the doctor gave her sulfur pill, which she should be taking with large amounts of water. Apparently, he did not mention to take extra fluids, so the sulfur crystallized in her kidneys and went into a shutdown. When I got there she was receiving IV fluids, and fortunately, the kidneys opened up and she was discharged after that. So, I stayed with her for a few days and I had to fly back. She stayed with her friends in LA for a few more days and flew back home.

During the subsequent years she kept herself very busy with several projects, even though she was talking care of all her rental units and etc. I forgot to mention when my father passed away. My father, Rev. Chan Ho Min, died on February 5, 1954. My mother continued her volunteer work in Hawaii.

She was so active. I was amazed at all that she did: she was with the Pan-Pacific

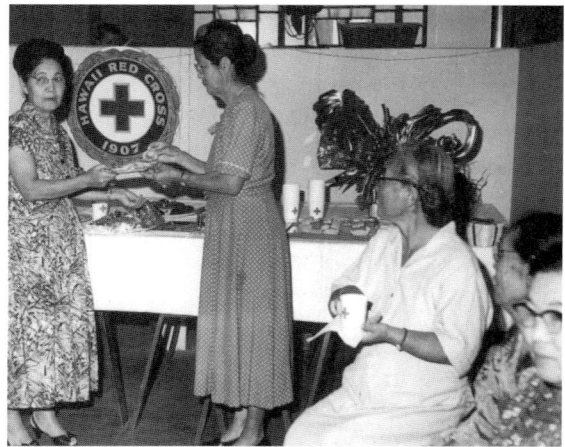

Mollie Min, receiving certificate award for work with the Red Cross, circa 1960.

Association, Southeast Asia Women's Association, YWCA, and the Red Cross. She was sent to Manila in 1954 to attend the Pan Pacific Conference. She was sent, also, to the 1955 World Brotherhood Conference in Belgium. She, also, went to the Southeast Asia Women's Association Conference in Australia in 1957.

In 1958, she wanted to see the whole world one final time, so she wrote to all the World Brotherhood Associations in all the Countries for which she'd kept addresses. She left by plane, first landing in Japan, where she was met by members of the World Brotherhood Conference, there. She stayed in one of their homes for about two weeks and saw a lot of Japan. Then, she went to India, where again, she was met by members there, and she stayed there another two weeks. She told me briefly, that she tried to visit Jerusalem and Egypt, but her flight was to land in Jordan at a major airport there, where she had much difficulty. When I learned of this difficulty, I wrote to my classmate, a Dr. Zukowsky, who was working as a doctor for a large oil company, flying all over for the company, from one oil well to another.

I wrote to him and said that my mother would be arriving in Jordan at a major airport and I was wondering if he could meet her and give her some assistance during that part of her travel. Later on, I found that somehow, he

Mollie Min with Senator Dan Inoyue and Red Cross workers, circa 1970.

contacted the major airlines and told them that Mollie Hong Min would be arriving one of these days and to let him know when. I learned that he was informed the exact time, when she was arriving and, he went to the airport and picked her up and took her to his home.

My mother told me that Dr. Zukowsky lived in a beautiful villa with several servants, and she was, really, treated very well. He helped her visit Jerusalem, which she had always wanted to see. Also, he helped her to go on to Egypt, where she met the World Brotherhood Organization there, and they helped her visit the pyramids, among other things. And I remember on one of those trips there's a picture of her riding a camel. She continued on through Europe, to France, Paris, London; finally, she returned to the United States and went directly, to California and Los Angeles, where again, she stayed with her good friends there, for several weeks; then, she returned home after three months of the round the world trip that none of us would ever dream of taking.

In May of 1963, she became an Honorary Board Member of the YWCA. She was, also, a volunteer worker for the Red Cross, since 1914 while she was on the Mainland. She, also, became a Gray Lady for the Tripler General Hospital for several years. In 1973 she received an Award of Merit from the Republic of Korea for her dedicated work in the Korean community and, also, for the huge amount of work and time that she spent during the Korean War to collect clothing to send to Korea. The last few years of her life was spent peacefully, at the Malady Hospital, when she became too feeble to do much walking and so on.

I know very, very little of the politics among Koreans here in Hawaii that went on in the community here. But, I know when my father was active in the school established by Dr. Rhee, there were some interesting stories that I heard. One of my very good friends, Dr. Timothy Wee, and many of the people of that generation, had parents who were working in the pineapple fields so they were put their children in this Korean Christian Institute (KCI), where my father was the Superintendent. I remember there was quite a large school building there. It had an upstairs floor- second floor; one half of the building was for boys and the other half was for girls.

They had a baseball team and the ladies formed an orchestra. Then some-how, my father, I don't know who arranged this, the boy's baseball team and the orchestra were invited to go to Korea and play against the baseball team in Korea. Well, Timothy was a, kind of a — well, I don't know, a horrent boy at his age. I think he was about 16-17 years old at that time. He was very playful and naughty at times, I guess, so my father actually, kicked him out of the KCI. But, he was the best player of the baseball team. So, when the team was invited to go to Korea to play at the Championship Games, my father asked Timothy to come back to the KCI school. Timothy did come back when he found out that the only reason they wanted him back was that they were going to Korea to play for the Baseball Championship game. So, they went to Korea, and they had a good time. The girls' orchestra went along, too. I remember Timothy, telling me some funny stories about that trip. I remember his story about Gertrude Lee's mother, cooking this huge five-gallon batch of jangjorim and making tons of rice. All they ate was rice and jangjorim! But they had a good time in Korea, they agreed on that.

In 1919, after Dr. Syngman Rhee asked Chan Ho to become the first Pastor of his new church, the Korean Christian Church, my father came to Hawaii. Also, my father became the Superintendent of the Korean Christian Institute. Two more Min children were born in Hawaii, Jesse on April 6, 1921 and Andrew on August 29, 1923. Both Mollie and Chan Ho taught Korean to the students at KCI. Simultaneously, Mollie became active in the Korean Women Society. Finding it difficult to raise a family of seven on a minister's salary, Mollie Min, took in sewing on the side to bring in extra money. She had high hopes for her children and worked hard to achieve their ambitions.

In 1929 or 1930 Chan Ho resigned from the Korean Christian Church. Mollie moved the family to Schofield Barracks, and they ran a laundry, catering to soldiers. The family lived there for six years. When as both of the older boys were attending the University of finally, the family moved back to Honolulu,. In Honolulu, she ran various enterprises, including a boarding house for university students, called the McDonald Hotel in 1939. The lived in the building, also. Finally, she converted that property in Punahou into rental apartment units and bought another property for their home.

On May 9th, 1963, she was elected to become an Honorary Board Member of the YWCA. Because Mollie Min dealt with the public so much, she was always dressed, immaculately, and always had an attractive appearance. From the time she signed up as a volunteer worker for the Red Cross in 1914, she continued to give her time year after year for the Red Cross and took every course offered except in life saving. She became a qualified surgical instructor and also served as a Gray Lady of the Tripler Hospital for several years. She was highly recognized for her 58 years of dedicated volunteer work for the American Red Cross.

Some of Mollie Min's dreams came true when the older boys graduated from college: Paul with an aeronautical engineering degree, and Thomas with a medical degree. World War II had ended the plans of Philip and Jesse, who had been attending the University of Hawaii. Philip preferred to marry early and become an appliance salesman and Jesse preferred to work for the Federal Government at Pearl Harbor. Andrew, also, went into federal work after graduating from high school.

In 1973 Mollie Min received the Award of Merit — I wished I had kept that large metal that they gave her, but we buried it with her when she passed away. It was a beautiful thing. It came from the Republic of Korea for her dedicated work in the Korean community. Mollie Min continued her very active daily, schedule of running the business of apartment rentals and do-ing volunteer work for the Red Cross on a weekly basis, until she as well over eighty years old. She regretfully gave up her volunteer work, when she became hard of hearing. Mollie Min's death on November 9, 1979 ended the era of a truly remarkable woman, devoted wife and mother. Her busy schedules never kept her from being a loving mother to her children. She was an aggressive, determined woman, and, like other women of her time, a devout Christian. Her capacity to help fellow men regardless of race was well-known and appreciated.

Q **What, specifically, was she awarded for by the Korean gov-ernment?**

A It's called: "Of Merit", something like that. Came on a huge metal. It looked like it was gold. I don't know if it's pure gold.

Q **Did your father visit Korea anytime he left in 1905?**

A No. My father left Korea in 1905, shortly, after my mother did, and he never did return to Korea, until shortly, before his death. He suffered a stroke and was unable to speak. My mother, knowing, that he would appreciate seeing his Country once more, did take him to Korea in the 1950's. Shortly after that visit, he went into Maluhia Nursing Home, where he died after three years.

My mother, when she was eighty, let's see, when she was about eighty-four, or five, it's hard to remember those things, she suddenly developed mental confusion, and in those days, there were no instruments like now. They couldn't scan and use MRI and what not, so neurologists could only say she probably had a multiple stroke… she was not paralyzed, but she had difficulty in speaking. Now, we can have better diagnosis of causes of mental confusion. She, also, went to Maluhia Nursing Home, and she was there for eight years, until she passed away.

Q **Did you once say that your father was in a ministry school with Dr. Syngman Rhee?**

A My father graduated from the same school with Rhee, so apparently, he was thinking about going into ministry, too. I remember the first time seeing Rhee, shortly, after my father came back to Hawaii in 1919. I've known Dr. Syngman Rhee personally, all my life,.

Q **Didn't he gave you a medal personally, at one time after World War II and he was the President of Korea at that time? What was that all about?**

A Not really a medal, but I did get something from him. When he was in Washington with Mrs. Rhee, they had what they called an Embassy, but that Korean Embassy wasn't recognized at that time, because there was no Korean government at that time. He stayed in that "embassy", and once, he drove up to New York or near somewhere I was. On the way, he stopped in Philadelphia to see me. Fortunately, once it was a Friday afternoon, so, he went into the Dean's Office at my University, and asked the Dean if he could take me down to Washington for the weekend. The Dean said, "Of course." So, I was called to the Dean's Office. There was Syngman Rhee.

We got into his car and he drove to Washington, and it was the most nervous drive I ever had. When he kept driving, he'd drive with one hand and he'd blow on the fingers on the other hand and, sometimes, he'd blow on two hands while still driving the car and it would go...I said, "Wait, wait, wait, don't do that." Then, finally, I asked him to let me drive, and finally, he did, thank goodness. I asked him, why do you blow your fingertips? He said that when he was in the Japanese prison, they used to torture him by placing burning bamboo sticks under his fingernails. I guess that was very painful and it probably damaged some nerves permanently. It was quite a habit with him. He just kept blowing there, from time to time, when he was driving and sometimes, he'd blow two hands at the same time.

Q **How old were you?**

A I was − let's see, I think I was a junior in medical school. I went to medical school a little younger than most of the others − I was, let's see, I was about 21 years old or so at that time. It must have been in the in the 30s. I remember that I was assigned to a general hospital down South and stopped in South Carolina. I wanted to go overseas so badly, especially, to the South Pacific because I understood that those of Korean ancestry who could speak Korean would eventually end up in Korea to help the troops. I thought, then, I could interpret for them and what not. So, I found that the only way to go in that direction was to attend Walter Reed where they had two-month courses in tropical diseases. The troops in the South Pacific were coming down with malaria and all these parasite diseases. No doctor in the United States or the Army knew anything about parasites and tropical diseases. They had this course at Walter Reed. So, finally, the General Hospital in which I was in, let me go to Walter Reed to take this course. I did spend two months, there. While we there, I looked up Dr. Rhee and they invited me to an "embassy" party. There was still not a real "embassy" but they were able to invite a lot of non top counsels. Rhee asked me to invite, and bring along several of my fellow officers. I did − a good party was going on, then.

Q **What about your father? You said he left the Korean Christian Church at that time. Was there anything about it?**

A   Well, the Korean Methodist Church was the only religion for the Koreans in Hawaii and Syngman Rhee decided to form a separate church which is now called the Korean Christian Church. My father was the first minister of that church. He was a minister for years there. I remember growing up as a little child, and we'd be driving from Kaimuki down to Rhee's church – the first church building was a small wooden building, and it got bigger, and finally, we have the present church now.

    When we drove to the church on Sundys, we would be driving a Model T, and four of the children would be singing Christian songs that my mother had taught us. Then, we would go to Sunday School, then, after Sunday School, all the other children would go home. We, Min children had to stay there for not only Sunday School, but for the whole sermon afterwards, which was a long deal for a Sunday, while all the other kids went home. My father preached there for a good many years up to the early 1930's.

Q   **Tell me a more details about what you know of your father's work at the Korean Christian Church.**

A   Well, apparently, my father was the first Korean Pastor for the Korean Christian Church because of Dr. Syngman Rhee's efforts to have him come back to Hawaii. And, he remained a pastor for many years. I remember, we were very young. Apparently, they had a good congregation for many years. Then, I think about ten years after Rhee began his church, it seemed to have split into two groups, as far as I know. There was – the other group – who was trying to bring Rev. Kingsley Lyu into the church. Things got pretty bad, I remember, right in Rhee's church. Once, the two groups sitting apart on both side of the aisle got into an argument, during church hours and got into a fist fight. Even the younger people of the Church. The police came and took a couple dozen of the young people that were brawling there to the police station. It was quite an embarrassing thing for the Church to happen there. So, when these things got to a point, my father decided to resign and then, he did resign, what year, I forgot.

    I believe he left the Honolulu Korean Christian Church, when we moved out to Wahiawa in 1932. It was at that time, because I entered Leilehua High School, when I was fifteen years old in the tenth grade. So, that must have been 1932.

Q   In Wahiawa could you tell us what your family did, what kind of work?

A   We stayed in Wahiawa Town just for a very short when my mother and father found that there was a laundry shop up for sale in the Schofield Barracks area, which they took over. To be close to our shop we moved to Castner Village, right on the edge of Schofield Barracks and did laundry for the military people there for the next several years. We lived and worked, there, and I recall it was very hard work. Even at my age of fifteen, I helped with the laundry and delivery of clothes to the Schofield Barracks and to the Officers' homes.

Finally, in 1938, we moved back to Honolulu. At that time my father was quite, elderly, and he retired from work, but my mother continued doing work chiefly as a landlady for various buildings that she owned and rented out.

Q   Do you remember attending any school, Korean school?

A   Yes, my father opened up a Korean school – a little school at a public school after the regular school hours. I believe it was an elementary school that he was able to rent it, and my mother taught Korean there, also. There were other teachers that taught Korean there, and quite a few young Korean boys went to that school. That was before 1932. I remember I was only about 10 years old when I went to that school for a couple of years. Then, after that, I forgot all my Korean until I began practicing medicine and met all these new immigrants from Korea, who knew no English at all, so I had to relearn Korean.

Q   You once told me you attended the Aliiolani School – when it was a Korean school.

A   No, the KCI at Aliiolani was a boarding place for all the immigrants' children who needed it, because the parents worked in the fields, the cane fields and pineapple fields. I did not stay there. Later on, when the school population grew smaller, then, the KCI was moved to someplace in Kalihi. The Public School Government took over the area and the Aliiolani School became an Elementary Public School, I remember, up to the sixth grade, yes.

Q **Then, after that boarding place 1 closed, what happened?**

A KCI moved to a smaller place in Kalihi because, as the early immigrants stopped working in the fields and built up their own businesses in town, they bought homes where the children could lived at home and went to public schools throughout Hawaii. So, the Korean Christian Institute became smaller and smaller and, finally closed. I don't know what date, but probably, not too long after they moved out from the Aliiolani area.

Q **Did you feel differently from the local people born here? After all, you were born on the mainland.**

A No, because I was just a little kid. I was born January 4, 1917, and I was only two years old, when I moved to Hawaii. I always felt that Hawaii was my home. The only difference probably I had, was that when my mother was being cared for during her second pregnancy with me, she thought so highly of her doctor − actually, he was not an obstetrician. They didn't have obstetricians during those days. They were all general practitioners who delivers babies. She liked him. His name was Dr. Sweet. I don't even know his first name. But, when I was born − she made my middle name, "Sweet", so, I was Thomas Sweet Min. That created a problem, when I was growing up in public schools in my second and third grade. When the teachers called on our names and they called my name, "Thomas Sweet Min", all the kids would shout "whooooo" and whistle, and so on. I used to get into fights sometimes because they were calling me sissy all the time. But, I think that was good for me in a way because it made me study harder than the other kids. I read more things because they didn't select me to join their baseball games and football games and things like that.

So, I had more time on my hands and on the way home, I stopped by the library and take home books. I read ten times more than any other kid in school and that was nice. So, I think that helped me, mentally, in a way, to be called a sissy.

Q **Who were your friends when you were in high school? Name some names.**

A   Well, there are a lot of names: Namyong Chung is still my good friend, we practically grew up together from that time on when my family moved to Wahiawa. He was living in Waialua at that time. We went to college together, and then, we went to the army at the same time. He is a Veterinarian.

Q **Did you experience any prejudice anywhere?**

A No, there was no prejudice at that time. Possibly, there was a little prejudice at Leilehua High School. It wasn't real prejudice. At that time, the Military did not have their own public schools, so, their children came to Leilehua School, a local school for Wahiawa. I remember about half a dozen Caucasian kids, boys and girls, attending our class. They were nice kids, and we tried to be nice to them, but sometimes, they − well, we never got very close to them like our own Oriental pals.

Q **Tell us about the organizations during that time, Korean organizations.**

A I don't remember any organization. There was a small Korean Christian Church that I attended every Sunday. I was even in the choir. I think the chief reason I was in the choir was that every Thursday night there was choir practice, and that was where we could meet girls and get dates. But, I don't remember any organizations. I was never knowledgeable about Korean organizations throughout my whole growing up period. Even when I got older, I did not know much about the Korean organizations. When I graduated from the University, I joined the Korea University Club, and that was the only Korean organization I ever belonged to.

Q **You don't know about Delta Frat?**

A I had some friends in Delta Frat, and frequently, I was invited to their meetings, and so on. But, I know very little about that society except that it was more of a social organization than the Korean University Club, which tried to be a little bit more educational.

Q **What are your general thoughts about Dr. Rhee?**

A I first knew Syngman Rhee when I as a little kid when we were living in the first house on Third Avenue shortly after we came from the mainland. I remember I was, I think, only about four years old and the Korean church, they came over and helped chop down some — I remember — two huge mango trees in the backyard. Someone climbed up and cut down these large branches and Syngman Rhee was there, helping to get rid of the log by pulling it out to the front of the house for the rubbish truck to pick them up. I remember he had this large log that turned on himself. I was running around him, and then, he suddenly tripped and the log fell on my leg and cracked a bone in my one leg. In those days, we didn't really go to the doctor's often, but apparently, a small bone, was cracked. I could walk around, but it was quite painful for about a month.

When we grew up, I lived up on Sierra Avenue. Syngman Rhee had a home way on top of Wilhelmina Rise. He had a Korean man living there with him who did the cooking and cleaning for him. He, frequently, asked my parents to send us boys up to his house on weekends to stay overnight with him. I remember being driven up to his place way up on Wilhelmina Rise, and having dinner with him. He had a large bed and the three of us would sleep in one bed. He would impress us because he had a rifle. It was not a shotgun and I was amazed looking at it. When I grew up, I tried to do the same thing, it was impossible. I think it was not a shotgun, but a shot bullet; he could actually, shoot birds, flying in the air with his bullet; that's an almost impossible thing to do. The bird would fall down and be dead.

The next time I met him was when I was in medical school. They had like an informal "embassy" in Washington D.C. with a nice beautiful home. Mrs. Rhee used to make Korean food and even kimchi, and once in a while, Syngman Rhee would drive back to D.C. after attending some conference in New York City. He would stop by my school. He would go to the Dean's Office. It usually, was on a Friday afternoon. He would tell them to have me come to the office because he wanted to take me down to Washington D.C. for the weekend. So, the dean would send his secretary to find me in some classroom. Then, she would take me to where Syngman Rhee was waiting for me. We'd get into his car and we'd drive back to Washington.

The other kids that I knew there − were good friends like Unsik Kang and Namyong Chung. We as children were never, closely, associated with most of the Korean organizations. We just knew they were separated and had different ideas. We, second generation, really didn't know too much about that. I was gone from Hawaii so many years. For one thing, I was gone to medical school, and then immediately, after that, I joined the army. In those days, when you left Hawaii to go to school, you didn't come back, until you finished school, so, I was gone four years. After I finish college, I started my internship in Pennsylvania, and when I finished my internship, I was drafted to the army and I was in the army three and a half years. So, I didn't get back home from the time I left, 1939 until 1946.

My name is Inez Baeksoon Kong Pai. I was born here in Hawaii, actually in Wahiawa on February 4, 1919.

My father was Kong, Chi Soon. He came from Yunan, Hwanghaedo in the years between 1903 and 1905, I'm not sure. He worked for a while, two or three years on the plantation on the Big Island. He took lessons while he was on the plantation on how to become a tailor. He had heard that the Military base at Schofield Barracks were hiring and employing people who could make uniforms for the soldiers, who were apparently, were preparing for the First World War. So, eventually he got a concession and moved to the island of Oahu. Finally, he got a tailoring concession at Schofield Barracks.

My mother came from Korea, during the same period as my father, but they did not know each other at that time. My mother was 27 years old when she came from Hongchun, Kangwon Do. She came as a widow, and through the help of missionaries, she came to Hawaii. From the very beginning, she didn't work on the plantation, but worked in the homes of well-known families at the plantation bosses' homes, where she learned how to cook all kinds of American foods.

My father was 34 years old, when he came. By the time he met and married my mother in 1925, she was 38 years old, and my father was 45 years old. A year later, my brother, John, was born, in 1916, and I came along in 1919.

My father even had a certificate called the "New York Cutting School", I remember the certificate he got. He sewed so well. This was, of course, prior

Chi Soon Kong, father; Sook Chin Ahn Kong, mother

to marrying my mother. My father even recalls that they had a tremendous earthquake sometime in 1923, when he would be going through all the plantations in the islands and taking orders for suits or clothing that he would bring home to sew. But by 1919 the Military decided to do away with all those tailoring concessions and all other concessions which were going on there inside the military base. What were they going to do? This was after I was born.

They gave up that tailoring concession and mom and dad bought a "Mom and Pop" grocery store on King Street in the city of Honolulu, which is where Aala Park is now. That's between Beretania and Liliha Streets in Chinatown. Of course, this is a very different place now. They had a big concession there. I must have been 2-3 years old. Mother and father thought that was not the best place to raise children. So, we got a farm. They decided to farm up here on Maunaloa Heights, where I'm presently living. The land I'm living on

Chi Soon Kong, circa 1905.

97

John and Inez Kong, circa 1923.

right now is the same land that my parents developed. We went through all kinds of things to make a living.

At first, they were going to make candy, I still remember: Yeut. They called that Yeut. They cooked this barley malt, and then, they make this candy and take it into town in the little four wheel cart and try to peddle candy. But it didn't make a living. I still remember how mother and father would pull the candy to make these nuggets of Yeut. They called that Yeut. If you go to Korea, they sell them on the streets. But mother and father didn't make money on that, too. So, they changed business so many times. The other thing was, they decided to become chicken farmers. So, the whole house was filled with egg mechanical hatchers downstairs. I still remember, turning on the electricity and trying to hatch the eggs, mechanically. Well, that was all right except that the problem was that the chicken would eat each other, they would pick on each other. The chicken didn't thrive so we tried making money on eggs. I ate so many eggs that we couldn't sell. So that didn't work out. It was a lot of work.

So, my mother thought—I don't know where ever she got the idea—of raising carnations to sell to the lei sellers on Maunkea Street at the Oahu Market place. I still remember such memories I am having now, since I'm starting to talk about it. They would bundle up in the carts after harvesting the flowers to

Inez Kong with Parents in 1919.

98

Sook Chin Ahn and Chi Soon Kong at their "Mom and Pop" grocery store in Chinatown, Honolulu, circa 1923.

sell, and at the same time we were cultivating around 50 acres, both sides of Wilhelmina Rise. Of course, now it's a different landscape. On the Ewa side of Wilhelmina Rise, I still remember we planted corn, watermelon – we had a lot of watermelon – and on the Kokohead side of Wilhlemina Rise, near where Kahala Heights is, we had carnation fields. Acres and acres of carnations. So, on the side, we raised tomatoes, cucumbers. Mother and father would pack my brother and me in this four wheel cart, and take us downtown with all the vegetables and flowers. They would wrap us up in a little bundle on the sidewalk, and they would go around selling their flowers. My father would drive and my mother would do the marketing. When we were all through with the wholesale houses to sell our cucumbers, tomatoes, corn, etc. in Chinatown, we would go to the Palama Market, where more recent immigrants lived. Now days, they call the area Palama Settlement.

At that time there was a whole settlement of Korean families living there at Palama Settlement. Many second generation Koreans remember that place even today. I still remember Subok Kim's, Kara Kim's parents living there. They had about 10 children in the family. My mother knew them well and so, it was her philosophy that if we sell all these vegetables, and we can't do anything with them, she would for 25 cents a bag, a paper bag, fill it up with tomatoes, and cucumbers and sell it for a very reasonable price to them. And then, we'd go back to Maunakea Street and do our marketing. One of the biggest treats in Chinatown, after the hard work, I remember, was when she would take us to the Chopsui house and order a bowl of rice and a bowl of soup, vegetable soup. We'd never ordered anything else.

As I said, I was born in February, 1919. It must be remembered that March 1, 1919 is a very historical day because tens of thousands of Koreans rose up on "March First" in Korea to declare the independence from Japan, and we who lived in Hawaii heard about it between that time and April. I was about two, three months old. In those days, there were no such things as cars or buses, so my father took my brother on his back and sometimes he walked a little bit, because he was only about three years old. And my mother carried me. Imagine, we walked all the way out from Wahiawa to Honolulu (18 miles apart) to participate in the mass meeting of Koreans that were held. I don't know if it was in the KNA building. I was, naturally, too young to know that. Don't know, but at that time there was a Korean National Association, very active in the work for Korean independence and eventually, the KNA split, I don't know details of the split, but my father was a supporter of Syngman Rhee. Eventually, I remembered the Korea National Association(KNA) building on Liliha Street very vividly. It was a tall, two story building with white trimming. They would have these meetings and I was present one time when the women, both of KNA and Dongji Hoi got mad at each other and started to beat each other up. That's the kind of remembrance I have of that occasion.

Yes, it was then, we were operating this carnation farm. Like my father, Syngman Rhee was also, born in Eun An Hwanghae Do in 1875. My father was five years older than Syngman Rhee. Syngman Rhee wanted the Koreans to get together and sort of form a community and do the work for Korean independence. This is as I know it and I saw it. The Korea Pacific Weekly Printing Press was brought up here. My mother and my father helped him set that up. My mother always took care of him. She was sort of a caregiver for Syngman Rhee, the times he spent here. I remember him very, vividly, because he would carry me on his back, and play with me, when I was growing up. He had a beautiful house. At that time, we just had a farmhouse, but his was beautiful, to my eyes. His home here was right below ours. We were neighbors so I was always running in and out of his house and he would call me, " Beksoona, Beksoona, 나 하고 놀자 come play with me." Really, so I grew up that way, very close. He worked very hard to establish the Korean Christian Institute in Kalihi, and also, establish the Korean Christian Church on School Street, that wooden building. I still remember Syngman Rhee very fondly. He was sort of like another father to me. I don't know any of the details of the differences he had with the community then. Eventually, I found out by studying the story and history.

I remember very vividly, when the Korean National Association was near Liliha Street. I remember the building because it was as I can picture it, two stories. It had a central stairway going up to the second floor. There must have been a basement downstairs, but it had a long hallway. I remember that this was at the time when KNA was breaking up because Syngman Rhee wanted his own way. He had his own political philosophy, or personal, political drive for power, or whatever it was, he decided to break away. What I recall, I still remember is, he felt the Koreans should not be under any kind of a mission board which belonged to the Methodist Mission. He wanted to be independent. The person I remember who was his sort of his enemy was a man by the name of Reverend Fry, and I remember Fry because well, it's a name you remember, Fry.

My father and my mother were very close to him, as a matter of fact, I practically, lived at the Korean Christian Church, which Syngman Rhee, eventually founded on School Street. It was a wooden building on sort of a marshland place. I remember going to Sunday school, teaching Sunday School, later, going to Wednesday prayer meetings. Imagine living way out here in the mountains of Kaimuki. We'd go to prayer meetings on Wednesday nights, then, Friday night, we had choir, cause I sang in the choir. I also at times played the piano as a substitute pianist. I was very active in the Christian Endeavor. I became President. I think I surprised a lot of people because I was so active.

In Public School, when I was in the eight grade, I surprised everybody by

New Prexy

New Student President Gives Aloha Message

Dear Students:
I take great pleasure in writing a few words of "Aloha" and thanks to the Liliuokalani student body and faculty for electing me as your president next year.
All I ask is the united support of you students next year and I am sure that with your cooperation the prospects for the Liliuokalani Junior High School 1932-33 will be bright. Pai Soon Kong.

To Coast Camp

Inez Pacsoon Kong sails on the Lurline Saturday as one of the two delegates representing the McKinley High School Girl Reserves to Asilomar, Cal., for the national Girl Reserves conference, June 29 to July 6. She was reelected recently to serve a second term as president of the McKinley High School Girl Reserves club and is the first Korean girl to represent the McKinley high club. Clara Leong is this other delegate.

Inez Kong becomes President of Liliuokalani School.

winning the Territorial Oratorical Contest. And the following year, I became Student Body President. When I think about it, I just can't believe I was so active. I remember I served at McKinley High School in what we called the Girl Reserve. I was the only one who served two years in a row, President of the Girls' Reserve. I remember being Chairman of the McKinley Carnival Festival that collected enough funds to build that swimming pool. That swimming pool, gosh, I can't believe it. We were so young and yet, worked hard and didn't sleep for three or four days. Just didn't sleep, we worked so hard on the carnival. I can't believe I ran a carnival. Eventually, I became brave enough to run a lot of things like, when the Korean War broke out, the bazaars and the relief drives, oh, we made thousands and thousands of dollars. We made Daegu and Kimchi to sell. At one point, I think we sent 13 thousand dollars to Korean charities in Korea.

Anyway, I graduated from McKinley High School and I went to the University of Hawaii for a short while, and then, I went off to the USA Mainland. And I went to Los Angeles City College, got involved with Korean

Inez Kong wins oratorical award.

ORATOR

Pae Soon Kong, who will represent Liliuokalani Junior high school
at the prohibition oratorical contest
to take place at Mission memorial
hall Monday night. She will speak
on "Prohibition — Its Observance
and Enforcement."

affairs. Oh, in the meantime, the most fantastic, the most fantastic thing in my life, actually, a turning point, was my what my mother died in 1935. In 1935, I was a junior at McKinley High School, the largest Public High School in Hawaii. At that time, I had my eye on running for the Student Body Vice President. But my mother said, – I really had an extraordinary mother, – I mean her life is a story on her own. Anyway, she said, "I don't want my children to grow up being nothing, not realizing their Korean heritage." So, she went to McKinley High School to talk to the Principal in May of 1935. School normally ended in June, but she told the principle that she was taking me and my brother to Korea before school ended. We were going through Japan, to travel in Asia. She said, "I want my kids to know who they are." I guess in today's words, she meant that she wanted us to realize our identity. She said in Korean, "You must know who you are; if you don't you are nothing." [여기서 기르면 아무것도 안돼], "You are not a person" [사람 안돼].

So, the most dramatic period of my life, there I was, in 1935, 16 years old, going to t Korea. We went by ship on the President Coolidge, I still remember. I still have pictures of that experience, too. I do. We went to Yokohama, and then, we went to Kobe. We got off at Kobe. My mother wanted us to see Nara, Kyoto, so we saw all those beautiful temples; I still remember how awesome it was, how beautiful Japan was in those days. Then, we went on to Shimonoseki, and we took a ferry, an overnight ferry to Korea. It was a fantastic experience. We didn't fly. Everything was by train and this was in 1935, at the height of Japan's expansion. Japan had already gobbled up Manchuria in 1931, and she was very active in the Korean Independence Movement in North China. So, we were considered like spies, you know, and we were followed all around in Japan and in Korea.

Then, imagine, getting into Busan! I've always compared that scene of the difference, of a beautiful, modern Japan. I had been in Yokohama, but I hadn't seen Tokyo. I saw Kyoto and Nara, all those beautiful places. And to land in Busan! to see the beggars on the street. I had never seen scenes like those in Busan. You would see poor people begging and in rags. You would see people who were beggars, but didn't have their minds, who were obviously insane, mentally very ill, dragging themselves around. I never forgot a woman who was in rags; the dress she was wearing was bloody. She probably, was menstruating or something like that, but nobody was caring for her and she was lying around like that. Huh! Can you imagine a 16 year old girl – me – seeing all that...

The trip to Korea was a turning point in my life. I was young and very impressionable, most struck by the way the Koreans were at the time, being oppressed by the Japanese. I saw so much starvation and hardships on the part of Koreans, and they lost of their freedom. So, I decided then, that my life's work would be to work for the independence of Korea. I'll do everything in my power to help in trying to work for the independence of Korea. It was something like a fantasy, because this was 1935 when Japan was at the height of her powers. So, it was a dream to do something. I decided to pursue the dream.

We returned to Hawaii in September. We came home late so that my school year had started, badly. I couldn't run for Student Body President election. However, somehow, I ended up Vice-president of the Senior Class. After McKinley, I went to Los Angels City College, and it was at Los Angels City College, when Pearl Harbor was struck. That's when I wrote to Syngman

Rhee, who was the Director of the Korean Commission in Washington. I still have his letter. I had been thinking of going to Berkeley, to matriculate at Berkeley University, but instead, Pearl Harbor was bombed and that changed my decision. Imagine being happy about Pearl Harbor. I knew that because of the attack, this is the beginning of Korea's Independence.

So, I went off to Washington, D.C. There, I worked for Dr. Rhee as his "gofer" (assistant secretary). At the same time, I registered to go to George Washington University. I was going to school, but after hours, I was doing all sorts of political things. Also, because of my speech making abilities, I went around to various colleges, making speeches. I have pictures of myself at Bucknell University, and that's the only one I remember, but where anyone spoke about Koreans, I was there to speak up for Korea's independence, and eventually, I ended up getting very much involved in the Korean Independence Movement.

At the same time, I got to know all these Korean leaders who were sent from the Koreans in the different Korean organizations on the Continental United States and Hawaii. Such people as

The Trip to Korea 1935, Inez, mother, John.

Jacob Dunn, I got to know Jacob quite well, and there was another man who worked for Syngman Rhee, who became Minister of Transportation, later, in Syngman Rhee's Government, when he became President. The other big man I knew was Warren Kim, who was very informed and knowledgeable of Korean affairs. There were only a handful of us Koreans in Washington D.C. at that time. My husband Edward Eui Whan Pai was in the USA Office of Censorship then. That's where, at that point, I began to break with Syngman Rhee. I was studying, majoring in Poly-Science, and I must have been a really kind of headstrong person because I didn't agree with Rhee. My personal experience with Syngman Rhee is really another dramatic story because he told me, "I don't want you to associate with those people." They were the people I just mentioned, previously.

He, also, mentioned, Kil Su Han. Kil Su Han was a very nice person. You must remember that I was, only, 23, 22 years old in 1941 or 1942. These men were in their 40s and 50s, so, I was sort of like a kid. And Rhee again tells me, "Don't associate with those people, they're Communists and traitors"... and so forth. I have to tell you this story because very few people know this, you know. So, Rhee really said: "I don't want you to be associating with them." I don't know if I should be saying this, but, I have to tell the truth.

At that time, when the war was going on, he wrote a letter to my mother, saying that, "Inez is associating with very undesirable people, infact, they're Communists." He was talking about Warren Kim and Jacob Dunn, and Kil Su Han. In my situation, no way are they Communists, traitors. They were working for the same thing, Korea's iIndependence. It was my personal conscience that rose and rebelled. But, the point that got me so angry was that he would tell my mother, write a letter to my mother, saying I was associating with undesirable people such as them. So in my impulsive anger, I called Dr. Rhee...here I was in Washington, going in and out of his office everyday... there were other incidents which turned me against him and I really turned.

On top of that, my husband, Edward Eui Won Pai was working for the USA Intelligence Censorship. He was reading all of Rhee's letters. Ed was in censorship of all foreigners' communications. Ed was a great follower of Syngman Rhee, until he found out all the terrible things he was telling the Korean people, you know, in the United States. Also, lying to the Korean Provisional Government in Chungking at the time when Kim, Ku and Kim,

Kyu Shik were there...

So, when Syngman Rhee said that I shouldn't associate with people like them, I thought to myself, no that's not true. They're not Communists. I know something about Communism because that was my subject in college. So, we all kept associating with each other because there was only one Chinese restaurant where all Koreans go. It's called Wings Café. It's famous, famous, because all the Koreans would go there. So, we'd all eat together. We all became friends.

So, one day, I don't know whose idea it was, the KNA people selected me as the courier. This was in December 1942. Also, I had applied to become a member of the troop of Korean women who were being recruited to go to Kook Min Hur. Right after the war, they didn't have the WAC (Women in the Military Corp) as we do now, and they didn't have the WAV (Women in the Navy), but they were picking Asian women, Chinese or Korean, not Japanese, to go to Kook Min Hur to man the office from which, at that time, that famous General Stillwell was flying over the Burma Road. Oh, that was so exciting. So, I applied with the help of the people whom I got to know on the American side, who were the "Flying Tigers". They were in and out of Washington and I met them. We socialized a bit and I said I wanted to register. One of the men's name was, as I recall now, John Davis. He was very well known in those days.

Anyway, I applied with the goal that I would be one of their recruitment of nine women. Of course, I had to go through a security check. In the meantime, they sent me to Canada, Monte Blanc, where the powers of the war were. The allied powers were getting together in Monte Dome. I carried a petition, because they were going to discuss Korean trusteeship. The KNA was against it, Syngman Rhee was against it. It was the KNA who sent me to protest it with the recommendation of a bunch of my friends: Kil Soo Han, Jacob Dunn, and Warren Kim who submitted my name to the KNA. I think Kil Soo had a lot more to do with that.

Anyway, they sent me up there. It was winter, December. There was snow all over from Montreal up to Monte Blanc. It was one of the most exclusive ski resorts, largest on that side of the world. So, I still remember going on the Tunable, I call it the Tunable train, the little rickety train that went to the lodge. When I got there, I was like an intruder. Who is this person? This is a kid. So, one group wanted to send me right back, but they can't send me back. The train wasn't going back right away, they had to keep me there. And the other one said, "Well, just let her stay. And she can go back when the train comes back. In time, she could go back."

I never forgot, my defender. He was very famous: Admiral Yarnell. He was the Head of the Navy, during the war. He came to my defense and said, "We can't personally blame her." Even though I stayed, I was not allowed to attend any of the sessions. I had to sign a letter saying that I was just there to perform…I think I still have that letter. So, all these body of men got together, and they allowed me to stay there. They sent me back the next day. So, when I went back, which was around early December, I had to report to all these Koreans who had sent me to Canada.

I still remember, Ed Pai was sitting there. When I first met Ed Pai, we had gotten into a verbal quarrel. It was in the late summer of 1942, when I first met Edward Eui Whan Pai. He had come to Washington to work in the USA Office of Censorship. Previous to that, he had come when the war broke out. This was in 1942. Only 4 months earlier, he had been working in New Hampshire, Manchester in a brokerage firm. When the war broke out, he came down to Boston to join the army because he felt this was a wonderful opportunity to participate in the Korean Independence. And when they found out that he could read, write, and talk in Japanese, they were amazed, pleasantly, amazed. They didn't recruit him into the army. They said they needed him much more, urgently, as an interpreter. So, they sent him out to Missoula, Montana, straight from Boston.

Edward Pai was from Kimhae, Korea. He was born in 1904 and had come to America under the sponsorship of George McCune's father. Incidentally, McCune's family is so well known in Korean missionary history. Edward Pai came back to America because although he had finished his studies at the Pusan Commercial College, he knew he didn't have a future in Korea under the Japanese. He wanted to return to America, I'm not sure when. Maybe it was in 1925 or 1927. And he went to the University of Dubuque. Also, he finished his studies at the New York University. He got his B.A. from Dubuque, and got his M.A. in international finance at NYU. He graduated at New York University in 1937. He was going to go to Shanghai and open up a shoe factory with a friend who is very, very famous now. He happens to be the founder of McCann Shoe Store. Two young fellows, imagine Tom McCann and he would go out to Shanghai. Can you see these two young fellows, 1937, going to a foreign country not knowing what was going to happen in September 1937? Shanghai was bombed, you see. They couldn't go to China. So, they decided to stay home.

Anyway, Ed Pai somehow got into stock brokerage work in 1937. This was in Manchester, New Hampshire. He was working there, and then, eventually, in 1941, the war broke out and Ed came out to his new life which I have already explained. Anyway, when he was in censorship, he began to read all those letters that Syngman Rhee was writing and was receiving from Chungking. Ed became very disillusioned with Syngman Rhee. One of the things was, Rhee was writing letters to the Koreans in the US, saying that the Korea Provisional Government is going to get recognized. This was something that was going on between Syngman Rhee with Cordell Hull, who was the Secretary of State at that time. Of course, the significant part of Cordell Hull's letter back to Syngman Rhee was that the USA cannot and will not recognize the Korean Provisional Government, without the consent of the people who were being governed. We cannot have a government outside the country which had not ruled the country be recognized as the legitimate government. However, Syungman Rhee was writing letters on the contrary. (The contrary information given to the Korean community by Rhee had a political impact on strategy plans.) Ed Pai realized that he was lying to the Korean people and all the time collecting money from them. He needed money and so forth.

Meanwhile, Ed and I had nothing to do with each other at that time. As a matter of fact, the first time we met in late summer of 1942, he thought I was some sassy Korean woman, Korean girl who thinks she knows so much. That was his impression of me. And I thought he was just a stuffy, fuddy-duddy, because he said to me, you need to just continue going to school little more so that you can grow up a little more. I took great offense and we never spoke to each other for some time. But, we always saw each other at the restaurant because we always ate Asian food at the Wing Café. Anyway, Edward broke away from Rhee. He had admired and respected, and almost worshipped Syngman Rhee before he broke away from him.

I broke away from Syngman Rhee in his office with that quarrel I had with him. I told him, "You should not get angry with me, they're not Communists." Actually, you don't argue like that with Syngman Rhee. However, when he wrote to my mother and said I was associating with that kind of people, I got so angry. I called him up on the phone and I said, "I know in your eyes I am doing things that you don't agree with, but why do you have to call my mother? Why do you have to call my mother and complain to her that I am not behaving myself according to the way you want? I think that's a terrible thing for you to do." That was the kind of thing that broke me away from Syngman Rhee. Of course, he regarded me as just one of the traitors, Communists. That's where the break began. However, I had another very dramatic encounter and break with him.

Rhee was very anti-Communist. That was because he had by that time married Francesca. She's Austrian. They had both traveled, and now, I realize why he became so anti-Communist. I didn't realize it at that time. He saw Russia when it was really, really in a very bad situation in 1935. He went to Geneva, also, in 1935. It was there where he met Francesca. He came back so anti-Communist.

Of course, he was a very religious person and Confucian at heart. He used his powers in a very classical Confucian way…in a bad way. The negative side of Confucianism is that there is no real democracy. You have to accept, obey, respect your father; you have to obey and respect your state; all these five principles of Confucianism. He literally, believed it. If he is the sovereign or the father of the house, he expects to be listened to, and if you are not listened to, it is not idealistic at all. If you don't obey him, then, you're persona non grata. That was his way of doing things. That was the reason for his eventual downfall. When I took the newspaper clipping about this Yeon Ahn incident to Rhee, I think the Communist were already there in China. I said to him that this article is about the KOPOGO President Kim (Kim, Ku) leader of the Koreans. He said this doesn't mean anything and he threw it out, I mean he threw it away! In my simple mind, I thought well a Korean is a Korean. Kim, Ku is fighting for Korean Independence right?

I wasn't Communist, but I, certainly, was "leftist." So we broke up over that. When we were in Korea, I was always afraid that when Syngman Rhee comes to power, we have to leave Korea. We're not going to stay. I was in the United Nations Commission. That's another story because I was teaching at school when I got to Korea. I was teaching school at Seoul National, also, at the Women's Medical College, Sudo Medical College. The Americans were so admired by the Koreans, so admired. Eventually, that feeling was changing after Syngman Rhee got elected.

Rhee wasn't doing very much for the people, and he was doing some policies that was going so badly. For instance,…I could give many examples,… such as, anybody who opposed him in someway, he, himself, personally, did not give that person the downfall, but he had them somehow… We knew, personally, knew people, who were very powerful in the political parties, who were eliminated by a third person. Certainly, a supporter of Rhee eliminated them, and he (the person who carried his wishes) didn't get punished. Kim Ku's assassinator was allowed to live. His name was Ahn, I think. We all think that he was killed because…what Syngman Rhee does…his modus operandi was that he never goes out to kill them himself, but his says, "Uum, Ah…"that guy, that guy "저런저런" like that. That was enough. And the people who just adored him went out and found ways to get rid of that person.

It was that year 1942 December which was such a momentous month. I can remember it so vividly because that's when Hitler and the German Army were turned back. They called the place at the time, Stalingrad, now, it's called Leningrad, and now, it's St. Petersburg. That was the turning point of the war and that's December 12, 1942. I had just came back from Canada. In other words, we had already had the Midway Battle, May, 1942. We had reached a turning point in the Pacific War. The European War had a turning point in the December of 1942. You see, I lived those days from day to day. We lived in a time that we couldn't have butter…we couldn't have meat, we used to wear silk stocking, but no silk stockings. You know, we went through the war and through the deprivation and rationed things. Anyway, that was the turning point.

We had this dinner, and there was Ed Pai, sitting there, watching me. I don't know what thoughts went through his mind. It was a few days after when he asked me for a date. I was so excited because he was one of the Korean men that I have met who was appealing, although I had this big argument with him. He seemed serious, and he, also, was nice looking. He was a gentlemen, really, a gentleman, not like some of these guys you date. They just want to proposition you, as most of the Korean men that I met,

Edward Eui Whan Pai and Inez married in Washington, D.D., circa 1941

people like... They were, too, old or I wasn't interested in them in any other way than working together in this Independence Movement, or whatever. Ed Pai was someone that I found rather attractive. So, he called me and we dated. I was living at the International House Dormitory on New Hampshire Avenue. Boy, we really got interested in each other. We were seeing each other for dinner at the Wing Café, practically, every evening. Then, he'd come home to the International House, and we'd play ping pong down in the base-ment. Eventually, he got so tried that he said, "I think you'd have to marry me."

In the meantime, I told you I had applied to go to "Kookmin." The first thing, when I came to Washington, was to apply to Kookmin. That was also when Philip Ahn's sister, Ahn Chang Ho's daughter was in Washington. This was after I was married. She went into "The Waves", the women's navy. Anyway, the permit came through and I was checked for security. There was another crazy thing I was doing. I was going to Maryland every week to fly, you know, an airplane. I had started flying, taking lessons on the Piper-cup. They called it the Piper-cup...small airplanes. I also, had been taking lessons in dueling, nine hours a week.

Since I was going to Kookmin, I wanted to learn how to fly. Oh, I was crazy. Anyway, I used to go down there. Ed just couldn't figure me out, too. The approval to go to "Kookmin" came through. So in the meantime, I was dating Ed. He took me on Christmas Eve to this most fashionable restaurant in Washington, the Balalaika. I never forget it. I never tasted such things as frog legs earlier. It's delicious. I had a bottle of wine and all that. He treated

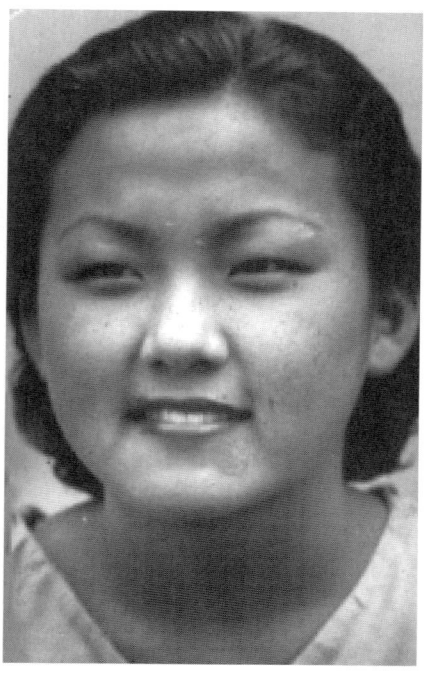

John Kong, only sibling of Inez, was an active counselor for her.

Inez Kong (Pai), accomplished writer, poet, and orator, circa 1940.

me like a queen trying to sweep me off my feet or something. Anyway, I liked him. It wasn't no long before I felt that I really fell in love with him. Anyway, this "Kookmin" approval thing comes through in February. So, I went to him and asked him, "What do you think?" He said, "Well, that's a decision you'll have to make. I think that you're going to be graduating in a short while. You should maybe get your degree first, but I want you to make that decision all on your own. Don't expect me to advise you." He didn't ever say he'd love me or anything. However, we were attracted to each other, right? Whew, I had to go through such connections on account of that.

At that time, the telephone line connections were made with Hawaii. I called up Honolulu and talked with my brother and I talked with my mother. My brother was just furious. Not really furious, but he could figure me out. He said, "What are you doing with yourself? When are you graduating?" I said, "Well, I'm due to graduate in June (1943), and he says, "Okay, if you really want to go, why don't you at least finish your degree?" That seemed reasonable enough. I didn't know what was going to happen. It was very exciting because I had been selected. I have all the newspaper clippings too.

My life went on so many different ways. I've done so many different crazy things since the time I was in Los Angeles just before going to Washington, D. C. Not crazy really, but when I think about it, in 1938 I went to represent LACC (Los Angeles City College) to the National Youth Congress in Washington D.C. Five of us from UCLA (University of California, Los Angeles) in Pomona, and others from USC, and LACC. I represented Los Angeles City College. They selected me as a delegate. Professors got together and they asked me if I would go and I said, "Sure". So, we took a trailer and went to Washington D.C. with a car and a trailer. I have all those pictures. In 1939, I was selected by LACC to represent LACC at the Japanese-American Youth Conference in Tokyo. We had to have the approval of the committee in Japan. They turned me down. They said it was because I was not an "Occidental American." That was the reason they gave, but I think it was when they found out I'm from a Korean background. So, I couldn't go, but I have, also, newspaper articles on that. That's what happened that let me go to Washington, D. C.

Interview with Agnes Pahk Kwon
husband **Manuel Kwon**

My name is Agnes Pahk Kwon. I was asked by Roberta Chang to bring back some of my memories of childhood and my life before and after I got married.

My father's name was Park, Duk Soon and my mother's name was Martha Han. I was born in 1913. I come from a family of mostly girls; there were twelve in our family, but the number of surviving children was eight girls and one boy. I'm second to the last. We lived our early years in Ewa Plantation and my father was one of the first whole families who came to Hawaii with three children. This means that the first three children were born in Korea.

When we lived in Ewa, my father was not like the laborers in the sugar fields because he was put in charge of cooking for the laborers in the fields. He was given a "Gok Sang" (kitchen), like a restaurant where he provided meals for the single men workers, when the workers came home from work.

My father knew how to cook for a large number of people because

Duk Soon and Martha Pahk, cirea 1920.
Greta Kwon Uyeki Aibum.

Duk Soon and Martha Hahn Pahk family. Left to right: Wallace, Duk Soon, Annie, Agnes (sitting), Nora, Rose, Hazel, Martha, and Stella, circa 1918.

when he was in Korea some missionary families instructed him on how to cook for a large number of people. The single men did not live in houses which have kitchens.

So, when I was a child, we spend much of time – our leisure time – helping in the preparation of vegetables like stringing the beans and cleaning the onions, stuff like that, which we enjoyed doing very much. My father and mother got up about three o'clock in the morning to prepare food for the men's lunch pails to take to work. My memory is not too good about the early days, but at the time of First World War, I was old enough to know that there was great need for food. Because my father was trained in the business of providing food, he had a whole room full of food goods, such as rice, stacked full to the ceiling. Because he had this Christian background, he really helped a lot of Koreans in those times of need.

I know that during the time when he was the cook, we were very busy. I believe he must been paid either by the plantation to do this work. I'm not sure. But, then, we didn't have a real need for food, you know. We were such a minority. We Koreans clung together. We had a church, a Korean church. The first Korean minister was Mr. Won Myung Chung. He was Willa Chung's husband. He was really not an ordained minister, but he was like a leader, and we all went to Sunday School under his instructions. We went to church, and we had Korean classes after public school. Because of this closeness with each other, we developed a great friendship among us Koreans.

It continued that way even after we left Ewa Plantation because of this Korean Methodist Church. It was not just a Methodist Church. It was a Korean Church. When we moved to Honolulu, I recall, very happy days because as children, we didn't see the things happening in the world, but I have very happy memories in Ewa.

The sad thing was that my mother died when I was five years old. My father continued to take care of the kitchen with the help of my older sisters. I was still very young, when my sisters were already teenagers. My oldest sister, Louisa, married Shi Dae Han,. They moved to California. I hardly saw her because she moved away before I was a year old. My second oldest sister, Lily, became the wife of Tai Sung Lee, who was a youth worker at the YMCA. He was very close to the Korean people.

My third sister is Nora Pahk Chai, who was one of the leading nurses at the Queen's Hospital. She was first Korean to become the Supervisor of nurses at that hospital for many years. These three sisters have all died. My next sister who is surviving today is Rose, the first in the family to marry a Caucasian. She's living in San Francisco with her children. And my other sister, Alice, who is living in Hawaii is the widow of Hyun Woo Lee, who was a chemist with the Hawaiian Sugar Plantation Company.

My sister Hazel is next; she is married to Rev. Euicho Chung, Pastor of the Methodist Church at Fort Church. They had an interesting life because they went to Hilo, and then, in the later years, they established the Good Will Industry in Hawaii. Hazel and Euicho went to the Mainland to head the San Francisco Good Will Association there first, before they established a branch in Hawaii. (The Chungs' life story is told by Hazel separately.)

My brother, Wallace, is the only brother I have. After my parents died, Wallace was sent to Los Angeles to be with my older sister's family because he was still very young. But he came back to Hawaii to live in Hilo because he was appointed as Manager of a hotel in Hilo. There he met Pearl Choi, whom he married, and they have, I think about, four girls and one boy.

Because we lost our parents when we were very young, my youngest sister, Stella, was sent to our older sisters' families. Stella didn't have any chance for further education. She lost her husband about ten years ago. Her name is

Stella Baptist.

Q **Your brother-in-law, Tai Sung Lee, is in our Hawaii history profiles. He was really an outstanding Korean community figure. Could you tell us what you remember about him?**

A Because we were such a minority, the Koreans clung together. Tai Sung Lee, who was, at that time, a YMCA worker, was very concerned about Koreans. And so, he organized little groups of students and tried to help those who didn't have a job.

Because we were very close and we had no welfare or anything, I was one of those who was sent to live with my sister, Lily and Tai Sung Lee. They happened to have a daughter about my age whose name was Daisy Lee. Daisy is right now living in California. She used to be the organist for the church. She was a very talented pianist. I forget when Tai Sung died, but after he died, there was a continuation of his work by Donald Yong Gak Kang. Donald took over the work that they began together.

Q **Tell us about what you remember about Donald Kang.**

A He was a teacher. And he was very active with the student movement, too. I believe it was during his time that Donald put out a school annual for Korean high school students. My graduation from the School of Nursing in 1934 is in that book. We had this annual of all the graduates of Korean ancestry for several years. The annual kept us closely connected to each other.

Q **What did your mother die of and when?**

A I think she died of cancer. She died when I was about five years old in 1919. That's what my older sister said, that she died of cancer. So, it was my father who really raised the younger children.

Q **Your father became ill when you were about thirteen. How old was he by then?**

A He was about sixty-five, I think in 1923. He had some gall bladder trouble. In those days, all people thought that once you went to the hospital, you're dead. So, he'd to go to a doctor, but he never wanted to go to the hospital. Through the grape vine, he found out that if you went to a masseuse, you would do better and would recover. But then, his gall bladder erupted at the masseuse, and following that, he died a few days later. At that time, my sister, Nora was in training at Queens, and she was very angry because our father listened to the other women who directed him to go to the masseuse, instead, of going to the hospital to be treated.

Anyway, he died, and so, that's why we younger children were sent to different homes among our sisters to be taken care of. I went to my sister, Lily. My sister Hazel was already kind of engaged and Alice was kind of engaged. My sister, Stella, the youngest in the family lived with my sister, Rose. So, this is how we all stayed connected as a family.

When my father was living, I was still in high school and was living with Lily, the older sister with whom I was very close. I went to McKinley High School, but she was at Roosevelt High School. When my father died, I was there and saw everything, and I made up my mind at that time that I would be never ignorant about sickness again. I wanted to know why he died. So, at that time, I volunteered to be a nurse like my sister, Lily. I wanted to know about the ideal

Burial Palace of Duk Soon Pahk and wife Martha Pahk, attended by noted persons in the Korean Community.

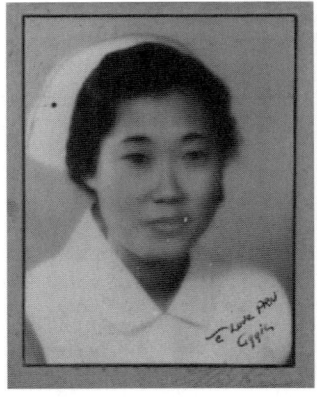 

Agnes Pahk graduation photograph, 1934.
Katherine Kwon, Manuel Kwon's sister-in-law.

health methods. It was from then, that I was health minded. Because we didn't have money, at that time and I was too young to be a nurse, I stayed out of school for one year after graduating from high school.

However, I was not behind in school level because I had skipped two grades in elementary school pushing me on a higher grade level – and that's another part of my history. My sister, Nora, was a teacher. I was living with her at that time, so I could see how she taught her classes. There were two grade classes in one room. So, if I were in the first grade, I would be listening to what was happening in the second grade. When the time came for promotion, they skipped me to the third grade, so I missed second grade. I think that happened to me at the fifth grade, again. So, I skipped two grades. Having graduated within a short time, I was too young to go to the Nursing School. So, I had to stay out another year to become qualified to go to Queens Hospital. The school age for entrance was age 18 and it was cut off in September. Since I was born in November, I was not not yet eighteen for entrance, I had to wait. Finally, when I graduated from Queens, I was still very young, not even twenty-one. I was always the youngest, also, the smallest in stature of the students in the class. I always had this complex that I had to be better because I was so small. I studied harder to be equal with everybody else. I felt much of these pressures because of these feeling, and partly, because of my feeling of wanting to be my own boss.

Before I graduated from Queen's Hospital, I met Manuel Kwon

Manuel Kwon, second from right, visited Korea to meet his parental extended family. Kwon is part Spanish, circa 1929.

on a blind date, not really blind date because he was at the University and he called the school of nurses' home. I didn't know who this fresh guy was. He called and wanted to talk to anybody, and I happened to be on the phone. He asked me to go to a certain dance party, whatever it was. He said that he was a Maui boy. I told the other girls in my school of nursing class that he called for a date and they said, "Go with him. He is really nice guy and he's smart." So, this is how we met, my future husband, on this blind date. Ever since then, it's been history.

We got married. Before we got married, Manuel was already teaching in Hana, Maui, and there was opening in Hana for a nurse, so, he applied for me. And because Maui people all knew each other, he told the Commissioners or whoever was in power there, that we were planning to get married, and he told them that I got to have this job at Hana Hospital. It was a two-nurse hospital, a country hospital, where we nurses did everything. I got the job and became an expert overnight, because we had to do everything. I recall the times when there was an emergency with big accidents. I would call Manuel because there was no other emergency help. He always rush over to help

Manuel Kwon's maternal family (*standing, middle*).

Manuel Kwon's father

me, but then, he was horrified to see the mess that was all around due to the accident, all that blood, broken legs and broken heads! I could see that he could hardly stomach that. Dr. Harold Patterson was the doctor there. On other occasions, Dr. Patterson would call on Manuel to help the surgeons. I recall one time, Dr. Patterson had to amputate a leg. He called Manny, and after he amputated the patient, he turned around and gave the leg to Manny. As Manuel was holding the leg and didn't know what do with the leg, his face became pale white.

There were many, many happy occasions in Hana. It is a beautiful town, more so during those early years in Hawaii because, Hana was something like Kahuku, a little isolated area. If there was a wedding, everybody in town went to the wedding. In a small place like Hana, the teachers and nurses had special treatment when they went to the movies. They had a set place for them in the theatre. You know your seat when you went to the movies. People went to play tennis a lot, there, too because it was a good place to play tennis, everybody played tennis. I did enjoy Hana. Today, when I think about tennis, I remember that we had wonderful times there.

There were people who in later years become well-known in their profession, even in the City of Honolulu, getting their internship in Hana. When we moved back to Honolulu, my husband, she and I became very close friends. We began to take dancing lessons. When our kids were about seventeen or eighteen, they were part of the group. And we still have many, many happy occasions at their patio. it was a large place, right next to the First Methodist Church. Even though these were far into countryside, we had great big parties, we really had terrific times.

Before I got married to Manny, my sister used to tell me never "intermarry," and my husband was part-Spanish and part Korean. That put a fear in me. There was opportunity for me go Chicago to take post graduate course in obstetrics, giving a chance to think it over about Manny. I went to Chicago and he remained in Hawaii, getting his final teaching degree in education. I thought if we survived the separation, then, we'd get married. We survived and married after I returned to Hawaii.

We had many, many interesting happenings after we moved to Honolulu. He became a full time certified teacher at Central Intermediate School, and I was certified in nursing.

Q **How many children do you have?**
A We have four children, one boy and three girls, my two older children are teachers and my son is in Samoa. He's with a Korean group, I believe, who are fisherman. He's connected with the Korean fishery thing there. And my youngest, Greta, is the only one living in Hawaii, and she's my real backbone for whatever I need. She's very willing to do whatever I need. And, I'm very fortunate to have her with us here.

Q **Could you go back and tell us about Manuel as a teacher at Central Intermediate School, and then what happened?**
A In 1941, he volunteered to go into the Military Service. When he enlisted, I didn't know what it meant. Later, I resented it very much because he left me with three children. I had to take care of these three children by myself. And because everything in the USA Armed

Forces was so hush, hush, he was sent to Fort Benny, Georgia without my knowledge. They took him away because everything was blacked out.

Q **Was this during the war?**

A Yes, war.

Q **What year was that he left?**

A 1942. And so, I decided I wasn't going to stay on the island. I was going to move to the USA Mainland, too. So, he arranged that I go there with our three children. My oldest was about six years old. I being born in Hawaii was ignorant about simple things that Mainlanders do. For instance, in Hawaii shoes were worn only on Sundays. I and the three children got very sick on he ship to the mainland. I was very poor traveler. My son also got very sick. I think we were on the ship, the USS President Tyler, which was an army transport.

The three children were Melvin, Laura and Irene. Greta was not born yet. She was born after the war. And as I said, Melvin was very seasick, and I got seasick and I wanted to die. The first three days, I wanted to die, but after the third day, I got a little better after I got some fresh air and we all recovered from whatever.

Then, we had this long train ride to Fort Benning, but we were given a place outside of Fort Benning because Fort Benny was overcrowded at that time. We were put on a train, again, and this train took about three days to get to Georgia. As I mentioned before, our kids did not wear shoes in Hawaii, unless it was a special occasion, so, half the time they were leaving their shoes under the chairs, or on other people chairs where the kids took off their shoes. One day we had to get off train to eat lunch because they did not have dining cars in those days. So, we had to get out of the train, eat, and dash back to the train. I remember at one time, this porter ran up to us to give us one of the children's brand new coat which they left behind on the train. My daughter told the porter, "My mother told me to keep my coat clean and your hands are dirty." The children didn't know what black person was. I was so embarrassed, but I didn't say anything. That was their first experience with black people. I felt bad because everyone on the train was very good to us. When they knew we were rushing with the meals for the kids, they helped me get food for the kids to finish on the train. They helped us a whole lot.

There, my husband had put this woman in charge of taking us to our hotel which they had found for us. When got there, it was so heartwarming. The woman brought blankets and brought flowers to us; I thought Hawaii was the land of Aloha, but they were even warmer, than we were, because we were just nothing, and yet, they were so good to us. When Sunday came around, this woman who took care of us, came to pick up our kids to go to Sunday school. She was so wonderful. They called her Sister Louise. Throughout the years we kept in contact with her, until she died few years ago. She used to write to us every Christmas. I think she was a great strength and warmth for people like us. Another thing, because we were Oriental – we weren't black, weren't white – people didn't under-stand what we were, because they didn't have Orientals in the South in those days, and people would stop us on the street and ask us to say something because they didn't know what strange animals we were.

Q **What year was this?**

A 1942, 1943? In Hawaii, I can remember, there was shortage of toilet paper and Kleenex. But where we were, the factories making those things were in that area. They had counters full of Kleenex and toilet paper. We just hoarded them, because back in Hawaii we were so used to hoarding goods like those things. It felt very strange to have more than one box of Kleenex, and people all crowd around us to wait on us because we were different. Sometimes, I think we were an education to them, and they were an education for us. We had never seen anything there that we were familiar with in Hawaii. I loved the things I saw. I was a little scared because I'd never seen so many black people in my whole life.

The white people would walk out of the store, when a black girl comes in. I didn't know they had such great prejudices. I've never felt that before, and it made me feel hurt, even though they treated me as a white. I was so used to mixtures of people in Hawaii where I don't think we have this extreme racial prejudices. After we left Fort Benning, we went back to San Francisco. Manny bought a car and we drove across from Georgia to San Francisco, where he was going to the University of California to take Mandarin language class, because he was going to be sent to China as an Liaison Officer with the Chinese army. We stayed in the USA. It happened that my mother-in-law had a place in San Francisco, and she had a downstairs apartment, so we lived downstairs, and Manny was able to go to school from there. But after he was through with that, he was sent to the China-Burma theater. He was able to use his Chinese language knowledge enough to carry on a conversation with the Chinese people there. He said that he had many happy and very unusual experiences while he was in China. He told me when he was dying for Chinese food, they would go to a Chinese restaurant in the community and they'd be sick later on. But, he felt it was worth it because they enjoyed the food.

In the meantime, I was in California. A new law was imposed on all travelers going to Hawaii. You must give proof that you have a job waiting for you before you are allowed to buy a flight ticket to Hawaii. It did not matter even if you were locally born in Hawaii. Even as a military veteran and a graduate nurse, because we did not have reciprocity in Hawaii with California at that time. So, they didn't even consider me as a graduate nurse. Maybe it was because in Hawaii our standards were different. So, I decided to go back to school again, because if I had to stay in California for a long time, I didn't want to be unable to work, if Manny didn't come back. So, I went back to school at Blow Mountain, which was a ladies' finishing school. It happened they had nursing education in advanced courses. I took that.

One day, I remembered a person by the name of Mother Rossie at a Catholic College. I went to her office. She asked me how I felt about Japanese, and I told her I had a very good friend who was Japanese, and I didn't have any prejudice against the Japanese, and she asked me if I was afraid. I said, no, I wasn't afraid.

That was during the war, and I experienced many, many good things and bad things. I remember one day I was parking on the side of a hill, and then, two women on the sidewalk said, "You better get out of here you "Jap," or something like that, very angryly. Because I was hot tempered myself, I came out of the car with my hands on hips and I said, "Don't you dare talk to me like that, my husband is fighting for you, and here you're talking to me like I'm a Jap. I'm not Jap, and to begin with, if I were Japanese, I wouldn't be disloyal." So, I was really angry. Another time, I was in the library with the kids, and a man stopped by us and said, "Who is this, are these your children?" I said, "Yes," and he said, "I didn't know Filipinos that young." So, we were called "Filipinos" and they call me a "Jap," and then, I said to myself, I learned a lot of things from being there, all these different experiences.

Manuel came home on furlough in 1945, and just about the time he came home, the war ended. He had a choice of either continuing on and he would be promoted to another rank or get out. He decided he had enough of the army. He got out. A problem developed. Here we were in California. What happened is that we found out we could not go back to Hawaii, until we could prove that we were able to support ourselves. I had to write to Queen's Hospital, and he had to write to his former employers to secure a position before he applied to return to Hawaii.

Q **I'm surprised, what do you mean you could not come back to your place of birth, Hawaii?**

A The Government in Hawaii did not want too many people coming to Hawaii, even former residents, that's why we resented it. The reason was that there was shortage of food in Hawaii because shipment to Hawaii from the Mainland was restricted and the land in Hawaii to grow its own vegetables became under the control of the USA Military Command. Many people were coming back to Hawaii and military families wanted to join their military husbands in Hawaii after the War. A regulation was put out that people who want to come to Hawaii must prove that they can support themselves.

Because of our connections in Hawaii, we were able to come home to Hawaii, but it was not easy and took much effort to get the clearance. I had my sister write to me about a job. Manny used his connections to get his job back. We even proved that we owned a house in Kaimuki. Incidentally, we rented that house to Song Hae Lim and his wife, Lily Ahn Lim. They rented the house and we had to tell them to move out because we were coming home. What was nice was that they were paying our mortgage for us, while we were away, so, the house was being paid for.

When we finally, came back, we got our jobs back. I did not go on a regular staff shift. I became what was called a "floater" nurse; they put me where I was needed, but I've been out of nursing so long, it was a big strain on me. Manny was assigned to Central Intermediate School as a teacher. Then, a year later, he was offered many, many different positions at different schools throughout the island of Oahu.

Luckily, we had a house waiting for us. Many interesting things happened when we returned home. We were invited to different places for dinner. One night, when we came home from a party with the three children, we were so tired when Manny took the kids out from the car. We didn't check with each other, if all the kids were in the bedrooms. Next morning, we heard something coming from the garage, "Mommy, Mommy," we thought Lorna had fallen out from second window, but she had slept in the car the whole night and we didn't know that. That is a fun thing to remember.

What happened to us next in settling back in Hawaii was that Manny was given certain seniority; then he could apply for higher positions instead of being a teacher, so, he became Vice-Principal at Central Intermediate School. They even gave him credits for the years he was away during the war. He was appointed Principal of Kipapa School, which was a very small school, and I had to make a decision what to do, rent a house again or what, so we decided move to Wahiawa, just a few miles from Kipapa. That's where he became Principal for maybe for four or five years, then, he was transferred to Mililani School which is a little beyond Wahiawa. After that he went to Nanakuli School. That's another interesting story because Nanakuli town is a Hawaiian community and the people were very different there. The Hawaiian people have a way to love people, they have certain loyalty, and you have to understand their way of loving. We had many, many warm friendship while in Waihawa, also. I remember one morning, when I got up, I found some chickens at my back room door and some pineapples, sometimes pies. People would bring us things like that, so nice. And in Kipapa, they used to bring beautiful produce, lettuce and string beans. There we had had many mango trees and all kind of the trees in our back yards. There were wonderful birds living there.

However, this was a time of a little trouble happening. My son and daughter were in the same classroom. My daughter got promoted, so she had jump a grade. That was bad for him. He felt inferior because they thought that he either flunked or did something wrong. But, nothing was wrong with him. It was the fact that because in the rural areas the schools were small and the school had to combine two classes. That continued when we sent them to Mid-Pacific School in Honolulu where they were still put into the same grade. That created hardship for him many times. Maybe this is the reason why he did not want to do certain things because he felt as if he was not as good as the others. But, he was fine, nothing wrong with him.

By this time, Manny had learned how to golf. He joined the Lion's Club, and became active with them, and of course, he had P.T.A. (Parent, Teachers' Association). He was very community minded which kept him very busy, and I used to think that he had no time for us with our children because he was too busy with the community. I guess he had to go out to coach basketball to make extra money. Those days everybody needed extra income for so many things.

We went to Nanakuli to help out people there. People in Nanakuli, as I said, were very soft and very warm, but you can see that they were one of the poorest people in the community, even though they're very giving. At the same time even the parents were like children; for instance, my husband and his vice principal had to go out in his Jeep to pick up the kids to come to school, but sometimes, it was because the parents were irresponsible. Once he told me that he had to get funds to see that the kids had breakfast. Many kids didn't have breakfast when they came to school, so they had to give them free meals.

Manny used his connections with the military to get help for the children in various ways. One example was getting musical instruments from the Military. Manny was able to get all these instruments, given free by the military. The well-known Mr. Hodoki started a band at poor Nanakuli because of Manny, which made Nanakuli really proud of their children's accomplishments. Up to that point, they had nothing to be proud of, there was just nothing.

Actually, Manny was not active in the Korean community when he was busy working at the schools full-time, particularly, while we were in Hana, Kipapa and Halemanu.

Q **How about you? Were you active?**

A Actually, I was too busy raising the kids. I was busy with the children, when they were all young. But then, the only contact with the Koreans was at the Methodist Church in Wahiawa because Euicho, my brother-in-law was the Pastor of the new building of the Korean Methodist Church on Keeaumoku Street.

Euicho Chung was married to my sister, Hazel. At that time, there was no real building for the church. The Korean Methodist Church on Fort Street was exchanged for a temporary house in which Euicho's family lived upstairs and the church was downstairs, until finally, a new church was built at the present place at Keeaumoku Street in Honolulu.

As I said, while we gave all our energies to our jobs, we were not active in the Church and in the Korean community, except for the Korean University Club and maybe, sometimes at the Lion's Club. Sometimes later, Manny joined the Korean Golf Club. Manny played a lot with Korean golfers. I think he was one of the First Founders of the Nanakuli Lion's Club. He was very active in all the community activities where he was the Principal of the various schools.

Q **What was the goal of the Korean University Club (KUC) at that time and what kind of activities did they do?**

A The KUC started in 1934 or 35, the year we graduated from college. I remember the Club, meeting at our house. We used to meet in different homes once a month throughout the years. We would get together to form some sort of activities to raise funds for scholarships for Korean students. The KUC was the first to start this idea of a scholarship fund. Of course, we did not do that well in the beginning. We had fashion shows and we had golf matches and other ways to raise money for the students. In the beginning, it was only for students from Hawaii, but we were getting more lenient and included others in this Korean scholarship program.

I believe it was about that time that they had this Friendship Mission to Korea. It was a program that the Korean Community Council was asked by the USA Eighth Bridged to select four representative to go to Korea for a "Friendship Tour" between Korean Americana and Koreans in Hawaii.

Q **Would you explain to us what this friendship tour is?**

A   Well it was an exchange between the Korean Government and Hawaiian Koreans. They wanted to exchange knowledge, information, and stuff between the two countries between the two groups of Koreans. So they sent about four persons to Korea and four from Korean in exchange. So, we had to entertain the Koreans from Korea and the Koreans from here were entertained by the Korean Government in Korea.

Q **This was in what year?**

A   I believe it was in the last 1960's and early 1970's. I don't know how long it continued, but I'm sure it was at least about 6 years that the groups had exchanged representatives.

Q **President Syngman Rhee was ousted in 1960, so all the exchanges took place after he was President. Can you give some opinion on why it took place after Syngman Rhee left and not before?**

A   I think it had nothing to do with politics. It was an economic, exchange. Because they would pick someone from the Community.

Manny was one of them as was Rosie Chang.

As far as Dr. Syngman Rhee is concerned, my earliest recollection was when I was a child and I would overhear people talking about this man who solicited funds from the Koreans and many times they resented this. And that was Dr. Syngman Rhee who was out collecting money. Did you know that? Well, anyhow, as I said I have not been in contact with this political movement because I was so busy raising our kids and going to the mainland and going to war and stuff like that, so I really don't know too much about the history.

I do know that there was a friction between the Liliha Church and the Methodist Church in Keeaumoku Street. I never knew the real reason. To me, I feel the Korean University Club has been able to bridge this gap between the young members from both Churches, and it lessened the animosity between the two groups.

So, I think that education is the door to the togetherness of the people.

Manny was the President of so many Korean organizations. One of Manny's last Presidency of a Korean organization was the Korean Community Council, which composed of representatives from all Korean organizations in Hawaii. They accomplished many project for the Korean Consulate. So you see, he was very concerned about Koreans and the Korean community.

6   Interview with Winifred Lee Namba
regarding her mother: Nodie Kimhaekim

Nodie Kimhaekim   Winifred Lee Mamba

My name is Winifred Lee Namba. I am to talk to you today about my mother, Nodie Kimhaekim Sohn. She was born in Hwanghae Do, Korea, in 1898 on October 29th. Her whole family migrated to Kimhae, Chollanam Do, the southern part of Korea. And from there, the whole family, consisting of my mother, her older sister, a younger sister and a brother had plans to immigrate to Hawaii in 1905. Her older sister, who was about to get married said that her future husband had promised their father that he would immigrate with them to Hawaii, and that was why my grandfather agreed to their marriage. But after the marriage, my sister's husband changed his mind and refused to go to Hawaii and remained in Korea with his new bride. My grandfather was furious, according to my mother.

However, there was nothing my grandfather could do because they were married. So, they had to leave her behind. He went on with the plan to go to Hawaii with the rest of the family which consisted of brother, John Kimhaekim; Nodie, my mother; and a younger sister, Mary Kimhaekim. They arrived in Honolulu 1905. Nodie was 7 years old. Unfortunately, Mary died in Hawaii, when she was 9 years old of small pox. My mother always said that Mary was the beauty in the family, and Nodie referred to herself as the "ugly duckling".

The earliest recollection I have of what my mother told me about

Kimhaekim family; mother Yoon Kuk Kim; father Yoon Chong Kimhaekim; left, Mary; right, Nodie; second right, name unknown.

herself was that she attended Kaahumanu School in Honolulu. It was a Public School. My grandfather, after working a while on the sugar plantation, decided that it was not the life for him. So, they left the plantation. My grandmother supported the family by being a seamstress and being a midwife. I was told that my grandfather was a very handsome man and he was quite an adventurer. He never really settled down anywhere. He was always off to somewhere. Then, suddenly, my grandfather decided to leave Hawaii for somewhere in China to seek his fortunes without us. He died in Manchuria. I have no recollection of him at all. Later, my uncle, John, moved to San Francisco and married there. He was like his father, going off on his own. So, I never knew my uncle. That left only my mother and my grandmother here in Honolulu.

I remember my grandmother very well. She practically, raised me until she died because my mother worked very hard, long hours at the school that Dr. Rhee founded. My mother never really talked much about her own early experiences. She always tried to raise me as a "you were born in America, so you are an American citizen, so you learn all about America."

At age 16 my mother became acquainted with Dr. Syngman Rhee, who became her mentor. After she graduated from Kaahumanu School, a public school up to the 8th grade level in Honolulu, Rhee arranged a scholarship for her at Wooster High School far away on the USA Continent in the State of Ohio to finish her high school level. But, there was no money for transportation. Rhee had even arranged a place of her to stay at Wooster High School

Yoon Chong Kimhaekim, Yoon Kuk Kim, Nodie Kimhaekim

in Ohio, where she could work for room and board. The problem was to get to Ohio. Determined to get an education, my mother went to the piers every day for weeks, asking anyone who was going to be on board ship, if they needed anyone to help babysit on the ship because she had to get to Ohio, where her scholarship awaited her. A Colonel and his wife who were going on board ship to California and travel all the way to the East Coast on land, hired her and took her with them. To this day, as far as I can remember what my mother told me, the Colonel's family remained good friends with her.

Nodie went on to Wooster High School in 1916, so, by then,

Nodie Kimhaekim standing 4th from left, Chicago gathering for East Coast Koreans, Chicago, circa 1922.

Nodie Kimhaekim and mother Yoon Kuk Kim, circa 1925.

she was 17 years old. When she got to Wooster, she worked for her room and board, and after she graduated from Wooster High School, she received a scholarship to Oberlin College in Ohio, where she also worked for her room and board. She graduated in 1922. After graduation and getting her Bachelor of Arts Degree in Political Science, she returned to Hawaii to to work for the Korean Christian Institute (KCI) and, eventually, she became the Superintendent of the KCI, which Dr. Syngman Rhee had founded. She was a very loyal supporter of Rhee, and she believed strongly in the Independence of Korea. She spent months lecturing on the USA Continent, trying to raise money to help the Korean cause.

In 1927, my mother married my father William Pyung Won Lee in Chicago. Very shortly thereafter, the marriage was annulled. From what I understand, the reason of the annulment was because they were on different sides of the political fence. She was a strong supporter of Dr. Rhee, and I assume my father was not. But after she came home, she found out she was pregnant with me. So, she had me: I was born on August 31, 1928 in Honolulu.

It was a very difficult year for my mother because my grandmother, meanwhile, had gone to San Francisco to take care of my Uncle John, who was dying of cancer. After hearing about my mother's pregnancy with me, my grandmother, consequently, hurriedly came back to Hawaii and took care of my birth. My uncle had died a month before I was born in 1928. And my grandmother brought his body for burial in Hawaii. His wife had asked her to

Sohn and Nodie family together. Left to right, front; Nodie, Eva, Syung Woon Sohn; back row; Peter, Winifred, Abraham

bury him in Hawaii. That is one reason why, although his family remained in San Francisco, his body is buried here in Honolulu.

Then, Nodie, my mother, returned to work at the Korean Christian Institute and continued as Superintendent in 1925 until 1935, Dr. Syngman Rhee had gone to Austria in 1931 or 1932. He returned with a bride, Francesca Donner, from Austria. When Rhee returned, Nodie left KCI because Rhee took over as Superintendent of the Korean Christian Institute and he and his wife lived on the Compound of KCI.

My mother, then, went to work for the Kim Furniture Store for five years. She became a very close friend with Mrs. Kim. In 1935, a year after my mother started working there, my mother became more acquainted with Syungwoon Sohn and they married. He had two children from his first marriage, Abraham and Eva. Eva, the younger child, was four years older than me. Their mother had died. Abraham and Eva were students at the KCI. That is where Nodie, my mother, and Mr. Sohn met for the first time. I was there at KCI, also. The classes were very small and we were all thrown together, just like a little classroom where the 4th 5th and 6th graders were all put together in one room; we had lessons together. Other than that, my memories of KCI are pretty hazy. I'm sorry.

I remember both Mrs. Rhee and Dr. Rhee at that time, because I was a little bit older, then, but I was a "day-student," so I would just go to KCI for classes and come back home. I remember one thing about Dr. Rhee. He used to love to have his head scratched with a comb. And several of us had an assignment to scratch his head every afternoon. I was one of them who had to scratch his head. We hated it. I remember another thing about Dr. Rhee. When he used to talk to us in school, he had a very nervous affliction of blowing on his fingers. We were told it was from the torture he suffered in prison. I don't think he ever got over that torture because whenever he talked, he always blew on his fingers. That's what I remember about him.

Q **While you were there at KCI, what did your mother actually do?**

A Well, I guess, she ran the school...KCI. She was the Superintendent. There was a boy's dormitory and a girl's dormitory. And there was the school building in the middle and the kitchen or cafeteria. There were, I remember, one, two, three, four buildings. The teachers always stayed in the boys' dormitory to supervise the boys. My mother sometimes stayed in the girls' dormitory and she supervised the girls.

I remember when Dr. Rhee came back with Mrs. Rhee from Austria, they stayed in the girls' dormitory. At that time, I did not stay in the dorm anymore. I stayed with my mother and my grandmother about half a mile from KCI. My mother bought a house in Kalihi, and so that's where we stayed before she married Mr. Sohn. After my mother married Sungwoon Sohn, we became a family and he and his children lived with us in Kalihi Valley. At their wedding, Mrs. Kim of the Kim's Furniture Store was my mother's maid of honor and her daughter, Daisy and I were flower girls. I was a good friend with Daisy. I knew the whole family. We would get together quite often for holidays and things like that. We were very close to each other because we were all Dr. Rhee's followers.

In 1940, my mother left the Kim Furniture Store and worked with my stepfather who was a shoe repairman. He had shoe repair shops in Schofield Military Barracks, Wheeler Field, Wahiawa, and at the Naval Housing during the war.

Eva was four years older than I, and Abraham was six years older. So at that time, Abraham went to McKinley High School and my sister, Eva went to St. Andrews Priory after she graduated from KCI. I went to Roosevelt High School. After my graduation, I went off to college in Michigan.

When the war ended, my mother and father went to Korea at the time when Dr. Rhee had become the President of the Republic of Korea. They came back very excited because now Korea was an independent nation. Upon their return to Hawaii, my parents opened what they called the Kalihi Gift Shop, bringing in goods from Korea for the first time. During this time, she and my stepfather remained very active in the Korean community. There were a lot of Korean organizations for which my mother chaired, many of them.

Meanwhile, I was at Michigan State University. It was there that I met and married my husband, Dr. Ryujin Namba, who received his Doctorate in Micro-Biology. While there in Michigan in 1952, my mother asked me to come back to Honolulu, quickly, to meet with her because she was going to Korea at Dr. Syngman Rhee's request, where he asked her to become a member of his Cabinet, as the Director of the Department of Procurement. She was not sure how long she would be there. She may not come back to the U.S.A. So, my husband and I hurriedly, came home from Michigan in 1953 to see her off.

It was at this time of her departure that my mother told me that no matter what others said about our family past, I must know that she was my real biological mother, not adopted. All these years I was not sure because of the rumors.

Then, when my mother went back to Korea, my step-father followed her and they purchased a home in Korea. They called it Chongun Dong. That's when my mother was formally appointed to Dr. Rhee's Cabinet. Since then, my mother had to come home to Hawaii every two years to renew her USA immigration papers because she was still a citizen of Korea. Because she retained her Korean citizenship, it was one of the reasons why Dr. Rhee could appoint her to a Korean Government position. But she did not want to lose her Green Card status in Hawaii, so she had to return every two years to Hawaii to reestablish her card. Then, she could go back and forth to Korea without a problem.

Q **Do you know anything more about Mr. Sohn, your father' background?**

A He was a very wonderful father to me. He was with my mother at the Korean Christian Church, very active in Dongji Hoe, and they were both very strong followers of Dr. Rhee because during the war Dr. Rhee was in Washington D.C. working very hard, trying to get the independence of Korea. During this period, someone else took over KCI. Mrs. Mary Lee, wife of Won Soon Lee, I think it was.

After some time in Korea my father, Mr. Sohn, who had gone with her to Korea, started to fail in health, so he returned home to Honolulu. When his health was pretty bad, my mother returned to Hawaii, also, to take care of him. After my mother came back to Honolulu to take care of my father, she retired from the Korean Government, and she retired from all Korean activities in Honolulu, except attend Church services. My step-father died in 1960, and my mother followed him in death twelve years later in 1972.

Q **When Dr. Rhee was here in Hawaii after being ousted from Korea in 1960, did your mother keep in touch with him here?**

A Yes, I chauffeured my mother to go and visit with the two of them, Dr. & Mrs. Rhee. And then, my husband, Dr. Namba, and I left in 1963 for Bangkok, where my husband had an assignment to do some kind of research on microbiology. My husband was still with the University of Hawaii, and we continued to go back and forth on a contract to several parts of the world, especially, Far East. When my mother was in Korea, we visited with her several times. The last time in 1965 or 1966, we were passing through Korea, after Dr. Rhee past away and it was finally agreed by President Chung Hee Park that Rhee could be buried in Korea. My mother was in Korea at that time, and very busy and active in helping with Rhee's funeral arrangements. They had flown his body to Korea to be buried there. We did not have a chance to see her at the airport, but she sent an official person to look after us when we arrived in Korea. We hadn't known that Rhee had past away. That's why there so much commotion at the airport when we arrived at the same time as Rhee's body arrived. So, she didn't meet us there, but we were able to go to his wake and look at the casket and all that. And we met with Mrs. Rhee, there, too.

Q **So you knew Mrs. Rhee as well.**

A Yes, in fact, after the funeral, Mrs. Rhee went back to Austria. We were in Iran on Sabbatical, then. On our way through Austria, we met Mrs. Rhee in Vienna. Even at that time, when we called her up, she would say that we'll meet, but she didn't want to meet in the lobby because she was still afraid of the Communists. So, she came up to our hotel room.

Q **Do you remember the time that Syngman Rhee came to Hawaii for a visit after he became the President of Korea? I have a picture of you with him when you were an adult. And, I heard stories of that emotional event when two of you saw each other for the first time after he became President and you had become an adult. Some even said that there was a deep emotional exchange between you two, especially, the way he looked at you and solemnly, nodded.**

A Yes, because as I said, my mother and father were very strong supporters of him, whenever he came to Hawaii and they had receptions or anything like that for Rhee, my father, Sohn, especially, insisted I

Winifred Namba shaking hands with Dr. Syngman Rhee, 1954.

Dr. Syngman Rhee and the Korean Christian Church, circa 1954.

come along. So, I would go.

Q Did you ever have special meetings with him?

A Not really, no. I just met him with the rest of the group. But, that was mainly, because I took my mother several times to see him. And my mother was very close with Mrs. Rhee.

Q You are aware of people's rumors about you and Dr. Rhee, aren't you?

A Oh, yes. Ever since I was little. I was always teased about... that he was my father. And for a long time, I thought that I was adopted by my mother. My mother had claimed that I was the daughter of a very good friend of hers. Finally, after I married and before my mother went to Korea, my mother did tell me that I was her biological child. And, she also told me that my father...the reason why they separated was because they were on different sides of the political fence. She knew that it would just never work. So, shortly after they married, the marriage was annulled. She said she was so upset, that she tore up the marriage certificate. Of course, at that time, she did not know I was on the way...pregnant with me. She told me that she was very happy that she did have me and I'm glad she did.

Q **So, she then told you way after you were married.**

A After I was married, uh-huh. She was going to go to Korea to work there indefinitely, so, she sent for me. She felt at that time that she probably would never come back to Hawaii, but after she got there, I think she changed her mind and decided not to give up her Green Card. And I'm glad she didn't because we had many very nice years together and she was able to enjoy her grandchildren.

Q **Do you have any reason why she held up the question about you, not her daughter, until you married?**

A Probably, because the marriage was annulled. So, as far as the Korean community and the world knew, she was never married. Back in those years, it would have been very difficult to have said that I had a child with no husband to show for it.

Q **She was a brave woman.**

A She was, she really was.

Q **Why is your name...Winifred?**

A Well, she told me that I was named after my father whose name was William, and that if females are named after someone who is William, the name should be Winifred.

Q **Did she ever offer to introduce you to him?**

A Yes, she did at one time. That's why I firmly believe that the rumors about Dr. Rhee being my father is not true. It was about 1958, 1959, when my mother was living with me, the phone rang. I picked up the phone and there was a man asking for Nodie, so, I called my mother, and she talked on the phone. After she hung up, she told me, "Do you know who that was?" I said "No", and she said, "That was your father. He was in town and so he called to see how everything was." And she said that she was going to have lunch with him before he flies off.

She said, "Would you like to meet him?" I said, "I'm not interested meeting him." So, that's why I firmly believe that that was my father.

Q **What about the airport? You mentioned something about the airport.**

A And then, when he was about to leave, my mother asked me again, "Are you sure you don't want to meet your father?" I said, "No," and she said, "He's leaving today and we can go to the airport and say goodbye." But I said that I did not want to go to the airport.

Q **So his name was William Lee?**

A Uh huh.

Q **No idea where he came from?**

A No, but she did say something about that he was an attorney and that he was not in good health. This was when she asked if I wanted to meet him. That he had problems with his heart or something like that. That he had married and I think she said he had a son and a daughter. So, somewhere, I've got a half-brother and a half-sister.

Q **At the last interview, you mentioned that your mother and he met in Chicago?**

A The reason why I said that is: once, I told my mother that I was staying at the Drake Hotel in Chicago. It was a time when I was in college, and during the Christmas break, my husband and I went to stay at the Drake Hotel. My mother made a comment to me: "When you told me you were at the Drake Hotel, I should tell you that's where your father and I spent our honeymoon."

Profile of
Nodie KimhaeKim sohn
as presented by daughter:
Winifred Lee Namba

Winifred Lee Namba, daughter of Nodie
Kimhaekim was born on August 31, 1928. Mrs.
Namba has been under the shadows of two
famous persons in her life: her mother, Nodie
Kimhaekim Shon and her daughter, Anne
Namba. Both latter persons are well known
Hawaii. In essence, this interview focused on her
mother, Nodie Kimhaekim Shon.

Regarding her mother, Nodie Kimhaekim
Shon, Mrs. Shon will always be a noted historic
figure in the early establishment of Koreans in
Hawaii. She was particularly, remembered as an
outstanding faithful follower of Dr. Syngman
Rhee and all that Rhee stood for: Rhee's church,
school and political activities. Nodie at age 16
was under the guidance of Dr. Syngman Rhee
in 1914 which afforded her higher education
and personal accomplishments. The relationship
lasted to the end of Dr. Rhee's life in 1965.
Through this friendship, Nodie became the
Director of the Procurement Ministry in Korea
when Dr. Syngman Rhee became President of
the Korean Republic. In this presentation of her
life story, the discrepancy of her child's birth,
Winifred Namba, should be definitively resolved.

Also, Winifred Namba is the mother of
Hawaii's foremost well-known fashion designer,
Anne Namba. Anne Namba's acclaimed fashion
designs reflect her mother, Winifred Namba, who
can be described as a refine and elegant person.

My father's name is Kim, Kook Kyung and my mother's name is Emma Cho Kim. They arrived together in Hawaii in June, 1904 with my sister who was about nine or ten months old. They may have gone to Ewa Village and, from there, they moved around the island of Oahu. They settled, I think, in Waialua on the northern side of Oahu for a short time. Then, they moved to Castner Village, which is outside of Schofield Military Barracks and Wahiawa Town up to around 1925. Since then, we lived in Wahiawa all of our lives.

Q   **Tell us about their first arrival from Korea; you said something about bringing their young baby, your sister.**

A   My mother told me that my sister was one of the few babies on board the ship, and a Chinese woman who was a cook on the ship loved to take my sister and play with her. When she came back to my mother with the child, she always brought extra food for my mother and father. She said that my sister was one of the few children on board the ship.

When my parents left Korea, they did not tell my mother's family about going to Hawaii. So, when her parents found out about it, her father rushed down to Incheon Port with a pair of Korean booties that he wanted to give her for my sister. When my grandfather got there, the ship had already left. So, he gave it to someone else that was going to Hawaii to give that pair of booties which my mother got

Kook Kyung and Emma Cho Kim family, circa 1935. Left to right, front row: Bessie Shin, Sarah Pil Soon Kim, Philip Shin, Robert Kim, Emma Cho Kim, Nora Shin, Kook Kyung Kim, Margaret Kim, Nancy Kim Shin, David Shin, Nellie Shin, Daisy Shin; back row: Ching Do Kim, Mary Shin, Harold Yon Do Kim, Millicent Chinogi Park Kim, Sung Do Kim, Elsie Yang Kim, Won Do Kim, Ruth Shin, Chun Do Kim, Kyung Do Kim, Esther Shin.

later on. And so, they moved around and they lived in a placed called Won Luk Camp… that's a pineapple camp in the back of Halemanu, where I was born. When I was three years old, we moved to Kunia, another pineapple camp, and they lived there a year. Later on, when I was about five years old, we move to Wahiawa, where we have been living ever since. They wanted to have a place close to the Elementary School so that I would be able to walk to school. My father worked at the Schofield Military Base for the army which was near Wahiawa.

Then later on, he worked at the nursery (growing plants) in upper Wahiawa. Many years later after World War II in 1948, he left for Korea to do missionary work. He wanted to start a church in Korea. Meanwhile, my mother stayed at home in Hawaii. When he got to Korea, he contacted Syngman Rhee's office. He had been a strong and faithful follower of Dr. Rhee in Hawaii. So, Rhee remembered

Kook Kyung Kim, circa 1940s.

him. Rhee's office people in Korea,... after Rhee had become the President of Korea...were instructed by Rhee in whichever city that my father was going to go, to assist him in anything my father was going to do. The staff would guide him and take him around. When the Korean War started, my father had to go to Pusan and when he was in Pusan in 1951, he caught pneumonia. Meanwhile, he had met my mother's niece on the streets of Pusan and moved in with her, and then, his pneumonia had gotten worse. The day he was dying, he told his niece, "Don't go anywhere just stay here," and he passed away. My father worked with the Korean Veterans. So, they helped to have his funeral in Korea. He was cremated and in 1952 a woman who worked with him brought his ashes back to us. He's buried now at Nuuanu with my mother.

Q **You told me that the reason he called on President Syngman Rhee, when he went to Korea was because they knew each other very well, and your father was Rhee's ardent follower in Hawaii. Could you tell us a little bit more about the relationship?**

A Well, I know that my father worked for him. I mean, he helped by going out to collect money, donations to support to Syngman Rhee in the early days when Dr. Rhee was living in Hawaii. After working at the pineapple fields each day, my father would come home and go out to Honolulu and go around to different churches and different places to collect donations. He worked with Dongji Hoi. He did a lot for Dongji Hoi, Dr. Rhee's organization. I remember seeing receipts for the burial grounds that Rhee set up for a new organization called ...I cannot remember the name of the organization...or whatever. My mother said that he was very busy doing church work for Syngman Rhee. So, he was very close to Rhee in that way. I believe I have a book that Syngman Rhee sent him about the Conference they had in 1946 in Washington D.C. regarding what they were going do in Korea, after Korea was liberated.

Q **Was your father at that Conference,?**
A No, he wasn't. Syngman Rhee sent him the book which Syngman Rhee signed about this conference. I have that book.

Q **How about your mother, was she active in the Korean Christian Church?**
A Well, I know that she went to church with the church lady society. But I don't think she was as active as my father was. My father would go to church on a Wednesday evening …perennial meeting…and he sometimes would be the only one with the minister there: Reverend Richard Kim…there was no one else, sometimes.

Q **Your parents, then, were very close followers of Syngman Rhee and the Korean Christian Church in Wahiawa.**
A Yes.

Q **Could you tell us about any special events that happened?**
A Yes, there was an unforgettable event in 1923. My brother who was attending the Korean Christian Institute (KCI, a school for Korean youngsters) was selected to be on the baseball team tour to Korea, arranged by Dr. Rhee. My oldest brother, Won Do Kim, was on that baseball team. My father also, went on that trip. They had gone to raise money for the KCI. My brother became a hero because when the team was playing their last game in Seoul, there was a condition that if they won, they could stay in Korea to have another game to win the final championship; if they lost, they would have to take a boat to Japan to play there. They wanted to win so that they could go on to challenge the last team in Korea the next day. That would make our team eligible to compete in the final championship game over all Koreans, if they won that game. In that game, my brother hit a home run and so, they were able to stay for the last game the next day. It just

The KCI baseball team and girls' orchestra visit Inchon Naeri Church, the site from which the first immigrants came to Hawaii. 1923.

so happened that on that day when they were supposed to have gone to Japan, if they lost, Japan had a big earthquake. I remember they were all so glad that they won not only the Korean Championship, but my brother saved their lives because the earthquake hit the stadium where they would have had to play in Japan the day of the earthquake. They said that the manager of the team just hugged my brother even more when they heard the news of the earthquake.

Q **My goodness! Tell us more about this brother. Was he also, very active in other activities? And tell us about the Korean Christian Institute which was responsible of taking the baseball team to Korea in 1923.**

A Well, my sister, also, went to KCI. She said that she used to work at Dr. Rhee's home to help serve meals and do things like that. And, she said that Dr. Rhee liked her very much. But, she had to leave and discontinue working there because she was having headaches, you know, migraine headaches. Although my mother wanted her to go on to school, she got married instead, when she was about 18 years old, to Phillip Shin who was working in a Waipahu store. After they got married, they started a tailoring business in Schofield Barracks. They also, worked in the medical section of the Schofield Barracks, but their major work was their tailor shop there for many years. After their tailor shop work, my sister tried a little bit working at a restaurant at Fort Shafter, and then, she retired from it.

Q **So, what about her husband, tell us about him and his family.**

A I only know that he and his father came from Korea, and he was an only child, so, he wanted a big family. They had seven daughters and one son. And he educated the seven children very well.

Q **How old was your sister when she died?**

A She was, I think 92 years old.

Q **How about your other sisters and brothers; totally, how many were there in your family?**

A Well, my sister was the oldest one, and there were six boys, and then, I was born...the last one... the "mak nae." My brother, Chin Do is ten years older than me, and he is the "mak nae" of the boys. My brothers all love to play golf and go fishing, only one brother fished, but five of them were golfers. They would get together and play golf.

Q **So, there were two girls and six boys. Ching Do is well known in the whole Korean community. Can you tell us a little bit more about him?**

A I guess he was well known since high school where he played sports well, and so, after high school, he went to the University of Hawaii. I think he was recruited by one of the University Board Members to play football. He played as a guard.

Q **Tell us what you know about leaders in the community. Who do you think were leaders in the community? Of course, you feel Dr. Rhee was a leader. So, tell me about him, start with**

Wahiawa Korean Christian Church

him.

A Well, I don't know too much about Dr. Rhee except what I've heard a few things from my parents. I know that we had the March 1st Celebration at our church every year. We would all say, 'Man Sei' at the church. Most of the people at the Wahiawa Korean Christian Church were followers of Dr. Rhee.

Q **What activities do you remember at the Korean Christian Church?**

A Our life was centered around the Church. We went to Sunday school and we had different holidays, Christmas, Easter, and then of course, "March First." At high school, we did different things that weren't so close to the church, but I know that we had Christian Endeavor for the young people. And many of us were in that activity.

Q **Particularly, what is Christian Endeavor?**

A Christian Endeavor is a society of young teenagers. They carried on activities when they did different things, like going on outings.

Q **Did you have any close relationship with the Korean Christian Church in Honolulu on Liliha Street?**

A No, when I was young, not too much. But as an adult, I've gone to their activities more frequently.

Q **What about the Methodist Church in Wahiawa?**

A No, we were friends with the girls and boys that were members of the Methodist Church, but we did not do too many things together that I can remember. We were good friends, though.

Q **What about other leaders in the church. Who would say were leaders?**

A We had Ji Han Park, Ji Na Park.

Q **What years would that be?**

A In the 1940s, he lead the young people and then, we had Duk Moon. He was very active. He was a leader for us in my younger days, when I was in Sunday School.

Q **What kind of organizations, Korean organizations did you belong to?**

A Four or five years ago, I joined Dongji Hoi. Before that there really wasn't anything.

Q **What do you do in Dongji Hoi now?**

A We support the scholarships that they have for Korean members, the youths. That's one of the big things that they do.

Q **So, Dongji Hoi... you joined five years ago. Did you hear**

anything about Dongji Hoi earlier?

A Oh, yes, when I was a youngster, my father was active in it.

Q **What do you remember him saying?**

A I didn't talk to him about that because of the language. I mean he spoke more Korean. I never talked to them about those things. Whatever I heard, I know about the family from my mother, more than my father.

Q **So, what did you hear about Dongji Hoi and some other Korean events of the time when they were living?**

A The only thing that I can remember is March 1st Independence Celebration. At church, I remember one thing, and that is, when they said that my father was going to the pulpit to pray, I thought of sliding under the seat because his prays were long, and it would start out in a monotone, and then, increase in volume and then, I would be very uncomfortable because I didn't understand the language he was using. I mean, he was speaking in Korean, and, it didn't mean anything to me. The discomfort is that his prayers were so long. That's one thing I remembered about my father in church. He always carried a Bible with an English and Korean version. He tried to learn English through that Bible. He would stop anyone, including his grand children, to find out how to pronounce a certain English word,...and he'd stop all of us, all of us, not only his sons but with me, also...but, mostly, he'd ask the grandchildren.

Q **That's a cute story. Tell us more stories like that.**

A No, I can't remember. I don't remember anything more.

Q **What kind of food did you eat, I mean, was your mother the cook? Who was the cook in the family?**

A My mother was the cook and she made very good Kim Chi, so did my sister. My sister was a good cook, and she made very good Kim Chi, people liked it. Reverend Richard Kim said that my mother's Kim Chi was one of the best he ever had. My mother used to cook for him during the war, when he was working at Wheeler Field. He would come over and have supper at our house and we would be there waiting on him.

Q **You mentioned once about Onyong Camp, where many Koreans lived, although the Camp was established for the Chinese; could you tell us a little more about this camp and what years they were?**

A Gee, that camp was there quite a while ago. It must have been in the 1920s or so, up to maybe 1940s...no, 50s. It was a poor area, I guess, when they demolished it. There were quite a few Koreans living there and my girl friends, two of them, lived there. In fact, my sister lived in that camp, and so did my oldest brother lived in that area. Later my sister and brother bought properties elsewhere, and they built houses in nicer places in Wahiawa.

Q **Could you describe Onyong section a little bit more?**

A It was in the middle of upper Wahiawa on Kalani and Cane Streets. It's around the center of those streets. They had duplex homes there. The rent was very cheap. I guess that area was owned by the Territory of Hawaii (Hawaii was a Territory before it became a USA State in 1950). All the homes there... my brother, my sister and my brother-in-law, after they married, lived in houses there years ago, where the toilet was inside the house. Other houses, the toilet was outside and the washroom was outside. My brother and my sister had a garage and had an enclosed yard. Indoor plumbing was a new thing in those days.

Q **Would you say that most of those living in that Onyong Camp went to the Korean Christian Church?**

A No, not all

Q **Was it a mixture of other ethnic groups?**

A Yes, they had lots of Hawaiians, Filipinos, Portuguese living in that camp...in that housing area.

Q **Was it in the 1950s that the camp was torn down?**

A Must have been in the 1950s. They were pioneers, new immigrants. They had a number of boarders working at the nearby companies, and after awhile, they demolished it.

Q **What do you do know about the Wahiawa Korean Methodist Church and the Korean Christian Church relationship? Do I understand that they have certain names for the two churches?**

A We used to say, "down church" and "up church". The Methodist Church was in the lower part of Wahiawa, so, it was the "down church". And Wahiawa, the Korean Christian Church, was in the up-per part of the Wahiawa which is the reason we called it "up church". That's only a nickname.

Q **Which was larger?**

A Well, I think the Methodist Church was. I don't know really because at one time we had many of the Korean's families centered around it. The Wahiawa Korean Christian Church, eventually, had many of the older ones. When the first generation passed on, the children were very few, I mean, I would say that only 20 or so of us were active in the "up church"...The Wahiawa Korean Christian Church.

Q **I'm surprise to hear that your father went to Korea with the Korean Christian Institute baseball team arranged by Dr. Rhee. Could you tell us a little bit more about it?**

A I guess my father went along with the group because he wanted to show my brother around Korea and have my brother meet his fam-ily...our grandparents. When I asked my brother, Won Do, what did he learn about our grandmother, he said he could not remember; he couldn't remember the relatives at all.

Q **Any personal things that your father might have mentioned?**

A No, I didn't talk, too, much with him. Because he spoke all in Korean, and our communication was not that close. Even with my mother, I would overhear them saying things. When my father was in Korea, I know that she called my father long distance on the telephone. She said that our father was in Kyung Joo, Kim Ga (경주 김가). That's where his ancestors came from: Kyung Joo, Kim Ga. My brothers didn't even bother with them; I mean they weren't interested in relatives there, until they got older, when one of their sons was going to marry a Korean girl. Then, he had to find out about the family background.

Q **Tell me about your trip to Korea.**
A Well, when I went to Korea in 1959, I took my mother to Korea because she wanted to see her niece and to thank her niece about taking care of my father, who then, was living in Korea setting up an orphanage. And my fourth brother, also, was working in Korea. So, when my brother said that we could go and stay with him, we went out there and we met all of my mother's nieces, her sisters, and I met my cousins on my father's side. There were about five girls and one son. We had a good time. It was nice to meet them.

Q **What was your brother doing there?**
A He was working for a game company that had pin ball machines and things in the NCO clubs, whatever.

Q **So, this group that you went with your mother, was that sponsored by the Korean Christian Church?**
A No, she and I just went on our own. We stayed two months. That was in the summer, June and July.

Q **Which reminds me, the trip that your mother took in 1936 and the one that your father went with the baseball team, did they ever talk about how they went there or what kind of passport?**
A You know, they never said anything. But then, just thinking about it, I am curious about what kind of passport they had, if they had any, even my mother, I don't remember. I guess she didn't have any

passport that I can remember, because they were Korean citizen. They never became naturalized. So, I don't think my mother had a passport at all. She also went in 1937. And that was when I was about 10 years old. I wondered why she didn't take me, but she said, "No, you would not be happy being there." I think it was because of the facilities they had there. I wanted to go because I had a cousin that was about my age in Seoul.

Q **What do you remember of Lee, Won Soon.**

A I knew Lee, Won Soon had a big business in New York City because when I went to school in New York, my niece and I stayed with his family because Velma Pyun Kim was there. When I got to New York, we called Velma and she told us to come and stay with them, before we left for a different destination. So, every vacation break I had, I would go down and visit with them. Lee, Won Soon had this big business, I mean he had this business in lower New York. He brought properties in different places. Then, he moved to Los Angeles, then, back to New York. And then, I guess he went to Korea after the WWII. That's where he stayed for a long period of time.

Q **Were you aware of any kind of activities that he was doing?**

A No, the only thing that I know is that he worked with the Olympics, too. That's about it. I was not interested in politics and whatever they had going on.

Q **Tell us about your brother's wife, Elsie Yang. Their son, Dr. Robert Kim, has always been proud of your father...his grandfather. But tell us about Elsie's parents...the Yang family. Her own parents were very refine and quiet.**

A Elsie was my oldest brother's wife. Elsie would have family "get-togethers" at her son's home...my nephew, Bob Kim's place for Christmas. Her mother and father lived close to our house. And I remember that her father was always an active man, moving around. Other than that, I don't know what kind of politics, what activities they did.

Q **Do you remember if she came from Korea or was she born here? When did her parents came from Korean?**

A No, I don't know. But I know that she has four sisters, plus, herself, five girls. There were two boys. Her older sister went to school on the USA Continent, and there, she married a doctor, a Korean from Wahiawa, too. And they lived in Pennsylvania.

THE STORY OF HA SOO WHANG
The Ha Soo Whang story is a documentary film.
The following excerpts were taken from the film.

Ha Soo Whang   Mary Whang Choy

Narrator:

Sometime in the 1930s when I first saw Ha Soo Whang, I was only 3 years old, but I knew she was a very special person in the Korean community. She was known as Whang, Ha Soo, because the Korean custom is to use the surname first. Her two nieces Elizabeth and Mary Whang called her lovingly, "Komo."

Ha Soo Whang was unlike the local Koreans in Hawaii. She always wore a hat, spoke with great confidence, and authority. She was always among so many people. Ha Soo Whang was born in Korea and came to Hawaii, via California, sometime in 1919. The Korean community was fractionated by political turmoil at the time she arrived, the story of which is a novel in itself. So, she came at a crucial time. It was Ha Soo Whang, the "YWCA woman" among few other leaders such as, Tai Sung Lee, the "YMCA man", and the gifted Donald Yong Gak Kang, who all together did extraordinary things to guide the immigrants and their children through the turmoil of assimilation and acculturation.

But, let's begin Ha Soo Whang's story from the beginning as told by Mary Whang Choy, a niece of Ha Soo Whang.

Mary Whang Choy:

My Aunt Ha Soo Whang was one of three siblings who came to America when they were adults. There were eight siblings, altogether, four daughters and four sons. But, only three came to America. One of them was my father, Rev. Sa Sun Whang. Her parents (my grandparents and other extended family members) were living in Uiju in the northern part of Korea...right on the border of China and Pyongyang. The northern part was not "North Korea" then.

Ha Soo was the second to the youngest, the seventh child in a family of eight children. Their mother died and their father died, when they were all very young children. The eldest sister became the head of the family. So, my Aunt Ha Soo looked to her as another woman of great strength and courage and independence. Her older brother, Rev. Sa Yong Whang, was number three in the family. He was the first to leave Korea and come to America. From that point, he was very instrumental and responsible for bringing out many of his relatives to America. He brought my father, Rev. Sa Sun Whang to America; that was when my father and mother left North Korea during the political turmoil there. They settled in San Francisco.

Following that, my Auntie Ha Soo, with the encouragement of Korean missionaries in Pyongyang, Korea, joined her brothers in America. The Whang family members were Presbyterian missionaries, basically. From Pyongyang, she went to Seoul, attended

Rev. Sa Sun and Tai Sun Chang Whang and children: Mary, Paul, Elizabeth, circa 1920.

Rev. Sa Yong, first of the Whang family to come to America, Circa 1917.

school there, and it was there, where she had the final encouragement to go to America. So, with the help of my uncle Sa Yong, she, too, came to America and went to school first in California and went on to Aspens, Alabama to attend the Women's College there. So, they were the only three, who came to America.

History about my aunt Ha Soo: she was a younger sister of my father, Rev. Sa Sun Whang and Rev. Sa Yong Whang. She left Korea as a young woman about 1912, went to Alabama, where she entered a woman's college, Aspens Women College, got her degree, and then, came to Honolulu, where she was offered a position with the YMCA International Institute. But first, I do want to mention how she worked in Alabama and attended the Aspens Woman College. She was very well received, very well loved. Still, she never, at any time, lost her consciousness of being a Korean woman. A picture shows her with her beloved Korean flag wrapped around her skirt.

She came to Hawaii between 1919 and 1920, and a year later, she was offered the position of Vice President of Social Workers at the International Institute. In that year in April, she went to San Francisco and brought me and my sister, Elizabeth to Hawaii to care for us during the time of great bereavement of my father because our mother, his wife, died. Aunt Ha Soo, we called her "Komo", brought us back to Hawaii with her so she could take care of us. Our brother, Paul, was left in San Francisco with our father.

Aunt Ha Soo was one of three ethnic social workers at the YMCA in Honolulu. She was the Korean Social Worker, and there was a Chinese woman, Mrs. Yi, who took care of the Chinese women, and Miss Kisimoto, who worked for the Japanese women. I would say they were the first ethnic

Ha Soo Whang displays her ethnicity at Atherton University, Alabama, where she matriculated, circa 1919.

social workers in Hawaii. They cared, they nurtured, they tried to meet the needs of the immigrant women who had come to Hawaii. Primarily, Aunt Ha Soo worked with women who were "picture brides." She helped them adjust to the many, many problems that they faced...their domestic problems, and often times, abusive situations. She would act as a court interpreter, go to court, and speak for them. She also, would conduct classes to help cultural affinity to the American society. That would be in the areas of English, homemaking, and also, at the same time, exposing them to American culture.

She also, developed a great interest in the Korean young people. In the early twenties, I would say, in 1925 or 1926, the Hyung Jay Club was organized by Aunt Ha Soo. Youngsters, young Korean girls from all the broad community of Hawaii despite the political cleavage among their parents, came and joined this organization, which was primarily cultural. There, we learned the cultures of Hawaii and the old folk cultures of Korea.

Aunt Ha Soo would bring into the organization Korean men and women, who more recently immigrated to Hawaii and were experts in Korean folk music, Korean dancing. She would have them teach us the Korean folk cultures of our native Country. From there, productions were produced. My Aunt Ha Soo would write the play, she would dramatize it, she would produce it, and she would bring in all the artists from Korea, the elderly people to perform. We, as the young women of the Korean community, would learn from the elderly and perform the dances depicting the old folktales of Korea

Hyung Jay Club, Old Folks Korean Culture at University of Hawaii, 1930s.

Hyung Jay Club performing Korean dance at the old Honolulu Stadium, circa 1930s. Left to right: Margarte Kim, Jayce Kim, Yealinae Kim, Sunbee Inn, Sarah Hong, Sarah Lee.

for the local people in Hawaii...very dramatic productions. That was a wonderful era for all of us, young people, because we never lost sight, particularly, for my sister and me, we never lost sight of the fact that we were Koreans, and

YWCA, front row,
Left to right: third
Ha Soo Whang, last
Esther Park

we had pride in our heritage. We credited my Aunt Ha Soo for her deep feelings for Korea to carry on the old culture, cultural ways, the music and the
dance of Korea to pass it on to our new generations, the Korean-Americans.
At the same time, she was still nurturing and caring for the women of Korea
who came to Hawaii in need of guidance.

I always think of the very dramatic production at the Honolulu Academy
of Arts. It was held in the Central Court with this huge arch. I have pictures
here of the early productions that were put on at the YWCA on Richards
Street. I have photos of some of the early productions of Korean dance and
Korean stories that were produced by my Auntie and the Hyungjae Club.
I have other photographs of the young women who learned to dance the
Korean dance, performing at some huge general community gathering. I
have, also, another picture of a production that was put on at the YWCA in
their hall and other photos depicting some early customs of a wedding, the
Korean bride and groom.

A few years later, this production at the Academy of Arts, which was,
really I think, one of the greatest productions at that time. It was held at
the Honolulu Academy of Arts, depicting again the culture of Hawaii. We
have Sarah Lee Young, pictured as a Korean bride. My sister, Elizabeth and

I, showed off some costumes worn by the Korean people for the Korean dance scenes. More members of the Hyungjay Club, who also participated in that production are in some of the photos that I have. The programs were so well received: the whole community, hundreds and hundreds of people present, the color, the music, the dramatic presentation of these programs were well written. If you go back to the Honolulu Star Bulletin or the Honolulu Advertiser, you would see many articles written about that very wonderful production by my aunty.

Personally, my Aunt Ha Soo was a tremendous influence on my life and my sister's life. She was a wonderful model for us. She reared us because we came here as very young children. I was five years old and my sister was eight. She reared us, she taught us, she educated us. We remained here in Hawaii throughout our lives, and we did not return to San Francisco to join my father and brother. In the meantime, my father remarried. But our lives, my sister and I continued here with my Aunt Ha Soo, who was family, who was both mother and father to us. With her strong sense of self, and her strong

will of independence and courage, and trying new things and being a forerunner of new attitudes, she was right there and without her, I'm not sure where our lives would have gone. We look back and respect and admire her as a woman, a single woman who reared, literally, reared, a family of two young girls.

Her work with the International Institute began about 1922, and she worked there until 1939 because at that point the YWCA decided that the

YWCA, front row, Left to right: third Ha Soo Whang, last Esther Park

International Institute was no longer viable. I'm not sure what the true reason was because they were the women who were offering great services to women of each of these ethnic communities. At any rate, the YWCA had decided to close the International Institute. At that point, my Auntie continued with the YWCA for about two years. She at that point made another transition in her life. She retired. She was also a very wise business woman and bought a place in Waikiki. Then, she would sell it and buy another place.

I think women at that time, very well known Korean women in particular, were esteemed for their sense of business. In many cases the women, the Korean women, were the ones who were, financially, responsible for their families and for educating their children. Evidently, my Aunt Ha Soo, also, had that very wise streak of good business sense. She started buying properties in Waikiki, then, she sold that and bought property on Dole Street across the University of Hawaii. There, my sister and I have many, many childhood memories. We went to the University High School, right across the street of our house. And then, she sold the property there and bought another place in Waikiki with a little apartment in the back so she was able to take care of herself, financially. She never depended on anyone for financial help, in fact, she was a source of help to other people, other family members or other people in the community. She was so compassionate. She was such a compassionate woman. Her self-interest never came into the picture. Her mind was always focused on the other. That is something I will never forget about her, her great compassion for people. But anyway, she lived very happily in her cottage in Waikiki with her little apartment in the back that gave her a little income. Therefore, she was able to live very fully.

Her last years, I would say her last ten years, she moved from the Waikiki area to the Punchbowl Area and involved herself in condominiums. There, her last ten years of her life were spent there. Her health deteriorated, but she was still pretty alert. We needed to care for her, but she was able to stay at home. She had a short stay in the hospital and returned to her home. We were there, when she passed away. So her life…she went very peacefully, a life of great, great fulfillment. She died, we think, about 92 years of age in 1984.

I did take a trip in 1989 to North Korea, to Pyongyang. A small family group, my brother and his wife made this trip to the North with us. My trip to North Korea in 1989 was a very symbolical trip for me. Our little family unit of my brother and his wife, of my own daughter here in Hawaii, and a niece in California— six of us made this journey to Pyongyang— to the home of my parents and my father's family. It was such a symbolic trip for me because my Komo, Ha Soo, my father, Sa Sun and my uncle, Sa Yong, their lifelong wish was someday they would be able to go back to their hometown, Uiju, which they never did.

So, my being there in Uijiu, I felt was in some sense, I was there for them. I think it was a kind of closure for them and their love for their country, my being there."

My name is Emily Kim Choi. I was born in 1919 in Kohala on the island of Hawaii in 1917.

My father was Hong Soon Kim from Pyung An Do and my mother, Young Chin Park, from Pusan. My father came to Hawaii as a bachelor in 1910. He was recruited as a laborer to work in the pineapple fields. I suppose he didn't like the life of a bachelor because he soon asked to have someone act as "go-between" to find him a wife. There was a friend of his who knew my mother and they started corresponding. My mother was a beautiful woman and she is 13 years younger than my father. She arrived in 1913 as a picture bride and they were married in Honolulu. She always thought that she could further her education in Hawaii because that was what was promised to her. But instead, she got stuck in a plantation where my father was working and they struggled to make a living.

I'm the third child in a family of five children. We had four sisters and one brother. My eldest sister, Rachel was born in 1914 on the Big Island; my second sister, Florence was born in 1917, also on the big island; and then, I was born as the middle child. Aida was born in 1921, and my brother Joe was born in 1923. As you can see we are all two years apart. My sister, Aida, pasted away in 1995. She was the youngest in our family and we all miss her terribly.

My father was never cut out to be a plantation laborer and there were many times when he would cut out from work. He really hated it. So, he would play "hooky" from work – not going to work. I remember my mother

Hong Soon and Young Chin Park Kim family, circa 1924.
Children, left to right: Rachel, Emily, Joseph, Aida.

saying that he was a very poor provider. He would stay in his room and help other Koreans with letter writing because some of the Koreans could not read even Korean. He would read to them what they received from Korea. My father also, taught young children the Korean language.

Wherever the family moved to a new place, my father looked for a place where there were jobs for women, too. So, if they needed a cook in a certain camp, my mother said he would try to move there and if they needed a seamstress to make slippers or fix clothes, my father would get a job there for her. Well, my mother helped out by sewing and cooking and doing things for the bachelors that the bachelors couldn't do themselves.

For a while, my father homesteaded on the Big Island in Kohala, where I was born. And although they didn't make a good living there, we were able to survive. Later on, he heard that life was easier in Honolulu, so he gathered the family, and we all moved to Honolulu where my father had a little grocery store on Liliha Street. My father started another business in Honolulu, the City Captiol because people told him that's where the money was. He started a loan business. He was a trusting soul and he gave too much monetary credit to many people who didn't pay him back. Naturally, he went broke. And so he had to close this business.

Then, he heard that Wahiawa was a good place for families to be brought up and to make a living, so we moved to Wahiawa. In Wahiawa, we went into

170

the laundry business. It was hard, a backbreaking work for all of us, but we managed. My sister, Rachel, being the eldest, learnt to drive when she was 15, I believe. And she could barely drive, but we bought an old Chevrolet. The first week after she got her license, we drove around the island. I wonder how we survived because we couldn't make the little white hill in Waialua. We practically, had to lighten ourselves to get over that hill, but we had a lot of fun, in spite of all the hard work we did.

Rachel became the driver of the car to pick up and deliver the laundry. She marked the different items of laundry, and she sorted them. My father and my mother did the washing. Florence, my second sister, also helped. I helped my sister Rachel do some of the marking and checking. And after the laundry was done and we pressed and put them in baskets. We would check the laundry again to see that all the pieces were there. Aida, being the youngest in the family, would do the cooking, simple things like rice and maybe soup. And she would hang up the laundry when it was time to hang up. My father helped out with the flat pieces, just as I did, and my sister, Florence, who was pretty good in ironing and doing things, did the uniforms and the dresses, and the more difficult things. And I remember that they all worked far into the night and my mother used to work until 2 or 2:30 in the morning to get the laundry ready to be delivered on the specified day. In those days, we used to do the bachelor's laundry, complete with uniforms, linens, clothing, everything you can think of for $4 a month. And yet, there was competition among the Koreans to do the soldiers' laundry, and sometimes we would lose a customer because someone else would do it for $3.50 a month. Those sure were tough days.

We, surely, didn't have any time for homework. We used to work in the ironing room until about 9 o'clock. We were excuse to go to our home which was connected, of course, and by that time we would be too tired to read or study, so naturally, most of the time, we would go straight to bed. We went to Wahiawa Elementary School, then, to Leilehua Intermediate School, and then, to Leilehua High School. After high school, I went to a business college in Honolulu, where I studied secretarial work. From there, I got my first job at Wahiawa Motors for $40 a month, which we considered was good pay at that time. But after about a year, I took a civil service exam and got a job at the Board of Water Supply for $105 a month which was real, real big salary at that time.

We were members of the Korean School at Wahiawa Korean Christian Church, but I think it was Reverend Park who taught us our elementary Korean. My father was, also, very instrumental in teaching us because he would reward us with candy or whatever he could get to encourage us to remember our Hanmunja (Korean alphabets), and he would give us tests. I remember he gave us all ten handicaps. Rachel would have to know the most, Florence would have to know the second most, which was ten less than Rachel, and I, the third, would have twenty less than Rachel. So as long as we could write the Hanmunja and tell my father what it was and how it was used, we would be credited for that many points.

When I was still very young, living in Wahiawa, most of my friends' parents had joined the Korean American Club, which at that time was "the thing" to join. The Korean American Club was quite prestigious in those days because you had to have a pretty large sum of money for the initiation fee. As long as you were Korean, I believe you could join the club, if you paid the initiation fee. Most of my friends belonged to it. I remember Mary Lee, Beatrice Moon, and Anna Kim. Those are the ones who come to my mind now, but it had nothing to do with Church affiliation. It was just an ethnic thing and I really envied them. They never flouted their connection with the Club, but when they say, "I'm going down to take piano lessons, or I'm going down to practice piano", I was very very envious. I'd wish our parents could afford that, too. I remember they had a piano there, and I wanted my parents to join the Club, real badly, because I wanted to go down and take piano lessons.

At that time, Mr. Owen was the manager of the store and he ran everything. He had a son who was called Philo (also, known as, George), but not the younger brother, who was also named Philo. He was nearer our age and we knew him well. I don't know how come they had the same name. But they were the "in people", meaning: well-known, modernized Koreans because of their father who was very stylish, himself. As the Founder of the Korean American Club, Mr. Owen made the Club fancy. We were quite envious of those who were in the Korean American Club.

While we were living in Wahiawa, we used to go to church every Sunday, Korean Christian Church, and my mother would give us each a penny. And

Clarence Choi, Emily Choi's
husband.

we would be so tempted to buy a piece of "Oh Boy" gum for 1 cent a stick, instead of giving it as an offering. But somehow we managed to hang on to it. Once in a while, my parents would give us two cents. And with one cent, I remember we would buy the dumbbell candy. It is one lollipop with candy on both ends of the stick. It was coated with chocolate. Boy, was that ever good!

As we grew older, we went to Christian Endeavor meetings, every Sunday. And after Christian Endeavor, we'd get together and wish that we could get a ride to Schofield Theatre, where we could watch some movies. The movies I think at that time were 20 cents. And we had to wait outside until all the GI's got in first and then, we were allowed to go in and sit in the back. That was really a treat.

In 1943, Clarence Choi and I were married at Wahiawa Christian Church by the Reverend Richard Kim. Clarence's family also, lived in Wahiawa, so grew up together. His family is known for their strong ties with President Rhee. Clarence's brother was the one who financed Rhee flight to Hawaii when Rhee was deposed in 1960.

My parents were very strong members of the Korean Christian Church. I suppose they were Christians in Korea; at least my mother was, they continued going to church here, and my father was even a lay minister at times. My father was a very broad minded person and he loved to read. He would read whatever he could, even opposing newspapers. By opposing, I mean views that were not Dongji Hoi views, but other views. My mother would ask him, "Why are you reading that paper?" Almost anything else outside of Dongji Hoi, according to my mother, was Communist at time. If you are not, Dongji Hoi, then you are a Communist. Or at least, it was how it sounded to me at that time. My father would say, "Well, I have to read both sides of the question. Otherwise, how can I make a right decision?" Of course, all his decisions had already been made because he has always been a staunch

Dongji Hoe member.

Whenever Dr. Syngman Rhee came to Wahiawa, he was greeted with much excited feelings. They were really happy to see him. No matter how poor the family was, we would try to invite him to dinner and he would come over and have dinner with us. He was, really, down to earth. I remember when I was born, and I must have been about 2 years old, the Korean Independence Movement had begun, already, and all parents would more feverishly, teach their children, even very little children about it. I remember standing on the table and my mother said I should raise both hands and say three times: "Mansei Mansei, Doklip Mansei." Of course, I didn't know what it meant, but our parents told us the story that if you were an Independence Fighter and waved the Korean flag, they would cut off your hand which was carrying the flag, and if you changed hands to waved the flag with your other hand, they would cut off that hand. She told us all about the torture the Koreans had to endure that she had heard about going on right now in Korea. I don't know how true they were, but these were the stories that we grew up with.

I personally, don't feel that strongly, about President Rhee. I admired him because of our parents' devotion to him. I guess, some of that must have rubbed off on us. As a matter of fact, I didn't join the Dongji Hoi, until just last year because Clarence, my husband belonged to it. I just went along with him to take him there to accompany him. The good works I heard the Dongji Hoi was doing – they were helping, for instance, by giving scholarships – ten scholarships each year, which grew and grew and grew. Now I think they are giving about fifteen scholarships to young college students. I think that's a real good project that they were working on. I think it's not for the Korean Independence that we are working for now, but it's working for the good of Koreans here.

I also, joined the Taeguk Club after I married Clarence. The Club started out as men's club and it was a fun club for young adults; yet, it was a service club because we tried to help the community. Any time the Wahiawa Community and the Korean community asked us for help in certain projects, we would send a small check or what we could afford. We also, sent money to the orphanages in Korea. We did quite a bit of service work in Hawaii, too. Whenever a project came up and they needed help, they would write

Clarence and Emily Choi, second-generation descendants of the first wave at the Korean Christian Church eightieth anniversary celebration, November 1998.

to us and we'd donate a few dollars. Our biggest project that I know of is the bath house that we helped purchase for an orphanage in Korea. From what I understand, the project in Korea is still going strong and with that project completed, the orphanage is self-supporting, mainly, because of the bath house. The members of the Taeguk Club composed of second generation Korean, and some recently, arrived first generation Korean such as Mrs. Sunni Song. She is married to Benny Song, an old time second generation. Benny pasted away. Mrs. Song is still, living, but I understand she's not very healthy now.

Other than that, most of the young people in Wahiawa, at that time, joined the club for social activities. Even though membership decreased, we still have parties, now and then, and there was always a lot of fun. Recently, we dwindled down, drastically, in the membership. We have just a few members now. It's just the same people that meet all the time. Now that we are old, we're not into fund raising. That activity dwindled quite a bit. We just meet at members' homes and have pot luck supper, and if there was any solicitation that we think is for a worthwhile cause, that is brought up at our meeting. We hardly do anything now. As for our children, we have a few third generation Koreans like Ruth Mack's family. We tried to get some of our other youngsters interested, but they're just not interested. Ruth Mack's children are members. Maryann's son came for a while, but ours never did.

Q **Tell us about your own personal life.**
A I worked for the Board of Water Supply, where I had a Civil Service

job. I was very happy there. I have three beautiful daughters and three wonderful sons-in-law and three handsome grandsons. There's one that finished college, one who is finishing this year, and another still attending college. I don't have much to say about my life. I think it's such an average life. We've had a good life and have no complaints about it. Clarence has been a good husband and I've tried to be a good wife. We've been married 55 years this past February.

My name is Helen Sonya Shin Sunoo. I was born in San Francisco in 1915. My mother came as a picture bride. She came in 1914 when she was 17 years old. Friends introduced them through a picture bride arrangement. My mother agreed to being a picture bride because she did not like the pressure under a Japanese controlled Korea.

My dad came from Pyongyang, Hwanghae-do. He first arrived in Hawaii in 1903. Later, he moved on to San Francisco about 1920, which he found it very difficult. It happened that he settled at Sacramento first. Sacramento's summers are quite hot. So, he chose San Francisco for his home. There, he decided to become a barber. He established himself for several years, and

Mother and father's house;
Helen Sunoo's father, barber.

later, he hired five barbers to work with him. They worked with him on a commission basis. The Filipino barbers were chosen because they were very artistic in hair cutting. He had Chinese barbers, also, because it was in the Chinatown. He felt that he should be a friend with the Chinese.

In San Francisco, usually, a shop is in the front, and there is a long hallway which often have five or six rooms and a toilet. There wasn't a bathroom at our place. Later, my father managed to have one ordered. At first, it was a basic wash tub. Later on, my dad ordered a stainless steel bathtub which was about five feet long and about three feet tall. Mother had a very unique idea. The bathtub was set up on a brick oven. The Chinese had this brick oven and place a wok on top in order to heat the food and cook it. My mother used it to make hot water. She would build a fire under a big wok with water and the water was heated on this brick oven. The water was very hot. My mother could use hot water, anytime. It was not a common thing to do at that time.

Q **Were the other Korean families in that area?**

A There were several Korean families. My parents lived on Jackson Street where my father's barber shop was located. Many other Korean family homes were above Grant Avenue. They lived in the alley. There were three families that I can recall. The Kim family: the older son was Philip Kim. I don't remember his mother's name. He had two brothers and one sister. Another Kim family: his name was Dong Gyun. I cannot remember the full name of the family.

Q **Did you form a community? Association?**

A No, we didn't form any kind of association. If there was a meeting and important things to discuss, we went to the Korean Church. At that time, the Korean Church was way down on Oak Street. There, we had a Korean a printing press. It was a hand press. Shinan Minbo was the Publication. Il Kyu Paik was the editor. The minister helped.

Q **So, the community was the Church, then?**

A Yes, the Church welcomed Christians and any one who came.

Q **Were your parents affiliated with this Church?**

A   Yes, all the Koreans would come to that Church. There was only one church at that time.

Q   **The name of it?**
A   Southern Methodist. We continue to have this one church until, later, we built our own on Powell Street. There was some controversy about the sale of it, later on, under a new minister.

Q   **Tell me about this Methodist Church way back in your youth. Was that purely Korean, only, or mixture of ethnic groups?**
A   No, it was, purely, Korean.

Q   **How many families do you think were going to the Church?**
A   My guess is that we had 25 families.

Q   **Spread out in San Francisco area?**
A   Yes, there wasn't any Korean town or such to find jobs. The cleaning shops were scattered in American districts.

Q   **Did you identify yourself always as Korean or did you just blended into the Chinese community?**
A   In Chinatown, as a family, we still identified ourselves as Koreans. My father was very patriotic to Korea. He said that we have got to remember we are Koreans. I remember he sat me in his barber shop because my mother sent me there because she was busy with the younger children. I was a chatterbox. My mother had three younger children than I. So, I was often sent out to the barber shop. At the barber shop, my father would teach me Korean alphabets. He even made me a notebook that he made with used financial papers of the newspapers. He couldn't afford to buy me a tablet.

Q   **What other kinds of Korean activities do you remember?**
A   Oh, I remember the most outstanding activity was March First; it is called, "Sam Il Ku". For years, Mr. Kim, Dongwoo, who read the Declaration of Korean Independence out loud to us. It was the time

that Mrs. Ha came from Colorado. She had a very lovely voice and she, also, taught Korean. Her daughter's Godfather was very learned. He taught Mrs. Ha to read the Declaration of Korean Independence. I remember she read it to us for many years at this celebration. While she read, all the Korean children and everybody in the audience paid attention, while it was read. And after she read it, everyone shouted, Mansei! three times. That response was led by Kim, Dongji at the Korean Church. That's where everything is done on that Independence Day. It was a special day that we would all be there, all the Koreans, no matter where they lived as long as they come.

Q **Do you remember what other kinds of occupation Korean families had?**

A Yes, around Chinatown half a block down, the Shin family had a coffee shop. Then, the block that was across Jackson Street was Kearney Street. There was a Korean by the name of Chun, Deukgu, who had a shoe repair shop. And next to the shoe repair shop, there was a laundry cleaning shop run by the Lee family.

Q **What years do you think these were when you knew them and when these things happened? What years do you think?**

A It was about 1920. I would like to mention that on the opposite side was Doriam Kim. Her parents had a restaurant there. And one more, there was a candy and tobacco shop.

Q **What outstanding leader was there at that time?**

A The Korean leaders? I wasn't into politics. I was just a kid. But I remember one thing happened. Kook Min Hur was strong in San Francisco. Lee Dae Wi, was the leader. Il Kyu Paik was another leader.

Q **What kind of activities did they have? What were their interests?**

A I don't know. At that time, we kids played upstairs.

Q **Not involved, right?**

A   Yes, too young to be involved.

Q   **Tell us about yourself about the time when you were growing up and when you went to college. Tell us about that.**

A   I went to San Francisco State College. I was interested in teaching in high school. So, I took several courses there. The day before graduation, the Dean of Women called me and said, "Well, Helen. I am sorry to tell you, you will never be able to teach in California in the position of a Secondary Teacher. So, you might as well think of something else. Did you ever want to be something else?" I said, "No. Teaching was the only thing I wanted." She said, "Well, I have a scholarship for you." That brightened my spirit at the thought of a scholarship. "And what is that?" She said, "It's a cosmetology study." My heart sunk. Tears rolled out my eyes. But then, what could I do? So, I accepted it. Scholarship to cosmetology school and to become a beauty operator!

Q   **Was this after high school?**

A   It was after college.

Q   **After college! Could you describe again what happened.**

A   After I graduated from college, I wasn't offered a school teaching job but a scholarship for cosmetology to become a beauty operator. That was the offer that was made to me. So, I had to become a beautician. Then, I did operate a beauty shop in China town.

At the same time I, also, attended as many of the child development courses I could and enjoyed doing that. And by going to college was I could make a living on the knoll. Then my advisor's said, "Helen, you have enough. You'll need to get a Masters Degree. Later, I enrolled in Santery University. I had met all requirements except residence. They required one year of residency.

At that time I was married and I had two children. I told my husband about this requirement, and he said, "Oh, no. You don't have to get that degree. You don't need doctor's degree because we will go back and live in Korea. And you can teach in Korea without a doctor's degree." That was my academic ideal, to teach in Korea. So, I did not go to get my doctorate. That's what happened. Later, my husband found a job. He was offered a teaching job in Missouri. In Missouri I was, also, offered a teaching job. This was at a college, so this was a quite jump that I had. I got a chance to teach both in a small college, and later on, I was invited to teach at the University of Missouri.

Q **What did you graduate in, what kind of degree, and what were you teaching?**

A Oh, I graduated in Child Development and I was teaching Child Psychology, Adolescence Psychology, and I taught Educational Psychology.

Q **Did you make use of those degrees in your work?**

A Yes. I was teaching what I learned in Child Development at the University, and they, also, offered me a job working at a home nursery, observing the children at different stages of childhood. They had a one way window. I observed one dozen students behind this with one way viewing window. Different play areas had a microphone and we could observe children at different kinds of play such as individual play or parallel play and all kinds of things. Children wouldn't know they were being observed, so they were very free. Then, I had students from a nursing school come into my classes. They could, also, observe the young children's ways and how they can solve problems.

Q **Was the life in Midwest different from California?**

A Yes. I thought it was quite nice in Missouri. We, as Koreans, didn't meet with prejudice in the Midwest. They accepted us very well. I think we lived there for thirty years.

Q **What happened to your parents? I mean, after you married, did they remain in San Francisco?**

A Yes. Mother remained in San Francisco until my father's death.

Q **When did he die?**

A In 1950.

東京月見少年会
1937. 10. 5.

Dr. Harold Sunoo
(right, standing).

Q **And your mother?**

A My mother passed away about 1980.

Q **How many were there in the family?**

A I am the oldest of four children. Three brothers and myself.

Q **Tell us about them.**

A They are very close to each other, two brothers, especially. They have been close all their lives... David and Anthony Shin. Anthony is the first son and an attorney. David is the second son, who married a girl in Honolulu. They settled in Honolulu and he became a policeman. He was a captain in the police force until he retired.

Q **What about your children**

A I have two sons.

Q **Let's talk about the Korean National Association (KNA).**

183

A   For a while, my father was President of the KNA. My mother didn't think much of it. She used to tease him and say, "There aren't many people so why don't you take turns being President?" However, she joined too, but …

(Husband, Dr. Harold Sunoo interjected: "She was a chairman of the San Francisco branch, also." Helen responded: "For a while.")

Q   **What about the general community? Were there other kinds of activities other than the Korean activities you participated in? I know it's been a long time since you've been in San Francisco. You spent thirty years in Missouri. Do you recall any peers at that time? Any Koreans at the same age with you at that time?**

A   When we moved to the Midwest, my Korean friends were brand new friends. They were, mostly, teaching in college or universities or they were doctors.

Q   **Mrs. Sunoo, you are well-known for the many interview you conducted among Koreans everywhere, the earliest historic stories of life of Koreans in America. Let's discuss the important historical interviews that you did. You are known to have made 80 interviews of Korean picture brides or Koreans in general, starting from many decades ago. Would you tell us about that?**

A   Oh, my goodness. At that time, I wasn't…didn't know how to interview really. I let them tell me their life stories…

(Dr. Harold Sunoo, interjected: "You left your job to do that project.")

Q   **You gave up your paid profession and interviewed these Koreans of the early days…precious history, without a stipend? You gathered the memories of the first Koreans in America as a community. Is that what you did?**

A   Yes. More on their own lives. I had to spend an awful lot time of time for each interview, writing down what they remember. I did not know what a tape recorder was.

I told them that if they said something they did not want me to know then, we can erase that. Oh, I spent hours. They did have confidence in me. They said, "Why you wanted to know so much about me? I didn't know things well." I am doing this because our children are very interested in history. Many of the interviewees would always say, "I led such a shameful life, shame myself." Then, I said, "You established 'Koreanness' in us. You taught us how to be Koreans and what you have suffered as a Korean. You have done tremendous things for our life in a foreign country."

Q **What do you suppose they were ashamed of?**

A Oh, they were ashamed of their life…the fact that they left their family because in those days, a good wife saved their mother-in-law, but the women these days who came here had to be very independent. They thought, independently, which was hard to do in those days. But, I said to them "You are admirable. You are very brave to have come and then, some of you suffered with the man you married." I think among the interviewees I found only two cases of divorce.

Q **Only two cases of divorce?**

A When I asked them how they were treated when they were going to be a picture bride, some say that the families that you joined as picture brides sometimes didn't accept them as their daughters. In spite of that, they came. They knew they would be damaged. I mean banished, but they came. When they came here, they got very disappointed. Most of the men couldn't afford a wife. Most of them, said that as soon as they got married, they had to go out to the fields and work.

Q **What kind of fields were they?**

A Those that came to California, the rice fields, and fruit farms, picking fruits.

Q **These people whom you interviewed, you said all eighty of**

185

them were picture brides?

A   No. They weren't all picture brides. They weren't all women. They were men too. My aim at that time, was that we were all getting old and ready to die. I wanted to know and find out about their lives for our future knowledge of our past.

Q   **What years were these taken?**

A   They were all taken in 1975. I travelled all the world and I had to ask who knew what...from the Northwest, from California, most of them from California. I found one in Denver. One in Chicago. (Dr. Sunoo, husband: Because of the urgency that they all were on the verge of dying, she quit her job to do this.)

Q   **Oh, my goodness.**

A   At that time, I was about 60 years old, and I thought, my gosh, they're gonna die. Here I am today, older than they were, and I haven't finished.

Q   **But you've done it and it's waiting to be edited and so forth. That's wonderful. That's really great. So, they were from all over the USA, as you were saying.**

A   I saw the urgency of interviewing the early pioneers and I quit my job to complete this mission.

Q   **Totally, you interviewed how many?**

A   I interviewed over 99 Koreans or something like that. All over the United States. No one was sponsoring me at that time. It was through aid from friends and family.

Q   **They were both men and women?**

A   I began interviewing the picture brides, but the people I interviewed were men, also.

Q   **What happened to the manuscript now?**

A   I have it.

I am Dora Yum Kim, second generation. My father Yum, Man Suk came to San Francisco in 1904. I guess he must have stopped in Hawaii, and then, he came to San Francisco, where he joined a group of Chinese men and went up to Washington State and worked on the railroad tracks. After his contract there was finished, he came back to San Francisco. My mother, Han Shin Kim, came over in 1920 as a picture bride. And I was born in 1921.

Q **Where were you born?**

A I was born in Manteca, California. Apparently, they went down to the southern part of California to see if they could do farm work. They decided to come back to San Francisco, and on their way back to San Francisco, they dropped in Manteca to see their relatives, and that's where I was born. We moved on to San Francisco and have been in San Francisco ever since.

Q **Tell us about life in San Francisco.**

A Well, we all lived in China town because we weren't accepted anywhere else. People don't realize that, because now there are Asians all over the City, not only in China town, but all the other districts like Visitacion Valley, and Richmond District. They are just all over.

    My father's first business was a cigar store on the corner of Pacific and Columbus Avenues. Then, about a year later, he moved down to

Man Suk Yum, San Francisco, circa 1918.

Picture Bride, Han Shin Kim.

Picture Brides. Dora Yum Kim's mother in middle, Han Shin Kim.

Man Suk Yum family: George, Man Suk Yum, Han Shin Yum, Henry, Dora, circa 1937.

Jackson Street which is the border line of Chinatown. He had a 24-hour restaurant and my mother worked there, and we did, too, when we grew up. We lived in an apartment on Jackson Street for many years. Then, in the thirties, he decided to buy a house, one block of from Powell Street, which was the West border line of Chinatown. I believe he was the first Asian to buy property on Mason Street. When he first bought it, the Korean community said, "Oh, he's gonna 'Manghae', he's gonna go broke." After quite a while, they find out that he was doing pretty well because they saw that he bought a building with four flats and sold two for double the price. Then, he bought six apartments on George Street, sold that and bought fourteen units on the corner of Broadway and Jones. At that time it was so funny. We got a letter from the Nob Hill Association which said, "Would you please come and join us to keep Chinamen from moving up here?" I should have kept that letter. I couldn't believe it.

Q **How many children are in your family? I mean how many sisters and brothers.**

A I'm the oldest and then, came my brother, George and my youngest brother, Henry who was born in 1928. And when he grew up, George joined the U.S. Army during the Korean War. He didn't want to go, but he was drafted and he went down to Fort Ord, California, took a leadership training, then, he took a test. A Sergeant said he passed everything and that he would be good in anything he did. So, they sent him to Officer's Candidate School in Oklahoma. He graduated among over hundreds of Caucasians; he was the only Asian face in the graduation picture. And that picture is in Korea right now at the Independence Hall in Korea. The researchers there came here and took the picture and said they will make a copy and send it back, but I never got them back.

Q **Tell us a little bit more of the past again, like Korean incidents when you were a child going to grade school. Were you involved and was your father involved in Korean organizations?**

A Oh, definitely. We had a Korean Methodist Church on Powell Street in

Oak Street, First Korean Church in San Francisco. Rev. Sa Sun Whang, left with child Mary, circa 1915.

San Francisco. That's where everything started. Patriot Ahn, Changho, that's where he started his Independence Movement. The Koreans in San Francisco were really on to the Independence Movement. You know that Japan took over Korea and tried to eliminate Korea from the map. They compelled the Koreans to speak Japanese. The Koreans were stubborn enough to keep their own language on top of the Japanese they had to learn.

Q **You don't remember the Korean Methodist Church on Oak Street?**

A That's the church where my parents were married on May 1st, 1920. I have a picture of that and the building is still there. It's changed but I remember that building.

Q **By the time you were growing up, were you at the Powell Street Church?**

A No, I was at Oak Street first. I don't know how they did it but the Korean Methodist Church got some money from a wealthy woman or something like that. And the Church on Powell Street was built in 1930. Then, we had a succession of ministers and, Rev. Sa Sun Whang was the longest minister there – for 25 years. His son, Paul, is still alive.

Dora Yum Kim
second from left,
Paul Whang, Ruth
Shin Whang.

His age is 70 years old, now, but he is looking great for his age.

Q   **Tell us a little bit more about Rev. Sa Sun Whang.**
A   I remember he had a laundry cleaning store on Mason Street. When
    his son Paul Whang graduated from State College, he couldn't find a
    job. He tried to find a job when he went back home in the City near
    Chinatown. The City was full of discrimination and that was a story
    of our life, growing up with discrimination. Someone said "Couldn't
    you have done anything?" I said, "What could you do?" I mean you
    can get beat up and what's the sense of that? So, we all had to keep
    quiet.

Q   **Can you remember any activities, specific activity in the
    Korean community?**
A   The Korean Methodist Church was the only a religious order, and
    it was a place for the Koreans to get together, socially. Only a few
    Koreans were in San Francisco. There were more than a hundred to-
    tal. It was more like a community where everybody knew each other
    and most of our parents couldn't speak English. The only way was to
    get together in the church. The children all went to Sunday School
    there and went to all the activities. Their parents went there.
        My father was the President of the Korean National Association
    and was a member of the "Hungsadan" (Ahn, Changho had es-

tablished the Hungsadan, an organization as part of the KNA Independence Movement program, concentrating on the educational needs of Koreans abroad regarding their homeland.) After my father passed away, I found his books that were printed in Korean and my father was in it, saying that there are eight Provinces in Korea. Since he came from Kangwondo, he was one of eight delegates from Kangwondo. Ahn, Changho was one of them. They were very active and, so, the children were active, too, along with their parents. We never said, "No" to our parents whether we wanted to or not. We took it for granted and went to church with them all the time. When Ahn, Changho passed away in 1938 in a Japanese prison, they couldn't hold a funeral for him in Korea because we were still under Japanese rule. So, my father who, was the President of the Korean National Association in San Francisco at that time, had a memorial service for Ahn, Changho with a big picture of him. I remember I was the piano player for that ceremony. I was the piano player when Rev. Whang, Sa Son was a minister there, also. So, we have many fine memories from the Korean Methodist Church.

Q **You mention that there were over a hundred Koreans thene. To your knowledge was that the largest number or...**

A That's the largest I remember before 1965. After the Immigration Laws were relaxed in 1965, the influx of new immigrants began. Now, there are over ten thousands Koreans here in San Francisco. It's hard to believe.

Q **Getting back to the old days, then, I understand the Koreans at that time dwindled down because of what? Why?**

A No. They didn't dwindle down.

Q **Ahn, Changho was here in San Francisco. And then, he moved down to L.A. with a lot of his followers, right? His family moved down to L.A.**

A Yes.

Q **Could you tell us a little bit about the group of Koreans in San Francisco moving down to L.A.?**

A Well, you know, all the Koreans were active together. Some moved down to Los Angeles like Ahn, Changho's family did. But I think he went to Korea soon after he went to Los Angeles and he was in prison in Korea. Yes? His family settled down in Los Angeles.

Q **Were there many other families who went down too?**

A That moved down? Yes, the Lee family had a family of ten children. They had a cleaning store on Canal Street and they all moved down to Los Angeles.

Q **Did quite a number of Koreans move down there?**

A There were still Koreans here.

Q **Was Syngman Rhee here also?**

A Oh, yes. Syngman Rhee was here.

Q **What do you remember of Dr. Syngman Rhee?**

A Just that he was a visitor here. When he was in San Francisco, he stayed at Yang, Choo Eun's home. So, when Rhee became President of Korea, he invited Yang, Choo Eun to come to Korea.

Q **Who is Yang, Choo Eun?**

A He was a man who had a restaurant on a Third Street which is in a not too good area. But he was good to the Koreans that would come by because after the 1924 Exclusion Act only scholars, ministers, and students could come over. He had to feed them because they didn't have money. He even fed Syngman Rhee. Of course, Syngman Rhee had done some great work in Hawaii before coming here.

Q **What other leaders were there in San Francisco?**

A The one main person I could think of is Rev. Lee, Dae Wi. He was a minister who married my parents and many others here. He was...I think...was the first Korean who graduated from U. C. Berkeley in

Uncle Sam shop owned by Choo Eun Yang in middle and his wife on his right.

1916. He actually, graduated from Portland Academy because his son gave me his diploma, an ornate diploma. He was a big help to all the Koreans here. He is well remembered. But he died an untimely death because he worked so hard for the Korean community. I remember once I met a man from Chicago who got his Ph.D. from some college and he said he came with a group of students and they were ready to deport him back to Korea. Then, Rev. Lee came down and did or said something, and they all got to stay here because of him.

Q **Were the leaders all connected with a church?**

A Yes. All began at that church. Ahn, Changho started his Independence Movement there. Many things started from that Korean Methodist Church.

Q **You mentioned something to the effect of groups giving money to the Independence Movement?**

A   Oh, the bachelors. We had a few bachelors here at that time. And then, they were working for wealthy families. They would get one day off a month. They wanted to make much money to give all the money to the Korean Independence Movement. They were really "gungho" (strong advocates).

Q   **Who did they give the money to for the independence Movement?**

A   I think it was the Korean National Association.

Q   **Can you remember any of the Presidents of the Korean National Association besides your father?**

A   Uhm. They are mostly local people. But I don't remember their names.

Q   **Do you remember any other activities that they did as members of Kook Min Hur?**

A   Well, we had picnics once a year. And all the Koreans would come.

Q   **Did you mention something about a language school?**

A   Oh, my father was like Mr. Choo Eun Yang. He felt sorry for the Korean students and scholars coming over. So, he said to them, "I'll feed you free if you teach my children Korean." So, we had to go to Kukeo Hakgyo [국어 학교], Korean Language School every vacation time. I guess that's how I learned Korean and I remember the Korean language. I can still read and write, but I don't understand completely.

Q   **What kind of hours did the school hold?**

A   I think just a few hours a day and during the summer.

Q   **Were they quite consistent?**

A   Uh-uh. Well, nobody wanted to learn Korean at that time. Naturally, because we were kids. But, we all had to, so we did. However, my younger brother, Henry, while in the USA Army and when he was sent oversees on his way to Korea, they pulled him out from the airplane in Japan and sent him to Camp Dewy to learn Korean and six months of training and he went to Korea. And he became an interpreter at Panmunjeom. Later, he went on to the USA Army Intelligence Agency in Washington D.C. By the way, he was the first Korean American kid to be drafted by the USA Army for the Korean War.

Q **Tell us about the families that you know who were pretty steady Korean families in San Francisco. Families that you might think were "icons" of the Koreans in San Francisco.**

A Well, if you go by outstanding figures in businesses my father had a restaurant and the Shins had a restaurant across the street. Above them was a barber shop run by Henry Shin. And there was another barbershop on Washington Street run by the Cha family, and there was Kim, Dongwoo on Clay Street. And there was a cleaning shop on Kearney Street, Powell Street, and Mason Street and Pacific Avenue. Pacific Avenue was where the Moon family lived. They had a hard time. But the brother became a doctor, Dr. Henry Moon. He was a well-known pathologist and very intelligent. The Chinese doctors said they were all afraid of him at school because he was so intelligent. And he got a grant for cancer research, and yet, he died from throat cancer himself. It was sad. His youngest brother's name was Shiny, but later he changed it to William because, if he kept "Shiny", his full name would be "Shiny Moon". Instead, he changed it to William Moon. He's an anesthesiologist in Britain, right now. And he's well known there, too, I understand.

Q **So, how many whole families were active in San Francisco that you mentioned so far...**

A The two Shin families, the Chars, and Dongwoo Kim was quite a leader, too. And there was a Chun family who had a bath house on Stockwood Street. We didn't have bathtubs in the 1920s. So, people would pay to go there and take a bath.

Q **Was it "foodoo" style, like a Japanese style, many people in one big tub?**

196

A   No. I know that there were individual tubs in each room.

Q   **Tell us a little more about descendants'children.**

A   They all had children. My parents had the least number of children…
     three. The Shins had five children; the others had four children, and
     there was a family of ten, the Lees on Kearney Street, who later moved
     to Los Angeles.

Q   **The Moon family moved. Did they have the descendants here
     too?**

A   They passed away here.

Q   **No descendents still here?**

A   There is one in Britain, and the girl is on Stockton Street married to
     a doctor, Dr. Philip Park, and he passed away. Most of even the second
     generation were beginning to move away.

Q   **How about the Char family?**

A   Oh, they moved to Nevada. I was telling their daughter that all I
     remember is that she was a cute little girl. And that their mother was
     beautiful. They moved to Nevada because the father was jealous of all
     the attention she was getting from the other Korean men here.

Q   **Did you know the Har family from way back? Tell us a little
     bit what you know about that family.**

A   They had two girls and two boys, also. They had a cleaning store on
     Fillmore Street. My mother and I used to go visit them there. But they
     were a sort of aloof. They were not too friendly with the community,
     although they participated. There was another Kim family with three
     boys and two girls. But they didn't come around too much until later
     in life, when they felt like they needed to be among Koreans.

Q   **How about the Shin family? Who did the Shins marry? Philip
     Shin's family?**

A   They had five children. One was a famous boxer, Richie Shin and he passed away. I guess he passed away from Alzheimer from what I heard was from being punched on the head so much when he was a boxer. Peter, the oldest son, is still alive. Helen, the oldest daughter, is still alive and there is Pauley. The younger son died. The parents are gone, of course. The others are still alive and they have children.

Paul Whang has a daughter, Gale, who is interested in Korean history. She went down to Mexico and wrote a short paper on what she discovered there...Koreans in Mexico, speaking Korean and Spanish.

Q **Now, let's get to the new immigrants. Do you remember the Consul General, the first Consul General Choo, Younghan?**

A Yes, he came from Gangwondo, the same province as my father. So, they became pretty close. But he wasn't popular among the new Korean immigrants. He used to invite me to all his affairs. When he had his first celebration, I helped him find the first building the Consulate bought. It still exists at 3500 Clay Street. I remember they paid only $40,000 at that time. It was in 1949 after the war. That was the first Consulate.

Q **He was not popular? Why? Can you give me your version?**

A I don't know what he was. He was sort of crude and rude. The students didn't like him because he didn't grant the visas fast enough or not at all. I didn't know that until after he passed away. With him, we participated in a lot of City community activities. We had the fist trade in 1949. It was the first time the Koreans were invited to participate, so we had all the Korean girls assigned to come. We had a float and we had a beautiful Korean girl, Laney Park, as a queen. So it was nice.

Q **At that time, there was an increase of new Korean immigrants in San Francisco. Tell us about how they assimilated?**

A Nobody knew what a Korean was when we were growing up and they always asked us, "What are you? Are you Chinese?" I said "No". "You must be Japanese." I said "No". "Then, what are you?" And I would say, " Korean". "Korean? What's that?" I would tell them how

Japan came over and murdered the Queen and annexed our country in 1910 and tried to eliminate Korea from the map, entirely. We were known as the "Hermit Nation". Remember, we could never find Korea on the map in our geography books, in our history books. When the Korean influx began, the teachers had a lot of Korean students. They could not speak English, Chinese or Japanese, and then, they realized that they were Koreans. But the teachers didn't know what Koreans were until the Korea War.

At that time, I was working for the State Department of Employment starting before 1965. Apparently, I was the only Korean speaking person. So, I had to do all the interpretation, translating, and giving the Koreans their first jobs. These were for the immigrants. I don't know how they knew I was working at the State Department of Employment. Someone said that she asked someone for help and they saw my name at the airport on the board for Korean translation. Koreans coming in today don't realize that there was generations of Koreans before them. Some would say, "Oh, we're the first Koreans here." I said, "Oh, no. You're not. I'm the second generation already." They couldn't believe me. The first applicant I had to work with was a Korean pharmacist. I didn't know that pharmacist, professional registered nurses, and engineers could come over without a sponsor. But they had a tough time. They could read and write English. But they just couldn't communicate, orally. I spoke with them in Korean. One would say, "Gee, you were born here. How come you have an accent from the northern province [평양도 사투리]?" I thought for a moment and I said, "Well, my mother came from Pyongyang ," and they'd say, "Oh!" I guess I learned that from my mother. It was really funny.

Q **Did you get a feel of where these new Koreans came from, what part of Korea?**

A All I know is all they came from Seoul.

Q **Tell us little bit more of growing up when you went to school. Were there other Korean students in your class?**

A No, I was always the only one. When I entered UC Berkeley, there were only two Koreans: Mabel Park and myself. We had to join that Chinese Club because there was no Korean Club. Now, I hear there are thousands of Koreans there in Berkley.

Q **How did you feel to be Korean among the Chinese? Were they good to you?**

A We were discriminated against by the Chinese at Berkeley but having grown up in Chinatown, we were accepted by the Chinese, there. So, we got along with the Chinese in San Francisco Chinatown. For instance, when I was called my Chinese friend on the telephone and her mother answers, I can hear her mother says, "Oh, your Korean girl friend is on the phone." The Chinese in Chinatown used to say. . ."Oh, all the same...Chinese and Koreans...all the same." So, that was fine in San Francisco Chinatown.

Q **What about the early days, did you know anything about Korea and being Korean yourself. I mean, do you know much about what was happening in Korea besides the Japanese invasion?**

A Well, we heard terrible the stories about what the Japanese were doing in Korea. I remember my mother telling me that the Japanese soldiers would come down the hill and the dogs would bark to warn them that they were coming. They had only one knife among three families or something like that. When the Japanese came down they took everything, and they killed their little dog. And she never forgot that...

Q **How about Korean history. Do you know Korean history besides the war?**

A We learned about history in the Korean school [국어학교].

Q **What did you learn?**

A The Lee Dynasty and Han Dynasty. And we learned the alphabet. They said the Koreans are stubborn like the Irish, you know, stubborn and like to drink, like the Irish.

Q **Tell me a little bit about your contacts with your father's family or your mother's family in Korea. Were there any contacts, besides the fact that there was a war. Was there any contact before the war began?**

A No. Up until 1924, I remember my father was sending money to his sister and to her family in Gangwondo. I have a picture of their family, but of course, I never saw them in person. When I went to Korea last time, I met the Mayor of Gangwondo. He said, "I'll take you to meet your relatives," and someone said, "No, you'd better not go. They all want to go to America."

Q **And your mother's family?**

A My grandmother, all I know is that I have a picture of her and her maid and that's all.

Q **Who were your best friends when you were youngster?**

A I think a Chinese girl. Because I was the youngest among the Korean girls here, I had to find girls my age. The Chinese and Korean friends all had sisters and I didn't.

Q **Do you remember hearing about an important person that came from Washington D.C. who was supposed be marrying into a descendent of the Korean Royal family, do you remember that?**

A Was that the one in the Min family?

Q **Yes. That's the family. Do you remember the family at all? How did you know about them?**

A I just knew that they were somebody here of royalty. But they never came around much. The only way I knew of any Korean is if they were here permanently and coming to the church. We would meet them at the church to get to know them. I don't remember them at all, except that the wife was royalty or something to that effect.

Q **What else would you like to tell us?**

A Just about growing up without all the things are happening with the new immigrants. Now, it's surprising to see all the Korean restaurants. We never had this many Korean restaurants before. You have to give them credit. They all are doing well. The new immigrants have better opportunities than we had, except for the English language. All my children were born in San Francisco, grand children and great grand-children. They can't speak Korean. They sort of always ask me, "Why didn't you teach us?" I never knew we had use for it or even have interest in it. Now, there are Korean schools here. My son, Tom, was the one who wrote the proposal for what is now the Korean Center. It was called the Multi-Service Center for Koreans at that time. Gale Whang was one of them. And Melanie Han, Dr. Steve Shon, and Tom Suh, the attorney, all got together. They wanted to do something for the new Koreans who were coming over. But, something went wrong. We noticed, Gale and I, we couldn't get along with the new Koreans. They were different. And so, we all resigned and that's when then they moved the office a couple of times and went to Margaret Street. Now, they are at Post Street.

Q **What was this about not getting along together? What? Why? What do you think started that not getting along?**

A I have no idea. At first, when we were going to meetings, all they were doing is fighting. We didn't like that.

Q **Was it miscommunications?**

A That had something to do with it because the third generation here couldn't speak Korean. The new Koreans would make fun of them. Their ideas just didn't match. When we lost that program, we opened the Korean Community Service Center. That's when I started the Korean Senior Meal Program. Later, the Korean Center took it over.

Q **I guess the new immigrants were in greater need for that kind of center than the first wave, but then, I know you, Dora, personally, worked hard there.**

My name is Eleanor Chun You, and I'm a third generation Korean born in Hawaii in 1918.

My maternal grandparents are Mary Chun Park and Mr. Park. They had three children, two daughters, Young Nani and Sela Won, who was my mother, and a son, KwonJin. They bought Young Nani and Kwon Jin to Hawaii. However, they left my mother, Sela, in Korea so that she could go to school there. Sela was left in Korea with a Korean family to finish her education. However, my grandmother found out through the grapevine that she was taken out of school and was being used as a maid. They were upset. They decided that my grandfather should go back to Korea and bring back Sela to Hawaii. And so he did. But, on the way coming back, he got typhoid fever on the ship when he was bringing Sela back. Unfortunately, my grandfather died and he was quickly, buried at the seaside where the grave site was. Shortly after burial, his coffin got washed away during a thunderstorm. It was awfully sad.

In the meantime, my grandmother was thinking of getting a husband for Sela, her youngest daughter. Before Sela ever had set foot in Hawaii, she already had a fiancé. Why? Because my grandmother thought that Chin Wha Chun, who worked on the sugar plantation on Kauai would make a good husband for her daughter. He was smart and industrious, although he was about fifteen years older. Anyway, Chin Wha Chun liked what he saw and agreed to marry her. So, they became my parents.

Chin Wha Chun with bowler hat and Sela (in front of him on his right) on the Koloa, Kauai Planation when Sela arrived in Hawaii 1908.

There were six children in our family: three daughters and three sons. My sister Hazel, Margaret, myself, and my brothers: Soon Ho, Soon Sung and Soon Tae. Soontae died at an early age.

After a few years my father took us out of the plantation on Kauai and bought a furniture store on Fort Street in Honolulu after saving all their money when they came to Honolulu. My two brothers, Soon Ho and Soon Sung would go to the furniture store and help unpack boxes of furniture parts from the Mainland and assemble the furniture. I also would go there after school to collect money for my father whenever furniture was sold.

My mother took all the laundry there to wash the clothes in the back of the furniture store. She was always there, cooking or washing laundry.

Hazel, Sela, Margaret, and Chin Wha Chun, circa 1918.

204

Chin Wha Chun family.
Left to right: Eleanor (You),
Margaret, Sela, Soon Tae
(on lap), Hazel, Soon Sung,
Chin Wha, Soon Ho, circa
1926.

Chin Wha Chun, circa 1915.

She was busy bringing up the family, seeing that we were brought up with the right disciplining. She was a wonderful mother. My father was very protective towards her. They all worked hard. We were so busy. My father later, moved us to Beretania Street and opened another store near Aala Park. During the war, there was no furniture being shipped to Hawaii, so my father retired from the furniture business. And instead, he invested in real estate and rental properties. Although we came from a large family, we had a comfortable existence from his wise investments and hard work.

In the meantime, when we were on the island of Kauai, my grandmother remarried. Remember my grandfather died when he went back to Korea to bring my mother to Hawaii. So, my grandmother remarried a few years later. She married Kim, Dong-gun, who was a good friend of her first husband. They used to know each other at the sugar plantation on Kauai. They later moved to Honolulu, also, and worked at the Goodale Estate, a remote area of Kapai on the island of Oahu. They were caretakers of the three acres that the Goodales owned there. Grandmother also raise chickens there. She fed the chickens "sanipies" (scorpions). So, we used to go and catch "sanipies" for grandmother. She gave us all a big tall glass to catch "sanipies" to feed the chickens. So, I happily went with my brothers to catch them cause we had fun catching them for the chickens. We would have a contest who would catch the most "sanipies" among my sisters and my brothers. So, it was a joyous occasion then. The poor chickens. Grandmother, also grew their own vegetables; our parents were very resourceful. They grew chili pepper, green onion, string beans, cabbage, and turnip.

Q **Where was this again?**

A Kapai. That's on Oahu. It's a remote area. Past Waialua. Every Sunday my mother and my father would drop us off over there every summer. They taught us how to catch crabs, also. My grandpa would get a big square can and plant it on the sand and he would put fermented seawater in the can. The crabs would climb in. We'd go off and play about two hours. When we came back and the can was full of crabs. My grandmother would would pickle them with soyu and garlic. It was so good.

Q **What did your step grandfather do? For a living?**

A For a living? He was a caretaker for the Goodale and that's because the Goodales would come every other Sunday to relax and play there. Then, grandfather would take care of the property while they were gone and would get the place ready for them and clean up after all that. We would help him rake the road leading to the beach house.

Q **Tell us about your father. What is his background?**

A He was just a smart man. That's why I admired him. He made something of himself. He loved his wife, my mother, so much. We loved them both so very much.

Q **Where is he from? Did he have any relatives here?**

A He had about five brothers in Korea, I understand. I have never been to Korea to meet them.

Q **Did they write? Or did they communicate?**

A Not that I know of.

Q **Was he active in the Korean Methodist Church?**

A Not really. He was active in this furniture store.

Q **What about the Dongji Hoi? Did he belong to the Dongji Hoi? Or Kook Min Hur? or the Korean Christian Church?**

A As far as I can recall, he may have been, but it doesn't click in my mind. He wasn't active; he was more a family man. The family came first with him because he loved my mother so much. My mother would cook some food and we would go over and eat it out in the forest. He was strictly family man.

Q **But you didn't go to the church yourself?**

A Yes, I did. I even taught at the Sunday school at the Korean Methodist Church. That's where I am from. I have been taught at Sunday School and I taught there when I grew up. I take my children to the church every Sunday.

Q **When did you start attending the Methodist Church since your parents didn't attend the church. When did you start?**

A No, they did go to the church, also. Methodist Church. My memory's coming back. They did go to church. They were very gracious, and loved to meet people.

At church when I was young, I remember my father would say to me, "Soonyeeya. You always sleep when you are in the church. Don't do that." Yeah, my memory is coming back. And he would say to me "Don't talk, talk, in church and don't look all over. You're always looking over see who is in the back of you. Don't do that. Just sit still in one place."

Q **Was your father a member of Kook Min Hur (the National Korean Association) or Dongji Hoi?**

A I don't remember. I don't remember those things, too well, because he was busy.

Q **Let's talk about your husband. Who is he and how did you meet him?**

A Dr. Richard You was my husband. Richard's father had a rooming house across my father's furniture store in Honolulu. He was young. I saw him for the first time across the street going to his father's furniture room to help clean it. I didn't know this at that time. But he told me after when we got married that he saw me, too. He went and cleaned the father's furnished room.

How did I meet him? He was in same room as my sister, Margaret from years back. She said he was a wonderful, wonderful boy. She always admired Richard You. He said he was going to become a doctor. Very ambitious. One day I was going home from school and I felt like somebody was looking at me. So, I turned around and there was this

Dr. Richard You.

Dong Men You, father of Dr. Richard You.

208

Dong Men and Mary You family, circa 1924. Left to right: Henry, Melvin, Won Young, Mary, Minnie, Katie, Dong Men, Wonsik, and Richard.

young man smiling. So, I ran home and told Margaret. "You know, there was a tall, good-looking boy, staring at me." She said, "That's Richard You. He is a good boy." Then, we started dating. One day he said to me, "What kind of flowers do you like?" I said, "Why? What kind of flowers do you like?" He said, "Tulips" I said, "Tulips?" He looks at my lips and kissed me while I said, "Two lips." And that was our first kiss. We got engaged. Then, he went away to go to Medical School. I waited for him for four years. When he came back, we got married.

(Richard You became a medical doctor and was appointed as one of the International Medical Doctor for the Olympics for many years.)

Q **What can you tell us about his father, Dong Men You?**

A My father-in-law. I remember him. Not too much. The only thing I remember of him is when I went to the airport to see my husband go off to Medical School. He was there, also.

Q **What do you know about him?**

A Not too much. All I know about is what his mother told me about him. They were sort of separated, so to speak.

Q **Let's talk about your childhood? What school did you graduate from?**

A Mckinley High School.

Q **Tell us about your brothers.**

A It makes me sad when I think about my brothers cause they died so young. My sister, Hazel married young to Peter Kim from Waialua. Margaret was married to Young Hee Ko because she wanted the richest man in Hawaii. Although his family sent him to Korea to look for a wife, he came back without a wife because he liked my sister, Margaret. They got married.

My paternal grandfather, I understood, had three wives back in Korea. He brought his favored wife, Mary, my grandmother to Hawaii. That's what I understood when I was young.

Whanjin, my youngest uncle went off to California for the gold rush before his father…my grandfather died. Then, he came back after several years to honor his father. But the grave site was washed away. So, he was very upset and he went back to California. We never heard from him ever again. He was very upset. That's what I heard when I was young from the family. He never came back again. So, my grandmother used to always cry about him, "What happened to Whanjun," she used to cry. She used to be so sad, taking about him. She talked about him all the time.

Q **Did you hear anything about the community activity and leaders such as Syngman Rhee?**

A Not really. That's a different group. We were Methodist. We were not affiliated with things like that.

Q **What about Kook Min Hur?**

A What is that? My father was too busy with that furniture store and family, as far as I can remember, the family came first with him.

My name is Agnes Eunsoon Rho Chun.

My father, Hee Chang Rho, also, known as Hee Gyeom Rho, came from Ong Jin, Hwanghaedo sometime in 1903. My mother was left behind. This is a story I heard from my mom.

My mother and dad married in Korea and had three children. My parents were very young when the children all died. One day, she was told that my Dad had gone to Hawaii with Mr. Lee, Hong Gee. I understand that Mr. Lee, Hong Gee was the one who was instrumental in getting my father here. My dad had come here with the understanding, I believe, that my mother was going to be taken care of by her sister who was quite wealthy in the same village, while he was gone.

Hee Chang Rho Chun, circa 1925.

Upon arrival in Hawaii my father was sent to the Kauai Plantation with Lee, Hong Gee. I don't know when they came out here, but they later went to Honolulu, the Capitol of Hawaii. After ten years my father sent for my mother to come here. She came here sometime

Family Photograph: Left to Right: Flora Keum Soon, Violet, Jung Sun, Hee Chang Rho, Jung Han.

in 1913 and lived in the Palama District of Honolulu. As far as I know, my mother had not had any experience on the plantation.

They had five children born here in Honolulu. My siblings were Jung Han Rho, my second brother, Jung Sun Rho, my sister Flora Keum Soon Rho Park, and my second sister, Violet Rho. Violet's name is actually, Violet Oksun Rho Cho. I was the last one in the family living. We had one other brother who was right above me who died very young. The first time that I was aware of the family chokbo [족보] which is the genealogy of the family, was in 1950, when my sister-in-law had a cousin who came from Korea and said that this document was a chokbo, a genealogy record. This chokbo was with my mother at that time. My father had passed away in 1935, when I was 9 years old. I was not aware of the chokbo, until I heard my mother say that she had given this chokbo to my brother so that his wife's cousin could do some translation on it, and I never saw since then.

Later on, I found out from my mother that this Jokbo was lost. Somehow, they lost track of it. That's what I heard. So, my mother went to her grave in 1953, thinking that this Jokbo was lost and she was very upset about it. However, when my brother passed away in 1997, my sister-in-law gave it to me and said that I should have this document because it is part of our Rho family tree. I was very surprised. I understood now that the Jokbo is a part of

212

Left to Right: Jung Sun, Agnes, mother, Jung Han, Hee Chang Rho, Violet, Flora.

each family in Korea. This Jokbo actually shows it as Seygye [세계], meaning "from the beginning". As far as I know, the first grandfather who is noted here is recorded to have lived in the Koryo Dynasty period. I understand there are several pieces here which indicate the family tree. There are some pieces that shows the names, and the date of death of the family members.

We have one item in the Jokbo which is very unique. I found out from Dr. Youngho Chae at the University of Hawaii that this is not usually part of the chokbo. We couldn't understand what this was, but evidently, I remember, according to my mother one of the family used to be a city clerk. From what I understand this appears to be a mathematical booklet, probably, for taxation purposes because it does indicate here the military taxes, other land and grain taxes. So this is very unique part of our Jokbo document. This is something that someday I hope someone we will be able to translate to let us know exactly what it is.

From what I understand, my grandfather, the progenitor of the Rho clan was very instrumental in helping the King of the Koryo Dynasty. This is supposed to be what is called Seygye. This is the main chokbo listing all of the members of our family and they, also, have it graded by class. First class, second class, third class. This one here is a taxation book.

Q **Tell us a little bit more about your father, what he was doing here and about his affiliations.**

A I remember my mother telling me that when my father came here, he worked at the Del Monte Pineapple Cannery. I believe he was also, a security guard. I know that he was contracted by the company for the stacking of cans. The modern way of doing it is to have it mechanized by having all of the cans come on palettes. But I understand in those days they had to have Pineapples stacked by hand. So, I guess my father must have contracted a few people to work with him. The funny part of this story is what my mother told me about my father's honesty. What he would do when he was in charge of a working group, is that when he got paid, he had to distribute the money amongst them. Whenever there were a few pennies left, my father would buy these horse matches... when I say horse matches, those were little boxes of matches with a horse printed on it. He would, then, divide the matches amongst them. My mother thought it was crazy. She said, "Why couldn't he just keep that few pennies?" But, he was that way, he wanted to make everything equitable.

Another story was that my father who was very good handyman. One day his friend recognized my father's potential in fixing things. The friend thought of fixing broken things and selling them for a profit. So, he propositioned my father to go into a second hand business with him. They embarked on this idea. The gentleman said that he would be responsible for collecting the items, and my father would be responsible for having them refurbished. My father went into the business, but my mother said after a while, they had to dissolve it because there was a lot of friction between those two. What happened was that my father could not see selling an item that the fellow purchased for 15 cents and sell it for like $2.50 or $3.50. The profit margin was so great that my father said it was very dishonest. That's the way he was. So, we were sure he would never become a millionaire.

In 1935 my father passed away after a long illness. My brother Jung Han who was the eldest was pulled out of high school in his junior year. My sister, also, was pulled out. They both worked to support the family. My mother, then, had to start to learn how to sew trousers. We had many other Korean friends who became tailors, and they were running the shops. They delivered trousers and my mother would sew them. At a very young age, too, I learned how to sew button holes and help my mother. She, also, worked at the Pineapple Cannery as a trimmer. During those days, we were very poor and were not able to even have my brothers continue school. My second brother became a tailor. My sister, also, did not finish school. My sister, Violet, and myself, we both finished high school. This was our history about education. Then, when the war broke out, we were not able to continue to high school.

Q **How about activities at the church? Tell us about the church.**

A As far as I can remember, I was a member of the Korean Christian Church on Liliha Street, since I was born. I remember going to the Church and the Korean Language School located on School Street in Kalihi. We had another church on School Street. That is where the present Korean Care Home is located. We had buildings there, which were torn down to build the Korean Care Home. That's as far as I can remember. Then, when we built the church on Liliha Street, I was there, helping them clean the yard, as far as I can remember. That was probably, in 1938 or 1939, when the church was first built. I've been going there since and during the war. It was very difficult for me to be at church, steadily, because I was employed full time at Pearl Harbor.

Q **What about your father? Do you remember him being active in church?**

A As far as I can remember, I was only nine years old when he passed away. I remember him, but I don't remember his activities. Looking at my papers that we have, I see that he was active in the Korean Christian Church and the Dongji Hoi [동지회], I am sure.

Q **How about your mother?**

A My mother was always very active in church, as far as I can remember. She was very active in the Ladies' Society, and she was always there for any kind of programs that they had in support of the Founder of our Korean Christian Church, Dr. Syngman Rhee. I can say that my family, actually, my mother, myself, and my sister, Violet, and my brother, Junghan, just those are the ones I can remember going to church.

Q **What about contacting relatives in Korea?**

A As far as I know, our relatives were in the northern part of Korea. They did come down to the southern part of Korea, but I lost track of them.

Q **Is that both on father's and mother's side?**

A I think it's only my mother's side.

Q **Do you think your parents had a lot of family members in Korea?**

A I am not sure. All I can remember is my mother saying that there was a very talented young man in that family. While he was very young, he may have been kidnapped, or simply, disappeared. He was so very talented, my mother said, that he may have been kidnapped by someone who knew of his real talent. Another thing is, I still remember my mother saying that my grandfather used to be Jusa [주사]. I guess, it was a clerk, like a city hall clerk.

Recognizing my heritage didn't start until after my mother passed away. I wish things like this had begun earlier so that we would be aware of these documents.

Q **Many people missed the chance.**

A Exactly, I had thought of interviewing my mother several times, but never got around to it. It was really sad. My mother was a typical house wife. It was when she came to Hawaii that she was able to read and write. She learned to do that all by herself.

One example was so funny. One day, I came home from work and she said, "Oh, I wrote a letter to your sister (who was in California and could read simple Korea characters)." I read it, and as I was going along, I said, "What is this?" [이거 뭐야] She said, "Sutoa" [수토아]. I

216

said again, "What is Sutoa?" [수토아가 뭐야?] And then, she told me, again indignantly, she said, "Sutoa". Then, it dawned on me that what she really, meant was a "store". So, I told, "Oh, my goodness! [아이구] Why didn't you write, "Jeombang" ("store" in Korean)? ["왜 점방 안 썼어?"] She was kind of she hurt, but, she laughed. This showed that all of a sudden, she was trying to use English words "store" instead of the Korean word, "Jeombang." I said to myself, "Well, at least she was kind of westernized in a little way." I was very surprised that through diligence, she was learning on her own, how to read the Korean newspaper, also, Dongji Hoi Sinmun, specifically.

So, that was a story that I carry in my heart about my mother ...

Q **The last time we talked about your neighborhood friends, you said they were, mainly, Episcopalians.**

A Yes. We lived on Pua Lane for many, many years in the Palama area of Honolulu. I realized now that many of the Koreans there, many, many Koreans, were mostly, members of the St. Luke's Episcopalian Church on Kanoa Street. They lived all around in the Pua Lane Area. I had so many friends in that area who were from the Episcopal Church. They were, also, store keepers. They had little shops on King Street. We had cleaning shops, shoemakers, furniture store and several Korean grocery stores on King Street.

Q **Why do you think there were many Korean Episcopalians in that area?**

A I really don't know. Could it have been that it was in the vicinity of the Episcopal Church that brought them there? And usually, later, friends who go to the same Church get to live there, also. Or it could be that because they already lived in that area, they go to the nearest Church. I think that's probably what happened there. I really don't know, for sure. That seems to have happened at the Korean Christian Church. We, more or less, made friends around the Church.

Q **Could you name some friends among the Episcopalians, there?**

A   Yes, there is Charles Choo family, Anita Choo. There is the Moon, Young-whan, who was one of the grocery store people. There is the Adam Lee's family whose parents' were running a cleaning shop. We had Molly Chung and Jonny Chung. They were living across us. We had Patsy Kim and Calvin Kim, Audrey Kim. Those families were there.

Q   **Were they all Episcopalians?**

A   They were all Episcopalians..and several others in that vicinity. I remember Mrs. Mary Kang. Her daughter was Rosline Shida. Her mother went to the Episcopalian Church, eventually, Rose came to our church.

Q   **I think you are old enough to have witnessed the turbulences at the Korean Christian Church in 1940 and 1960.**

A   We had a couple of them, I remember, but like I said, I was playing low-keyed about politics most of the time. During the first disturbance, I was busy working. In fact, all along, I was working, so I never did take an active part in it. I remember many of the incidences that happened there. Going back to the incidences at the church, much of it was, I think, was among the older group that were involved in the turbulence there. As I said, I was working, and hardly went to church, regularly, at that time. So, I really don't know, too, much. I knew the outcome of the actual disturbances, but not much about reasons for them. I know that we had these disturbances at church which was very unnerving at times. I remember my parents, my mother, especially, were more involved in those incidences. The second incidence, as far as I know, had to do with the Minister again. I really can't remember the very specific incidences that happened. It was sort of a general feeling amongst the people that this was going on. The elderly persons were key players in the Liliha Church.

Q   **Tell us about the arrival of the new immigrants after 1950's. I can recall a rather large number of them went directly to the Korean Christian Church.**

A   Oh, yes. I understand what you're talking about. When the war broke out, I believe most of us were in the busy down town and in the Makiki areas.

For a long time, Honolulu City was small. As the circumference of the City widened beyond Kaimuki and Kahala, the new areas beyond Aina Hina came up. Koreas who were in the more wealthy circle moved to those areas. As the years went by, we noticed many of the children of the original immigrant families were moving outward from the immigrant areas. Many of them decided that it was too far to come to their original church and their working hours did not allow it. So, many of them joined local churches within their neighborhood. We, who remained in the old area, noticed that our membership was growing smaller and smaller, until the newer immigrants came, I guess, in the late '50s and early '60s. We noticed that many of the new immigrants joined our church. The congregation was getting bigger in the way of the new immigrants versus the locals. I guess many other churches, too, this was going on. We had a good report among new immigrants who joined us. Although, many of the immigrants felt that our church was not as warm in some ways.

Q   **Back to the past, you were beginning to tell us that the church was started by Dr. Syngman Rhee. Tell us a little bit more. Why did he split?**

A   From what I understand, through the years, Dr. Syngman Rhee was not happy with the Methodist Church hierarchy. We were told that many of the the Methodist decisions were made at the Methodist National Office on the Mainland. Rhee felt that for the Koreans this was not enough for them. So, I guess he left the Methodist Church and started his own group. I believe my mom and dad were one of those who went with him and have been with him, throughout the years. We stayed with him as part of the Korean Christian Church.

Q   **Any other historical events that you could remember? You were born in the 1920's. You were in Honolulu where most of the activities were taking place, whereas, lots of other Korean**

families were still on outside island.

A   Well, as far as I am concerned, I tried to become a part of the Korean community, also. I was very active with the Korean Community Council and I joined the Korean Chamber. This was back in the 1970s that I joined the Chamber. I've been with the Chamber, until couple of years ago. I don't believe I am still on their roster. I just kind of, slowly, gave up. The Chamber's membership is now mostly young people and so, I just kind of dropped out. The Korean Community Council had many activities in which I was very active. Whenever they had any kind of programs, I was always there for them. That's all I can remember.

Q   **How about the leaders of the Korean Christian Church? Who were the leaders way back then, way way back?**

A   I can remember old names like Dr. You Chan Yang, Nodie Kimhaekim Sohn, Syung Woon Sohn (Nodie's husband), Dr. Y.K. Kim (the Ambassador from Korea to the Philippines, appointed by Dr. Rhee after WWII). We had Sung Dae Choi, You Sil Lee, Inez Kong Pai, and her mother. They were very active, too. I remember those people. And there is this Mr. Ahn, Hyun-Kyung, Salome Han's stepfather. I know they were involved in a lot of activities for the independence of Korea. We were just youngsters going to the church at that time.

My husband, Soon Ho Chun, was a member of the Methodist Church when I married him. When we met, it was just getting to know each other, and I don't think there was any distinguishing Methodists from Korean Christians. It was nothing like that. We got married at the Korean Christian Church. He eventually became part of our Korean Christian Church. Women are stronger than men.

Q   **Last time you mentioned something to the effect that there may still be some sort of negative feelings between the two groups among the young set, as well.**

A   I think so, but very subtle. I think they still, considered them as Methodist or Korean Christian Church members. I think there is still the subtleness.

Q **Can you tell us little bit more?**

A You mean the differences? Okay. When you talk about our age group, this is the second generation now, we have older second generation, too, which I think are more knowledgeable about the split, right? But with us, the younger second generation, we still once in a while talked about Rooke Avenue, the Headquarters for the Korean National Association (also known as Kook Min Hur), as versus, not the being a member of that Association. The KNA was associated with the Methodist Church.

Q **Could you explain Rooke Avenue?**

A Rooke Avenue... I believe it is the meeting place for the Methodist Group, I think, who bought the Rooke Avenue building.

Q **You mean, Kook Min Hur.**

A Kook Min Hur, which is equivalent with the Dongji Hoi for the Korean Christian Church. It's a political association, right? Kook Min Hur are the Methodists, and the Korean Christian Church are the Dongji Hoi. I think Koo Min Hur has their headquarters for meetings on Rooke Avenue. I've been there, I was invited to attend one of the gatherings. But, the third generation, probably, would not have made any distinction between the two organizations. Even I, a second generation, didn't know too much. I never knew that there was such a thing as a Korean Military in Hawaii out here, sponsored by Kook Min Hur. That was way before my time, as far as I can remember. Only, after I got involved in the 75th anniversary of the Korean immigration to Hawaii, and the 90th anniversary that I realized that there was military organization of Koreans out here in Hawaii.

Interview with Hazel Pahk Chung
speaks about her husband Rev. **Euicho Chung**

Euicho was born in Korea, I think in Busan, and came to Hawaii with his parents when he was about 2 or 3 years old. The Hawaiian Islands were wanting laborers for the cane fields and his parents joined the immigration group. Euicho's family was assigned to the island of Kauai. So, he grew up on the Island of Kauai. His mother and father opened a tailoring business.

Ho Young Chung family, circa 1912. Left to right: Euicho, Ho Young, Margaret, Ellen, mother.

Euicho Chung, circa 1922.

When Euicho came from Korea with his parents, Korea was under Japan. And so, he was considered as a Japanese citizen. For all those years that he went to school in Hawaii, he was classified as a Japanese because as I said Korea was under Japan and all children born in Korea during the Occupation and Annexation by Japan were automatically, Japanese citizens.

After going to grade school in Hawaii, Euicho's parents wanted a better education for him, so he was sent to Iolani School which was an Episcopal school. The Principal of the Iolani School felt that this young oriental boy had much potential. After graduating from Iolani High School, Euicho and his parents agreed that he should still further his education. Euicho went to Oregon University.

Euicho's father was Ho Young Chung (정호 영). His younger brother, Choon Young Chung (준영) came from Korea, also. I remember that the first thing when Euicho introduced me to his father was that his father asked me what church I attended. I told him that I attend the Korean Methodist Church. He didn't say anything, but apparently, he must have been a part of that church, too. As far as I can remember, I don't think the family ever was members of Kook Min Hur.

When I got married to Euicho, I automatically, lost my American citizenship because of the law about marrying an alien, even though I was born here in Hawaii. And through the years after I married Euicho, I was registered as a Japanese citizen because the male spouse's citizenship determines the wife's citizenship, according to the American Law. Being a Japanese was sort of a handicap, but still, it didn't make much difference to me. In spite of that, I decided to get married. I had to go to Kauai to get married because his parents were living there. His mother and father were very upset that he was getting married to me because he was a college graduate and I was just a high school graduate, so his parents kind of frowned on me. It was felt that he could have done better, than marrying a girl not well educated as he was. He got his Master's Degree in North Dakota, living with Norwegians up there. We got married on Kauai.

Q **Why was it difficult to be classified under the Japanese?**

A I think the difficulty was just between the Koreans and the Japanese, not the whole Islands. We lived in a camp, a Korean camp. There were Okinawa camps, Filipino camps, Japanese camps. And somehow, as I remember, we were classified, when we were going to school, as a Japanese. My parents did not like the idea, but we couldn't help it. And it went on and on like that until we finished high school.

About the time I was living in Hilo on the Big Island of Hawaii, my sisters in Honolulu wrote to me and said that my two sisters who were born in Korea were becoming naturalized Americans because of a new immigration law, the Walter McCarran Act. I didn't know what "naturalization" was. My sisters explained that I needed to go

Rev. Euicho Chung and Hazel Pahk Chung family, circa 1932.

to the U.S.A. Courthouse in Hilo to apply for American citizenship, called "naturalization." They said that it would be easier for me to apply where I lived. So, I went to the U.S.A. Court in Hilo to be naturalized, feeling confident that all will be fine.

Something funny happened there in court. Because Hilo was a small town everybody knew each other. Even "big people" and "little people" would go to the YWCA and play games, like badminton and tennis and things like that. I had been playing badminton with Judge Frank McLoughton. He was the "big judge" in the town of Hilo. Imagine, me playing with a Judge at the badminton court nearly everyday. When my sisters from Honolulu wrote to me and told me that I could be naturalized easier in Hilo because my name was already mentioned in their naturalization papers, all I had to do was go to the local courthouse in Hilo to be sworn in and sign the paper. So, I went to the courthouse to be sworn in. When I got to the courthouse, I was told that I had to sit up there on the witness chair. I went up and sat down. And of all things! The judge walked in the room and it was Judge Frank McLaughlin. So I said to myself, "This is going to be easy for me." But Judge McLaughlin pounded his gravel, "pong pong" and he said, "Stand up, Mrs. Chung, I didn't give you permission to sit down." I felt so embarrassed in the whole big Court Room of the United States of America. So, I stood up straight. Then, after he asked me questions, he told me I could sit down. I sat down and I said to myself: "Wait till I get him at the badminton court tonight."

So, I was naturalized as a American citizen which I insisted I always was. That was a funny, humiliating incident. I liked Judge McLaughlin very much, but I was ready to scold him that night at the badminton court. After I arrived at the YMCA, I leaned against the wall where I usually wait my turn. I had my crossed with my badminton racket in hand. Then, Judge McLaughlin came by and he tapped me with his racket. I said, "Don't talk to me." The Judge said to everybody out loud, "She had the audacity to sit down. I didn't give her permission to sit down." Everybody there all laughed. We were friends again.

My stay in Hilo was very, very nice. However, my husband was called by the Methodist Mission Administration to go to the

Honolulu Methodist Church because they needed a young English speaking Minister. We were losing a lot of young people in the churches everywhere at that time. Our church, the Korean Methodist Church on Fort Street, was the largest in Hawaii.

Q Do you remember what year you went there?

A I can't remember that far back. I know our kids were little. I have pictures of our children there when Rachel was about 4 years old in front of the church sometime in 1934.

Q Tell me about the early relationship between the Methodist Church and Kook Min Hur and the Korean Methodist Church.

A That was long before my time. However, I remember Dr. Rhee. He was head of his Korean Christian Church after he left the Korean Methodist Church in 1918, and his followers were there at his church on Liliha Street.

As kids, it seems to us that the older people were so nationalistic. Mainly, in the beginning they were against only the Japanese. When Dr. Rhee came here, it seems like he divided the Koreans. At that time he wanted all Koreans to go to his church, but my sisters felt that we should stay where we are, with the Methodist Church. Religion had nothing to do with being Korean or nationalistic things. A church is a church. So, we stuck with the Methodist Church. But Kydokyo (Korean Christian Church) which is the other church on Liliha Street, I know it divided a lot of Korean families, like my father-in-law. He stayed with the Methodist, but some relative became Korean Christian Church members. It's one of those political, plus, national and Christian thing.

I remember so clearly when we were living on a plantation (it was after Rhee had become the President of the Korean Provisional Government), everybody began singing, "Dr. Rhee is leading the Koreans, leading the Koreans." And we began singing that, too. He is leading the Koreans because he was against the Japanese or something. We, as kids, didn't know what it was all about.

At Liliha Street, that's Dr. Rhee's church, and the other church, which was the Methodist Church, we had quite a bit of conflict, in the sense that we were told by Rhee's side that we were joining the "white people." I don't know what they had against the white people, but we were told if you wanted to be a Korean, you have to go to Rhee's church. And I still remember that on the plantations where I grew up, the whole group of Korean children would come and sing the same thing, "We're Koreans, we're Koreans," but we didn't know there was a separation of churches. We just stuck with the Methodist through that fight, right along. We weren't nationalistic. We were more Christians. The Korean Christian Church members worshiped Dr. Rhee as God. When we visited that church on Liliha Street, we noticed that they had a Korean flag instead of the Christian flag. Christian flag is what we felt that we were Christians, not this Dr. Rhee's thing. So, that's the way that division stayed. So, living on the plantation you had two divisions: Dr. Rhee's on one side and the Koreans who stayed with the Methodist. According to the other side, the Methodists were the Americans. That's how much I remember about the division of the churches. Our family chose to stick with our church on Fort Street (the Methodist Church).

We had nothing against Dr. Rhee, other than the fact that our parents felt that church should not be mixed with politics. Kook Min Hur is the people against Dr. Rhee, but we were not politically inclined in that aspect, either, but then, it became that way when the politics came in with the mixture of churches. So that's how I stayed with the church and with my father and mother-in-law on Kauai, to this day.

But still, my mother and father had Dr. Rhee's picture up on the wall, you know. (This was because Rhee was elected as the President of the Korean Provisional Government, 'KOPGO', in Shanghai 1919. His portrait was given to every Korean family in Hawaii. In respect for the Korean Independence Movement, Korean Methodists accepted the KOPOGO election). They considered him an important man, but we didn't consider him as Christ, you know. And that's why we just went to the Methodist church.

Q **Tell us anything that you remembered of other Korean leaders in the community when you were young. Do you know Pak, Young Man?**

A Yes, he was the leader, the opposite leader against Dr. Rhee. He was impressive, but we were more interested in our own life and our own education. However, there is something I remember as a youngster on the Ewa Plantation about Pak, Young Man. I remember the Korean men who followed him carrying some wooden things on their shoulders like it was a gun. And before that some young men people would come to our Korean camp to meet there, and then, they would shout "Mansei, Mansei 만세, 만세], and being kids, we wouldn't know what was going on. Pretty soon, they would have drills with the wooden guns, going back and forth on the main streets. What was happening? As kids, we didn't know. It seemed like they were going to invade Korea or whatever. We didn't know what it was. We didn't know what was Kook Min Hur or what was Dongji Hoi.

Q **Let's talk about your family members.**

A When my sister, Nora, became the first Korean graduate of the prestigious Normal School of Education (where a person is trained to become a teacher), they assigned her to the Island of Kauai, as a teacher in the public school. She was the first Korean graduate of the Normal School. They didn't have to go to college for a degree. When she was assigned to the island of Kauai, my father said you cannot go alone; you have to take one of the younger sisters to live with you. Later on, Nora was told that because she was born in Korea and therefore, an alien, she could not teach in public schools. This was way before the Walter McCarran Naturalization Act was passed. So, Nora went back to Normal School to become a nurse. She was the first Korean Nursing Supervisor in Hawaii.

My father and mother were one of the few people who came as husband and wife with children. The plantation didn't know what to do with this wife and two children. They had decided that the bachelors, the Korean bachelors in Ewa, had to have someone to cook for them. So, my father and my mother became the cooks for the Korean

Pahk Nora Graduation.

camp at the Ewa Plantation. I remember as a little child, we had to stretch our little arms out and get all the pile of wood for the burning stoves. One big wok was for making rice, another was for making soup. We always had soup. The other wok was to make a fast stir-fry type of vegetables and things. So, we had three big woks on that thing, and under the thing we had charcoal burning, wood burning and at the end of the day all the laborers, the single laborers would come and have dinner made by my father and mother.

Korean men who emigrated to Hawaii to work in the sugarcane fields were much older than the men from Okinawa or Japan. Ewa Plantation had segregated camps: Japanese camp, Korean camp, and Okinawa camp. But we didn't have any Filipinos in those very early days. Korean men would send their pictures, their young pictures of themselves to Korea with somebody who was going back and forth to Korea. The women in Korea chose to marry men who would pay their way over to Hawaii. This is why there were many young, pretty girls who married old men. One of them was my uncle. Many women ran away and went to other camps. So, that's how I suppose they began to have interracial marriages. But some women were very conscientious, and they stayed with the men with whom they were supposed to, that had paid their way over. They became very good housewives on the Eva Plantation, where a lot of Koreans were.

They built a long house for these Korean men, when the brides arrived in Hawaii, and I remember personally, that lots of those pretty ladies were so young. Some would be crying all the time and always crying. They would have to cook on the wooden stoves and men would come after work and chop the wood. So, my mother was like the Mother Superior to the young brides. Some of the young brides stayed like the one with my uncle. His wife was very, very young, pretty too. He started right away with a family. Those who stayed all did well, all educated their children, and they all did very well. That's just about what I remember of the picture brides other than the fact that the Methodist Church was packed with the young brides.

It was nice because my father was already established. When we were kids, we were always doing what you call "shim burum"-errands, just doing this and doing that. I recall so plainly, many things after my mother died. We were still very young: Stella was only 4, Agnes was 6, I was 8, and my brother was 10. We were all two years apart. Anyway, I remember that when my mother had died, lots of these women friends would come to our house, and even single, widowed ladies, whom we called "Ah Ju Ma"–Aunty. They would come and give our father something to eat and say to us, "Give this to your father" [아버지 드려라]. And for some reason, we felt very suspicious, we wouldn't give it to our father to eat; we would eat it all up. And we would wash the plates and take it back to her, and the 아주머니 lady would say [아버지 드렸니], "Did you give it to your father?" And we would say [예] "Yes" and we'd just run away. My father never knew who ever gave him anything. We ate it all up. This is what our oldest sister told us to do, because we didn't want a stepmother. We younger ones didn't know why, but we just did what the older sisters told us. Those were incidents that are very, very vivid in my mind.

Q **What do you know about the Korean Christian Institute, the girls' dormitory.**

A KCI? I don't know very much about that. I know that KCI was a very good thing for young Korean girls. As for the Methodist families, a lot of the Korean Methodist girls went to the Susannah Wesley Home, on Liliha Street. (It was the first Boarding Home and School for girls, started long before KCI began.) My sisters went to Susannah Wesley. There was a dividing line, I guess. It seems that at Susannah Wesley Home there wasn't any conflict of any kind at all.

Q **What was Susannah Wesley all about?**

A Susannah Wesley was a Methodist like an orphanage home. They use to accept young girls from all the plantations to live there and learn English, a trade, or something, sewing, cooking or something like that. A lot of Koreans went there. John Wesley, the Founder, was a Methodist Preacher, so many Methodist people are at Susannah Wesley. When our older sisters went to Susannah Wesley from the plantation, they learned to sew, learned to cook, and learned all those domestic things. You could learn more in that atmosphere than you could at your own home. Today, Susannah Wesley stands as a recreational center on Liliha Street.

Interview with Mary Kim Halm
Howard Halm, son, was present

Picture bride Chu Chi Lee longed to see her parents and left Hawaii with her firstborn, not knowing she was pregnant. Japanese passport for her and the children's return in 1921.

My name is Mary Kim Halm. I was born in Korea and brought to Hawaii when I was two years old, under an unusual circumstance. Upon arrival in Hawaii, I had to register for immigration papers, although my parents lived in Hawaii when I was conceived. Upon receiving the citizenship certificate that was granted to me, the USA Immigration Bureau requested that we write down what we would like to be known as, legally. So, I omitted my Korean name and just used "Kim" which was my surname and "Halm" my married name.

My father's name was Si Ho Kim, a bachelor, who arrived in Honolulu from Pyongyang in 1903, as was in most of the cases with the other Korean bachelors who immigrated to Hawaii about the same time. They

Marriage certificate of parents: Si Ho Kim and Chu Chi Lee, 1917.

were lonesome living by themselves, so they wanted brides. From what I understand from my mother, the men sent pictures of themselves to the women in Korea. They appeared quite young in their pictures, younger than what they actually were in age. Their pictures were disseminated in the village where they lived. Her parents granted their permission to accept Si Ho Kim's proposal for their daughter as a picture bride.

My mother's name was Chu Chi Lee. She arrived in Honolulu, Hawaii in 1917. I think she was in her teen years. She met my dad at the pier, and of course, she was a little disappointed because he didn't appear like his picture. He was a little older in years. But, they were married anyway, and they went to live in Wahiawa, Oahu. Before she arrived, he was working in the sugar fields, and lived on the plantation, as far as I know. I can recollect my mother saying that. Later, he left the sugar plantation and moved to Wahiawa, which was near pineapple fields where he worked. While there, she said, he was injured one day with the spikes of the pineapple leaf near his eye. Sugar and pineapple fields are very different kinds of work.

My mother was very lonesome when she first came. She eventually, became pregnant with my sister, Martha. Martha was born in 1918. Her Korean name is Guiyeom which means "loving and adorable." My mother was so busy raising my sister. My mother also worked. I think she helped working on the plantation for a while. She didn't write to her parents in Korea for two years. Her parents were quite worried, wondering what happened to her, whether she was alive or dead. They wrote to her one day and when she received the letter, she was so sad and so shocked. They thought that she was not alive. So, in spite of her financial condition, she somehow scraped enough money to return to Korea to visit her parents. She didn't know she was pregnant with me before she left. My older sister who was three year old went with her.

233

My father remained here in Hawaii when she went to Korea. When she arrived there, she discovered that she was pregnant. She stayed with my grandparents, until she was about six months pregnant then she tried to return to Hawaii. When she came to Japan, she went through customs, but they wouldn't let her go on the ship fearing that something would happen on the ship with her pregnancy. She was sent back to my grandparents' home in Pusan, Korea. There, she gave birth to me; therefore, my name was "Oesu," meaning "Whai Kut Jip" meaning, the home of the mother's parents. My mother stayed there, until I was old enough to travel which was about six months or so. She brought my sister and me

Left to right: Pildeok Lee, mother Chu Chi Lee, Youngsoon Lee.

back to Hawaii, and according to what she told me, there were a lot of other picture brides on the ship coming back with her. They helped take care of my sister because she was about three years old, running all over the ship. They had to help take care of her.

When she arrived at the port, she heard my father calling and calling me because he had learned of my name. He called all over the port until the ship landed. My parents were reunited. I forgot to mention that my mother said she was so lonesome living in Hawaii, that she asked her parents to send her two younger sisters to live with her in Hawaii. So, her two sisters were, eventually, sent here as picture brides, also. When they arrived, they lived together near each other in neighboring places. I don't know what city or what town. It could have been Wahiawa.

Q **How old were they when they arrived?**

HOWARD HALM, SON OF MARY ANSWERED   I think that my auntie, Youngsoon Lee, was probably, about 17 years old. Her younger sister was, maybe, 15 years old or so.

A   I was born in 1921, so they came a little after that.

Q   **Please, tell us the name of these two sisters…your aunts.**

A   My middle aunt's name was Youngsoon Lee. My younger aunt was Pildeok Lee. They treasured their surnames. I guess most of the Korean women from Korea like to keep their surname. My aunts used their surname "Lee" throughout their whole married life until they died. I've never seen "Kim" used, but, officially, they had to use "Mrs. Kim".

I don't recall too many things about the early years when I grew up. The earliest experience I remember was when we moved into the big city, Honolulu. At that time, I guess my dad had fulfilled his contract with the plantation and was able to move us to Honolulu.

Somehow, picture brides and other immigrants gathered in the area near St. Luke's Korean Mission. The Church at that time was called "Mission". They all lived in cottages around the Church. Therefore, we..the children…of the immigrant women, became very good friends like one big family. We all went to the Church very religiously, with our parents. My father really didn't go too often, but my mother did with her sisters. I recall going to Sunday morning services and Sunday evening services. Before St. Luke Church was built, we went to St. Elizabeth Church. I think I was about 4 years old when I was enrolled at the St. Elizabeth Preschool. It was a Chinese Congregational Church. But, our St. Luke's Church, which was built later, was purely Korean. So, we fitted in with each other after it was built. I recall being very frightened when I went to St. Elizabeth Preschool because I was asked to recite the alphabet by the teacher. On the next day, we had to know how to write and read the alphabet. I was very nervous, so I didn't go to school. I asked another friend of mine to go to the park and pretend that we went to school. At that time, there was the Palama Settlement playground, where all the immigrant children went to play with the equipment. My friend and I were happily riding swings all day. And then, my mother came and caught us, fetched us, and took us back home. Of course, I had a good spanking, and so, I went straight to school the next day.

Somehow, I survived that year. When I was six years old, I was taken to Kalihi Elementary School, a Government Public School, which was in our neighborhood. I was given a test to enroll. The Principal, I recall, was sitting on a chair at the desk. She asked me to read from a book. I read about four or five pages, fluently. So, they sent me straight to the third grade, instead, of the first grade. I was very frightened, when I went to the third grade class because they were sitting at desks, individual desks. I wondered why they were all putting their heads down on the desk. I thought that they were crying. Later, I found out that it was rest period. I must have done well because from the third grade onward, I was promoted and I graduated from high school at age 16.

Then, I enrolled in Nursing School. I thought that I wanted to become a nurse. It was at that time, I met my husband. I was about 18 and a half years old. He was already finished with his dental school education. We dated for about half a year before he said he wanted to get married. I said, "No, I have to finish my education." He said, "Oh". We couldn't get married then, because of the nursing school rules which did not permit students to marry while still a student. It's not like now. The nursing school rules have changed since then. After much thought, I decided to quit nursing school and we got married. Then, my husband said, "Why don't you go to the University of Hawaii?" It was a good idea, so I did enrolled at the University in the Teacher Education Studies. We were married in 1940. Howard, my first child, was born in 1941.

On December 7, 1941, World War II broke out. My husband was instantly, called into the activated Military Reserves because he was already in the Reserved Officers Contingent at the University of Southern California, where he attended dental school on a scholarship for the Military Reserves. And from then on, he was in the military services, until the end of World War II in 1945. In the meantime, my daughter was born two years later. Then, when my husband returned from the war, he started a private dental practice. He always wanted to return to California to practice dentistry. He had taken his dental examination there and he passed it. He came back here (Honolulu) just to look around more or less, to make a final decision where to set up his practice. He thought of Honolulu because this is where he had grown up and lived for many years. While in Honolulu, he took the Hawaii dental examination and passed it. So, we decided to stay and work at the Dental Clinic at Palama Settlement. But, he always wanted to return to the Mainland, so, he had to persuade me to return to California because I, being an island person, too, didn't want to leave. So, he took us on a vacation trip in 1956 to the Mainland. We enjoyed it very much. The next year in 1957, we moved to California. Howard, our son, was close to 16 years old at that time.

Q **Tell us about what happened to your sister and your aunts. When and whom did your two aunts marry?**

A They married "picture husbands"…men who had sent their pictures to my aunties just like my mother and father. When they chose their husbands and moved to Hawaii, we all lived near each other, and they were very close like real good friends throughout their whole lives. My Mom died first, then, my youngest aunt, and then, Aunt Youngsoon Lee.

Q **Who were the men… their names? Do you recall?**

A Phil Gu Rho was Aunt Youngsoon Lee's husband. I think it's Sang Ho Kim for my other aunt. I don't really recall. I think the tombstone will tell us.

Q **Were these two men also first immigrants who came to Hawaii before 1905?**

A They must have come before 1905 because they were old enough. I think most of the age differences was about 20 years between the men and their brides. The men would be 40 years old and the women, 20 years old. Then, as they grew old, the men died first, resulting in a lot of Korean widows.

Lee Donohue with his mother, Pil Deok Lee, first right and his aunts.

Q **Do you know where they lived? Did they lived near you?**

A We were always living close to each other, not in one house together, but always different houses in the same area. So, we cousins were like one family.

Q **I see. So, then, those two uncles' and aunts' familie were already settled in Honolulu by the time you were growing up?**

A Yes, my aunt, Youngsoon Lee, had one daughter, and Pil Deok Lee had four children. Then, her husband passed on and she remarried and had one son.

Q **Tell me about the ages of your parents, and what Province they came from.**

A My father came from Pyongyang and my mother came from Pusan. And her sisters came from Pusan also. Where the other men came from, I don't know.

Q **Exactly, how old do you think was your father when they married?**

A He must have been close to 40. Maybe 38. And she was about like 17, 18, I think.

Q **Tell me a little bit about growing up. You said you were pretty active at St. Luke's Church when you were young. How long and until what age do you think you were active?**

A I was active until I left the Islands to live on the mainland. I didn't go to St. Luke's Episcopal Church in Honolulu all the time because when we married, we moved to the other side of the island (Kailua) and went to the Episcopal Church there. We've been Episcopalians ever since. And so were my husband and his parents.

HOWARD, SON **Let's talk about the Korean School.**

A My mother enrolled me, in spite of the hardships, at an American language school in third grade at age 6. My mother sent us to the Korean language school, also, saying I must learn her language. So, all the neighborhood Korean children attended the Korean language school. And I was about 7 years old. I think I went there until I was in the 8th grade. I learned a lot of Korean history and Korean geography in that school. I must have excelled because I won perfect A's in my report card. My mother was real proud of me. But, it was a lot of rote memory type of thinking. The children came not only from the neighborhood, but from

Lee Donohue became Chief of Police of Honolulu.

other areas also. They walked to school from far places. Then, there was a choir at the church that came from the language school. A lot of activities emanated from this language school group. I have pictures of the group taken at the language school.

Q **Tell me about outstanding leaders of that time, Korean leaders.**

A Well, I can't recall. I've heard only Dr. Rhee's name often. My father-in-law was very active. He was always sending money to Korea or whatever organization for the Korean Independence Movement.

Q **So, he was the supporter of Dr. Syngman Rhee?**

A No, I don't think so. He was the supporter of the Korean Independence Movement, not of Dr. Rhee. It was another faction, I can't recall the factions.

Q **There's Kook Min Hur.**

A Yes, and what other faction?

Q **Dongji Hoi.**

A Kook Min Hur. That must be the one. That's the one that my aunts were very active in it, especially, my aunt Youngsoon Lee Rho, who was one of the officers' in that Club, very actively. As far as Korean politics, I was not interested. So, I didn't keep tracked. My father, as I recall, was not interested in Korean politics, also. He was a well-educated man in Korea. He loved to read. All I remember is that during his spare time he was reading Korean books. My mother actively, participated in Kook Min Hur with her sisters. But, my father-in-law was the one who was more actively involved with financial support and activities of Kook Min Hur. He didn't talk much about it, though.

HOWARD, SON **Let's talk about the country-side Koreans and the town-side Koreans.**

A What about them?

HOWARD, SON **About how difficult was it to know town Koreans and country Koreans and vice versa?**

A   I don't recall any difference.

Q   **So you were not aware of what was going on in the community, then? Did you join any Korean organization?**

A   Not when I was a teenager. After I married, we belonged to the Korean University Club. And the Delta Frat Club…two social organizations. When I was a teenager, I was more involved in Girl Reserves which Miss Ha Soo Whang was the counselor/advisor. After school, she came to our elementary school and gathered us up and took us to the park. When we had our meetings, she brought some desserts and refreshments. We enjoyed ourselves. I always considered her as a real much older person. Another incident I recall was when Miss Whang recruited me as a 6 years old into the Korean Dance Group. She came and asked my mother if I could join a Korean Dance Group. So, I had to practice and practice, I think, once a week. I learned how to dance the Korean dance. And, when we had performances, I recall my mother really giving me a good bath and cutting my hair and putting on my Korean dress before going there. I don't know who we danced for. That's the big cultural thing that I was involved in because Miss Whang wanted me to be in it. It was such a long time ago. I would say I was only 6 years old then, or maybe about 7 years old.

Q   **Did Whang, Ha Soo, herself teach you?**

A   No. It was another woman. Ms Whang's nieces were in it. Mary Whang (Choy, married name) was in my class. I think Mary was a few years older than I was. I think I was one of the younger ones. I recall going through emotions while dancing.

HOWARD, SON **Talk about grandmother's theatrical productions.**

A   I recall, vaguely, going to see my mother's productions and I recall the ladies…they all said that they came from the same Province in Korea, so they were very close knitted. They dressed up in costumes. They gave benefit shows. My youngest aunt, Mrs. Rho, was very active in it.

Q So what other personalities do you recall?

HOWARD, SON **What about Moksa Pyong Yo Cho, the leader of the Korean St. Luke's Church? (Moksa...a lector but not an ordained minister)**

A Pyong Yo Cho was Jackie Young's grandfather. I don't recall too much, but I know that he was sometimes substituting at St. Luke's Church, when Rev. Noah Cho went to Korea on trips to visit his family. Rev. Cho's family lived in Korea so, once in awhile, he went to visit his family. His father died in Korea. Pyong Yo Cho took his place in Church when Rev. Cho went to Korea.

Q Do you recall if there were any intermingling between the youngsters from the different churches?

A As I recall, there were the Korean Methodists and there were Korean Christians. We were the "St. Luke's Episcopal" Koreans. The church group youngsters never saw each other socially, except at the public schools. Even then, we weren't close. We really didn't know each other. I think the other churches had their own Korean language school. So, we mingled within our own group of friends in the neighborhood and with the children that went to our church and at the same language school.

Q Were you aware of any kind of cleavage in the Korean community, any kind of clash in the Korean community?

A Well, I would hear once in a while that they had clashes in the Korean Christian Church because they were trying to have the minister leave or whatever. But our church focused a lot on religion. We didn't have social problems like the Korean Christian Church congregation, as far as I can understand. The Methodists, some of them were my high school friends. But we really didn't socialize that closely.

Q What high school did you go to?

A I went to Mckinley High School.

The Korean students were an entity by themselves but were separated from each other because they went to different churches. And more or less, they did not focus on their religion when at school. But, the Korean Christian Church students were kind of focused on Dr. Rhee and Dr. Rhee's politics.

Q **Any other thing you remember about Dr. Rhee and his wife?**

A All I can remember is that they stayed at our good friend, Wilbert Choi's house. Wilbert Choi took care of Rhee, when he was ill and when Rhee ended his presidency.

Q **How did you become a friend of Wilbert Choi?**

A We became friends at Delta Frat Club.

Q **Did you belong to the Delta Frat, too?**

A Yes. I was an officer at the Korean Delta Frat Club at one point. We just went there to enjoy ourselves. Frat Club was mainly a social club for young adults, second generation Korean-Americans, who already graduated from high school. We met once a month at different homes. We had dinner after the social meetings, and we played Mahjong and poker and bridge and whatever. It was a social club with a short business meeting. It was unlike the Korean University Club, which gave out yearly scholarships for deserving students to attend the university.

Q **Tell us a little bit more about the Korean University Club.**

A The Korean University Club (KUC) as far as I can remember, the members had to be university graduates, except for "Associate Members" who didn't graduate from the university, but they were the spouses of members. At this present time, I understand, the membership has changed. A lot of the members are now newly, arrived Korean immigrants from Korea, but still highly educated. The purpose of the KUC is the same: to raise funds for higher education scholarships for young Koreans.

Q **In the old days, aside from raising funds for scholarships, what kind of activities did you do with the Korean University Club?**

A   More or less like Delta Frat Club, a social group except the KUC members were university graduates...with professional occupations. At the KUC meetings we talked about scholarships and the usual procedures about money in the treasury, then, minutes of the past meeting, and so forth. We had an elaborate inaugural banquet once a year at one of the hotel ballrooms.

Q   **Was your husband a member of the Korean University Club, also? Was he a strong active person in it?**

A   Yes, mostly he loved to go and play cards there. With all the men, they stayed and enjoyed themselves, playing cards. So, after the formal meeting breaks up, they just go in groups to do their own thing. It was a Club that focused on scholarships for deserving Korean students.

My name is Dorothy Kim Rudie. My Korean name is Bomsik Kim. I'm the third child and third daughter of the family. My father's name was Kim, Kyung Bok. I believe he came from Kangwha, Korea, and arrived in Hawaii in December of 1901.

It so happened that when the book, In My Footsteps, was being published, there was an article in the Sunday Star Bulletin Newspaper about the book. My husband went to the bookstore to purchase that book. It was, then, that we found that the Koreans in Hawaii were celebrating its hundred anniversary of arrival in Hawaii since 1903. I was stunned to see that they had no information about the few men that came to Hawaii in 1901. I have a document, saying that my father had come to Hawaii in 1901.

So, we quickly went to the Hawaiian archives to try to check the manifest of the ship that he told us that he came on. There was no mention of him or the passenger list. I believe that he came over in 1901 as a worker on board ship because he was a sailor when he lived in Korea. He left his family because he was an orphan at an early age and lived with his aunt. I don't know in what village in Korea, but they had chestnut farms because he told us that they had chestnuts at home. Then, he ran away from his aunt and went to sea. He knew a great deal about the sea because Kanghwa is an island. Then, from there, he came to Hawaii, passing through Yokohama, I believe.

At that time, there were no Koreans here in Hawaii, so he gravitated to the Chinese community. I found among his personal possessions, Red Squares

Kyung Pok and Aki Kim family. Left to right: Daisy, Kyung Pok, Dorothy (Rudie), Andrew, Aki, Rose, circa 1928. After Kyung Pok Kim, a seaman, jumped ship from the SS Mongolia in 1902, he remained in Hawaii. He continued working as a seaman on inter-island ships. He married a seventeen-year-old Korean picture bride at the age of thirty-five in 1913.

with gold lettering on them. I asked him what was that gold lettering? He said he belonged to a "Chinese Tong" which was an organization like "Hoi" means to Koreans. He joined that group because there were no Koreans here to form a group. He, naturally, gravitated to the Chinese, while he still continued working for steamship lines here in Hawaii, going to other islands along the Hawaiian Chain of Islands. The last company that he worked for was the Inter-Island Steamship Lines Company as a fireman.

My father retired from sailing and worked in the rice fields with the Chinese people. I remember my father's friends whom we called "Paki" (Chinese grandfathers) because when my father had a rice plantation in Kaneohe, I was born on that rice plantation among his closest friends who were all Chinese. He worked with Chinese workmen there, cultivating the rice fields. When he gave up that rice field work, he and a lot of Chinese bachelors, then, went to the Kapahulu area and had truck farms. So, we would go on a three-day break time to Kapahulu to see our Paki grandfathers. They would kill a chicken and cook it with peanuts which was strange to us. It was the first time we ate peanuts with meat. Then, they would take us to the corner grocery store to buy us animal crackers so that was a nice outing for us. There were, also, younger Chinese bachelors whom we considered as uncles.

After some time in Hawaii and after other ship loads of Koreans came, my father wanted to find a Korean bride. By then, there were more Koreans coming to Hawaii who were bachelors like him. He got to know the new arrivals, and they all talked about getting Korean brides. The Methodist Church helped such an arrangement, but there were not enough Korean women in Hawaii. Then, the Church and friends helped the men arrange picture brides from Korea. My father finally, found a young picture bride willing to marry him.

My mother came from the Pusan–Masan area in 1913. In those days, it was a tragedy because many of the girls were only in their late teens. Their husbands sent pictures of themselves when they were young and not as they were then. So, when my mother got off the ship, she said she was very afraid. When she found the man that she was supposed to marry, she was very pleased because he was only twice her age, not like the other couples. Twice the age, still, seems rather strange to us, but, my mother said he was so handsome and did not look too old. We giggled and laughed to hear our parents talk that way about when they first met, married and had children. The first three children were girls, not too happy, for Korean families. They were married on the same day that they got off the ship because there was no way that she could stay, unless they married, immediately.

Q   **What year was that?**

A   That was 1913, I believe. I gave you a document pertaining to that. We three girls, the first three children, used to question my mother about the past while our father was away at sea. He would be gone for two weeks at a time, and when he was on his free time, he would throw great big hooks over the ship and catch fish. Big fish. So big that it took two men to bring it home. When we were children, we didn't realize what a luxury that was to have such delicious fish. All we'd say when fish was served was, "Uh, fish, again". We didn't realize that it was a luxury. Even our neighbors all loved it, when our father went fishing because everybody shared in the fish. Now, that I am older, I have to pay $20 a pound for fish…that was quite a free feast at that time.

As a whole, we knew and saw very little of our father because he was gone to sea most of the time. A few times when he came home from a trip, he wanted to see us right away because he missed us so much, but sometimes school was in session. A couple of times, he would come to the school directly from the ship with a switch in his hand and ask the teachers to let us out of the school. He would tell the teachers that he must see us so that he could discipline us about something. While my older sister, who was a very obedient girl would go with my father regardless of what she saw — that switch, thinking that she's going to get spanked, and she would go with him, anyway. But I would refuse to go with him because I did not want to get spanked for something that I didn't do. So, I wouldn't go with him. Then, after school, when I went home, my sister would tell me, "Oh, you should've gone with me because we went into town, and Papa bought me lunch…he bought me this and that. He didn't spank me. He just wanted our company because he missed us children, while he was away overseas." He would pull pranks like that on us many times.

Other times whenever he was in town for a long time, he enjoyed time with his closest friend who was a Hawaiian man, his drinking companion. He was used to being a very good friend of Hawaiian men because he was in Hawaii for two years when there were no Koreans around at that time. After 1903 when many Koreans came, he made new friends. After he married, he met more Koreans.

When my father died, I asked my mother how come he had one of the largest funerals I ever saw in Hawaii. It was so large that the service couldn't be held at our normal size church at St. Luke's. It had to be held at St. Elizabeth Church, which was very large. Mother said that he was well liked because every man in that church owed my father money. I couldn't understand how they owed him money when we were so poor. We couldn't possibly lend them money. Later on, I realized what she meant. The Korean men owed him because he helped them get settled in Hawaii, since he was here earlier than thousands of Koreans who arrived in the next four years. He would give them things and help them understand their new environment.

My father was able to die happily because there were Korean immigrants around him. He was only 25 years old, when he first came here. He was on his own for many years during the prime of his life, when he traveled as a sailor on foreign ships before he first came to Hawaii. So, he was able to guide these people around in Hawaii. That's why people remembered how he helped them and why he had such a big funeral. That's why in mother's way of thinking everybody owed him money. But, it was more than that, he was well liked.

When he and my mother married him, the first three children were girls. My father was very disappointed. Since my mother had come to Hawaii as a very young picture bride, the men were much older than the women. I asked my mother how come so many of their contemporaries were divorced. She said you must realize that these were arranged marriages. Then, after two years of living in Hawaii, the woman knew their way around in Hawaii. There were shortage of women. So some divorced their older husbands and married younger men. She told us life in Korea was very different from life in Hawaii. My father was more Americanized by the time the other men came. From 1901 to 1913 he lived as a bachelor in Hawaii. Things that he expected of my mother was contrary to what she was brought up... such as when they sat down to table to eat in Korea, the men would be served first. But my father insisted that she eat at the table with him. She was embarrassed at first. She would take a bowl of rice, and then, hold it in one hand and get the panchan [반찬] to put it in the rice bowl. She would, immediately, turn her back to him and then, eat her dinner that way. He made her change her ways to be modern.

We would tease her about having only girls born to her... the first three were girls...and we'd tell her teasingly, that we wanted more sisters. We, also, wanted to hear more about her life in Korea. We'd giggle and roll on the floor laughing, when she tells us about these strange customs in Korea. We told her that we wouldn't be shy eating with men, especially, husbands; we would sit there and eat with him. Then, she told us that while it may be strange to us, we must realize that she was brought up in the old way and not the new way and that our father was Americanized before 6,000 Korean immigrant men came to America with the old way of life.

Our father still went to sea and left her in Kaneohe with the Chinese farmers for two weeks at a time. She was still shy enough that when she saw him after a long trip coming up the road over the mountains...because those days they didn't have good road, they only had a kind of trail, going up the mountain. She'd get flushed and excited, seeing him coming home. She got embarrassed looking flushed so that she'd run to the neighbor's house. She didn't want to face him because she knew what was going to happen...that he would want to have sex with her, immediately, and something like that. He would go home, and she wouldn't be there. So, he would go to the neighbor's house and out in the yard, he would call out in Korean, "Send my wife home." Of course, she would have to go home. She was still young and embarrassed.

Then, we asked her about what her life was like when she first came before we were born, and she said that when she was pregnant with me she had a craving for mangoes. You could find her sitting under a mango tree, eating mangoes like crazy. That discussion about pregnancy went around to talk about sex because we asked her how come...if he lived in Hawaii for twelve years before you came, how come we don't have any half Hawaiian brothers or half sisters like other Korean men had before their picture brides came. She scolded us; we shouldn't be talking like that. We laughed, persisting to ask her what happened when she was pregnant and couldn't take care of him. She said that she sent for a maid. "He was a good man, and I can't take care of him when I had so many babies. So, I sent a maid." We began to realize that their culture (Korean culture) was so different from the one in which we were brought up. Mother said that while she was pregnant with me, my father felt sure that I was going to be a boy. In preparation, he left a standing order with a butcher in Kaneohe, where there was a piggery, to send the pig's feet to my mother. A boy needs to have pig's feet right away. We didn't know what kind of Korean custom it was.

Even though our parents were not educated people, they went to school in Hawaii and learned things that we'd learn in school. They had their basic common sense because they knew that when she was pregnant with me that the mother has to have good food and certain kind of food if you expect to have a healthy child. So, when I was born, my father was very disappointed that I was girl, even though I was my mother's biggest and healthiest child that she had. You must realize that he got married so that he could have sons. When my brother came after my birth, of course, he was very pleased about that.

Mother told us that her mother said that if she left Korea, she may never see her alive. That came true because my grandmother had passed away in the meantime. By the time my mother did go back to Korea to visit, she had been in Hawaii about ten years. The life span in the Orient was much shorter, then, what it is now. These things which we learned from our mother was contrary to the custom with which we were brought up. However, I will say this: that whatever we were taught in school and come home and tell my mother about it, whether it was about health, or social science, or geography, she would question us about it to learn the new ways herself, because certain subjects were not discussed back in Korea. Also, she was trying to make sure that it was not something what we were learning would hurt Korean customs. We told her that we learned these things in school so, it was all right. As long as we learned it in school, it was okay to discuss it.

When my father retired as a sailor-merchant marine, he became a landlord. He leased rooming houses. My sister and I... would spend quite a bit of time with my father when we very young at the rooming houses, playing or helping him while he did the maintenance. I was about 10 years old. We learned how to fill out receipts, how to pay taxes, where to go for the City Water Department, where to go to find the Electric Company...all of these things were taught to us by him. We would be his assistant because we could read and write English. We learned business at a very early age and, we learned how and who paid the rent and who didn't pay the rent.

He still kept his Chinese friends, even though he had many

Korean friends after they arrived. But, his very close bosom buddies were the Hawaiian men that he knew so long ago. The name of one of them was Kealoha, his drinking companion, and then, there was this Chinese man at Alapai Street, a part of Chinatown where the rooming house was. They had a lot of Chinese restaurants there. He used to eat or get his meals there near his rooming house when we were not with him because sometimes our mother made us stay home. Sometimes, my father stayed at the rooming house over night.

Just before my father retired, he decided that he would take my sister and me to see the ship that he was working on. He knew his plan was to retire was soon, so he took us to the harbor. He was working at that time on the Island Steamship Line. We had to go down to the haul of the ship on a iron step ladder. We kept going down and down to the bottom of the ship and there were huge boilers that he had to use as gauges to feed oil in it. There were "catwalks" between the boilers. Nowadays, you would have to be a certified engineer to do that kind of the work, but in those days, if you can handle it, that was your job. Life then, was different. They had captains who would have the first cup of coffee from the pot they brewed. The lower officers would have the second cup, and then, the crew would have the third or fourth cup made from the same grounds. They had salt water showers for the men to cool off. He didn't work all the time because they worked only when they were going from island to island. Then, on his day off he would do some fishing – deep sea fishing. They used great big hooks.

He told us once that he almost drowned because the men were on the deck gambling. Those that didn't gamble were standing around watching them gamble. At one time when they were gambling, there was a brawl. My father just happened to be there, and they threw him off the ship. Life on the ship was different from life on shore, but he liked that. He worked at sea so long that we could recognize his footsteps...a sailor man's footsteps. He had that sailor's walk, bowlegged, you know, so we could recognize him anywhere from the noise of his bowlegged footsteps.

Q **Tell me about the church. You said something about being an Episcopalian from way back. Could you tell us little bit more?**

A Well, I was told that a lot of the men came from Gangwha and they were Episcopalians because that is where the Episcopal missions were. The Episcopalians had a strong hold there in Gangwha. A lot of the other men came from around Seoul and Incheon, but they were Methodist. Whereas, the women came from the far southern part of Korea. We children went to churches where we were told to go only by our parents.

Q **So, it was your father who seemed to have influence the family to go to the Episcopal Church.**

A Yes. My father's choice was that we go to the Episcopal Church. In the other two churches there was a rivalry between them.

Q **Which churches, name them?**

A That was the Methodist Church and the other church on Liliha. And that church on Liliha Street was about four times bigger than our church. But the thing is, the Episcopal Church we belong to was part of St. Andrews. We were a mission group of St. Andrews Church, the main church for Episcopalians from which we received support. But as far as the Korean community was concerned, St. Luke's Church was our father's choice and where the whole congregation was Korean.

However, our mothers...the pictures brides...because most of them were brought up in the Methodist Church, it was their choice that the children be brought up in the Methodist Church. But we were brought up by my father's religion. So, that's how come we were Episcopalian. But, my father went to church only once a year. I couldn't understand that. We all had to go to church and observe all Sundays, holidays and everything. But once a year, I remember on the first Sunday after New Years, my father wore a beautiful gray suit with his dressy shirt which was silk. Then, he'd go to church and the minister would be so glad to see him. And he'd be out there, visiting with him...that's when my father took care of all of the "ties" (church money collection) and my father paid all the tuition that we owed the church for the Korean language school. We didn't realize what my father's background was before he married. Later, we found out that even though he went to the church only once a year, he was very much respected by the ministers for the many things he had done in the past.

Q **Do you remember any leaders among the Episcopalians?**

A I forget. I was gone away so long from Hawaii. There are no Koreans in Minneapolis, where I lived. There was no contact at all, after I married and left Hawaii. I forgot faces, people and the language and everything because there was nobody to talk to when I left Hawaii with my husband who was Caucasian.

Q **But you remember going to school there . . .**

A I remember going to language school because my two sisters... they were older than I... three of us went to Korean language school. The two younger boys, went sometimes. A year after my father died, she married a Filipino man. It was a common-law-marriage because we children objected very much to a Filipino man for a father. We would have objected to any man that came to the household because we remembered our father. Nobody could step into his shoes. So, we protest it, and so my mother made arrangements for the three of us to go to Korea. I being the oldest who supposed to have gone, had to memorize all the birth dates of the family, I had to memorize all the birth marks that they had, just in case the documents were lost or stolen. I could prove that we were who we were.

But, one week before we were going to sail off, I put my foot down. I said that I was not going. I absolutely, refused to go. I refused because someone told me that if I went to Korea, my mother was going to arrange a marriage for me, since I was 14 years old and old enough to marry. She said that there were lots of Korean men – wealthy people that want their sons to come to Hawaii. Since there was a chance that I would be forced into a marriage and come back to Hawaii with a husband, I said that I absolutely, will not go. And my mother knew from time I was born that I was very stubborn. I was her worst child that she had. I was the most stubborn child. So, I didn't go.

My two brothers went to Korea, instead. They were there for two years during the Japanese Occupation. When they were ready to come home, my aunt in Korea took them to Japan, where they had to go first to return to Hawaii. She put them on a ship there to return to Hawaii. We were surprised to see them in Japanese school boy uniforms when they came back. Black caps, and black cotton outfits. They completely forgot their English. Instead, the teachers in Korea wanted to be taught English by the boys. They taught their teachers English what they could which was difficult because the boys were only about ten and eight years old. If I were there, I would have been able to teach them a little bit more because I was in Junior High that time.

I learned from my brothers that their life in Korea wasn't so bad because they were American citizens. In that small town, my mother sent enough money so that they could buy their own bicycles in Korea. That was a luxury for them. Every now and then, she would sent crates with sugar... delicacies to the children. My brother told me that there was a bully in that village. Remember, we were under the Japanese rule, and the police officer's son would try to intimidate my brothers. But, they couldn't touch my brothers because my brothers were American citizens. So, they got away with a lot. They had maids because I was told that the maids in Korea at that time would work for their meals and one suit, new clothing a year. That's how poor the country was. When they came back to Hawaii, they got into the habit of "Get me a glass of water," or "Do this for me" and "Do that for me." We'd look at them, as an older sister and we'd say, "Remember, you are in Hawaii. You want those things, you get it yourself. You are not in Korea anymore." My mother laughed.

There was a woman living in our neighborhood. She was a picture bride and she had a son about my brother's age. They would fight like children always fight, they play and fight. Then, the mother of the neighborhood boy would come out of the house and scold my brothers in Korean for fighting with her son. Since my brothers were fluent in Korean at that time, they could talk back to her in Korean – word for word. My mother inside the house behind the door just laughed because she knew that the woman was stunned that my brothers could match her word for word in Korean. As time went by, however, my brothers lost a bit of the Korean language, after they have been back for a while. They were in Korea for two years. It was only because of the Japanese Occupation in Korea that my mother had them come back to Hawaii. Years later, one of my brothers remembered some of the cousins who were their playmates when he returned to Korea after the Korean War. My brother said that he went back to check on the family tomb to see that whether it was properly cared for.

Q **You mentioned that when one of the boys was just about a year old, you remembered that your mother took that boy to Korea even at that very young age. Tell us about that story.**

A   That must have been about 1924 and 25 when my brother, Yongsik, the second boy was about 6 or 9 months old. My mother took him to Korea. She stayed there quite a long time I think, anyway between 6 and 9 months. When she returned to Hawaii, the immigration officer thought that she was bringing in another child; one that was born in Korea and not a child who was born in Hawaii. So, she was detained at the Immigration Station. To see her, we had to go to the Immigration Station because they would not let her out. Minister Father Cho of the Episcopal Church, busily, got proper documents saying that the child was born in Hawaii. It took about a month before she was released from confinement. My brother-he is now 74, does not know that he was confined in the Immigration Station for that period of time. That's how strict they were about the immigrants coming to Hawaii under unsure passages.

Q **Tell us more about your mother and her relatives in Korea.**

A Her name was Kim, Ok Hee. She was sometimes called Soon-hee. My sister took her name, Soon Hee. But on her legal documents and everything else, she was always Ok Hee. She came from Pusan, Masan area. The last time I was in Korea the road between Pusan and Masan was being built. There was heavy construction going on because of the 1988 Olympics going on. I had relatives from that area visit me in the hotel, when we were there in 1985. One girl cousin and one of my boy cousins came to visit us in the hotel. So, I still have relatives in that area.

Q **When you were growing up, your mother tried to match-marry you? Tell us more about it.**

A There were Korean families that wanted to immigrate to Hawaii because the Japanese close the doors for Korean immigration. They were wealthy families willing to pay the family in Hawaii money if they let the children marry. If I married a boy in Korea, then, I could bring him over to Hawaii because he would be my husband. Even in 1983 when I went to Korea on a tour, one of the tour members in my group, who was a divorced Korean girl was approached by the tour guide to introduce her to a man who offered $11,000 to marry her so that he could come to Hawaii with her as her husband. She told me about it, and she asked me, "Should I do it?" She said it's very tempting for her to do that. The plan was that after he spent a year with her in Hawaii, they could get a divorce. I told her, if she accepted the plan and if the authorities found out it was a false marriage, it would be you not he, who goes to prison, because he does not know the American laws. You know the American laws that this is a fraud. I said that she got to weigh the fact that she may go to jail. So, she chose not to do that. There were lots of such cases in Hawaii and at the West Coast of the USA Mainland.

Q **Tell me just a little bit more what you remember about Episcopalian Korean language school. Was there a big group of children same as your age? What year were you born?**

A I was born in 1920. There was a language school at St. Luke's. They took the children when they were school age. We would go to public school first. Then, at 2:30 or 3:00 o'clock we would be dismissed and go home to get a bite to eat. Then, we changed into Korean uniforms.

Black skirt and white blouse. Later, they modified it and it had a button for us so that we, as children, could button the blouse to make it easy for us to play. They put us according to our age group. We learned reading, writing, and Korean history. That was up to about eighth grade.

Q **What public school did you go to?**

A We went to a public school in the Palama area, Kaiulani School. It still exists today. It's across the street from Kamakapili Church. St. Luke's was on Banyan and Kanoa Streets. My mother's last home was on Banyan Street. We were in that area. I remember that Father Cho would be upset with us because we had explicit instructions not to go to school through the the Parish house yard of the Kamakapili Church. He had plum trees in his yard and we were told not to pick the fruits. When we came back to the classroom, we all had to stick out our tongues. If we had purple tongs, we got scolding. Picking and eating the plums was the only way we could have gotten our tongues purple. He had the right to scold us. You know how children are.

Q **Where did all your friends come from? Did you have any friends from the Korean Christian Church and the Methodist church?**

A Yes, we had friends from the other churches because we all went to the same public school. The Korean community was very small. Even our parents knew the other parents, although they belong to different churches. Particularly, the women knew each other well because they were all picture brides mainly, from the southern areas of Korea; they had something in common. Others came from the Seoul area. They would get together every now and then. During the New Year's holidays, they would make Juk, and Muk, with the green beans and stuff. Also, they would make different kinds of Yakbab. Even though they could cooked those things by themselves at home, they got together at the church or clubhouse and make those Korean goodies together. I remember as a child eating some of those foods. These women all knew how to prepare them. By that time, we children were all old enough to understand how to make them ourselves. At that time, they had been in Hawaii about eight years or ten, so they still cooked the things that they cooked in Korea. Our diet was more Southern Korea than Northern Korea.

Q **Tell us about your marriage.**

A Oh, my marriage...my mother didn't want me to marry a Japanese. We young girls were old-fashioned enough that before we got married, our fiancé had to ask our parents' permission, particularly from our mother to get married because my mother was the head of the household even though we had a stepfather. We had to get permission from her because my sisters wanted to get married pretty young. Rose got married at age 18 and I think Daisy got married at either 19 or 20, and I got married at age 19. During those days the legal age to get married without parents' consent was 21 or over. We had to get our parents' consent because we were under 21. My husband and I had to talk to my mother about it. I told him that before I married him or even went out with him, I had to know what his intentions were. I only started dating my husband after we were engaged because I wasn't going to trust a "Haole" (white man- Caucasian). So, he told me his intentions, and then, he went to ask my mother. My poor mother, did not know who I was dating. She didn't know if I ever went out with him. He bravely, went and ask my mother for my hand. My mother gave her consent. At first I was afraid because everyone said it wouldn't work out being a mix marriage. We were more determined that it would work out. We were mature enough to "make it".

My husband was a volunteer on December 7, 1941, the day of the Pearl Harbor attack. Every military person answered the emergency call, including him. I did not see him for three days. My daughter was at Children's Hospital because she was exposed to my niece who suddenly died from an unknown cause a few days earlier. Nowadays, we call it SID, Silent Death Syndrome. We didn't know what my niece had died of. It was a precaution to put my daughter in the hospital, also, to be under observation because they played together, closely.

When December 7 came, our first thought was to get her out of the hospital to be with me. It so happened that it was a Sunday. The previous Saturday I had done my weekly grocery shopping so I had plenty of food at home. We got our daughter home quickly. Then, my husband left to do volunteer work at the Military Baracks. He knew the Pearl Harbor area well because he had served in the military during the "thirties" (1930's). He liked Hawaii so much that when he was discharged, he came back to Hawaii as civilian. He became our neighbor; that's how come I met him. He drove an ambulance and evacuated the wounded at Pearl Harbor. What he saw that day, he tried to block out in his memory. He began to have amnesia. It was decided to evacuate us away from Hawaii, so we went to Minneapolis to the Mayo Clinic which is in Minnesota. Before we left Hawaii, he was told that he should go to Minneapolis because his mother lived there. That was the best place for him, the doctor told him. But, he wouldn't go without me. His mother came to get him and me. We were evacuated in 1942. We came back to Hawaii after a few years. Then, we returned to Minnesota, permanently, in 1965.

I had a very good life in Minneapolis, but there were hardly any Asians there. People there thought I was Chinese, Filipino, Indian or everything else. They didn't know what a Korean was. Nobody knew what a Korean was until the Korean War. They even didn't know a nation like that existed.

My social life in Minneapolis was very good because my husband belonged to the Masons and, he belonged to the Shriners. There, we belonged, also, to St. Lutheran Church, which is the largest Lutheran Church in the United States. I sang in the church choir. We had about five different church choirs. As a senior choir member, I was the only dark haired woman in the whole choir. Anybody can spot me in the big church. Also, I stood out when we go to my husband's Shriner parties. We belonged to various organization within the Shriners. People knew us because we were the only odd couple. Mixed couple. They were very nice people. They were curious and asked us how we met and all of that. Everybody knew us even though the membership was huge. Even though I cannot not remember all of them, they remembered me everywhere. I entertained them at my home; we had many private parties at our home.

I worked at the Dayton's Department Store in the sales section where we did all the billing. Eventually, we computerized the data. I was well respected because I learned it quickly. My co-workers at the office came over to my home often because I had a "rickshaw" (oriental decorated) home. They came there for skating parties, New Years parties, and things like that. So, I had a very good social life there in Minneapolis. It seems that the more educated people are the more tolerant people. The people at the Shriner's were a very tolerant to non-Caucasians. There were a few isolated cases who were not friendly. Those people were more curious rather than being rude. I did not have a problem with that there.

Q **Once you told me that you liked being different.**

A Yes, no way can a person like me can hide the fact that I am an Oriental. Most of them thought I was Japanese.

When we went back to Minneapolis, we were on a troopship that was converted into a hospital ship. We were supposed to land at Los Angeles, but Japanese submarines were attacking the coast of California. This was in October, 1942. Our ship, then, diverted down to the Gulf of Mexico. We went hugging the coast line and landed in San Diego. San Diego was not prepared for us because we were supposed to land in Los Angeles. When we came into the harbor, all of us were so happy to be getting off the ship. Then, we saw on the sky line, anti aircraft balloons with cables hanging down. They had submarine nets to entangle the submarines, if they came close. All of us people went on the shore side. The ship tilted. Then, the captain got on the speaker to reach everybody to go back to the state room. When we landed, the Red Cross assisted us to leave San Diego. We had to take a train cross country until we reached Minneapolis.

Whenever we went home to Hawaii, I would have Chinese and Korean dresses made, then, take them back to Minneapolis. I would wear them to Shriner parties and other functions. My husband was very proud of me, wearing them because everybody knew he married an Oriental. People knew him and knew my name because we were an odd couple. He didn't mind that at all. I remember he encouraged me to wear my native costumes all the time. We went to parties at other homes or other places and I had no problems at all social functions.

The first time I went back to Hawaii to visit, I met my mother's insurance agent, John Kim. Suddenly, I remembered him. I asked my mother "Did he come from California?" She said, "Yes. He was the young man that when you all were children, you spent summers at his family home in Kaneohe." I remembered, now, his father told us that he and my father had decided that John and I were going to be married when we grew up. As American teenagers, we don't even think of letting our parents arranged marriage for us. But John and I got along very well for a while. Then, we started fighting like cats and dogs because we did not want to get involved in an arranged marriage. During that time Korean parents tried to arrange marriages. My mother arranged my older sister's marriage. In our family there were only two children among the seven who married Koreans. The rest of us were allowed to marry whomever we chose. My mother realized after the first arranged marriage that we were right, and that she should not interfere with our choices and we've been all successful. We all have been celebrating our 50th wedding anniversaries. Only the one who married a Korean through an arranged marriage did not.

Q **About your father...being a good cook?**

A He could cook Chinese food. When my mother was sick, my father would take over the kitchen and we thought he was a better cook than my mother because he cooked elaborate Chinese food with lots of different vegetables, and mushrooms, delicacies that he learned from the Chinese men. He knew his way around the kitchen very well because he was a bachelor for a long time, until 35 years old. So, he survived that very well.

By the way, those days when you were sick, you didn't go to the hospital. You go to the hospital only when you are dying. The life time of my mother and father was very different. Another example of being different because I was brought up in their culture, was that when I got married to my husband, I used call him by his last name. My mother, too, used to call my father, "Kim Si." My husband did not like that, calling him "Rudie." He told me to call him what his mother called his father. So, I asked, "What does your mother call you?" He said that his mother called him "Honey." So, I called him "Honey." But, when our daughter was just a toddler and she'd go around the house calling him, "Honey, honey," we decided that this can't be, so, between my husband and me, we got to call each other "Mommy" and "Daddy" because the child was picking up "Honey" when calling her father.

Another funny thing was that it struck me when I came back to Hawaii for a visit, my mother asked me what my name was. I was stunned to find out that she didn't even know what my name was. I was her third daughter and she had been calling me by that title, "third child"…(in Korean: 'Setjae dal'). This revelation happened when her friends came over to visit her while I was there in Hawaii for a visit. They had never seen me before. So, they asked my mother in Korean who is she? My mother never mentioned my name, but would say that she is "셋째딸"–"third daughter," I kidded her and asked her is that my name, "셋째딸" all these years? I was always 셋째딸 to her. Even in 1947 when I visited her, she asked me what my real name was. I looked at her and I said you mean you still don't know my name – I was still 셋째딸? I guess that is the way we were brought up, living in both cultures. I don't regret it. I think it was nice. And fun.

Q   **Tell me about your mother's second marriage. You said that he was a Filipino.**

A   Well, he was a Filipino man. A widower. He had a wife who died in child birth in the Philippines. He left his daughter with the grand-parents and immigrated to Hawaii without relatives. My mother was only 35 years old, when she became a widow. When they first met, he came over to help her, to do the laundry and to cook for the family. He began wooing her. This was a real love match. Circumstances were different. We, children did not want a stepfather, regardless, who it was. It was only after we were married ourselves that we were willing to accept another man in our mother's life. My mother was ostracized by other Koreans because of marrying a Filipino. However, later on, their marriage made it easier for us children to marry outside of our race, too, because she did that. Strange, she didn't like the idea that we married outside of our race at first. But, she knew what it was like, so she permitted us to do that. When she saw that we would better off with our own choice, she agreed that it was better that way.

Q **Did you see the difference in people marrying Caucasian and a Japanese? How did you feel about that?**

A Well, the first boy that I was going with was Japanese. He was the youngest in the family. So, that meant that I would have to cater to all his older brothers. His older brothers were already telling me what I should do, how I should dress, how I should laugh, and how I should behave. I wasn't even engaged, formally, engaged to him. I resented that bitterly. Also, my boyfriend and I could not announce our engagement or plans to get married, until his older brother married. So, I thought, alright if he doesn't want to get married first, and he's has to wait until his brother gets married first, I won't wait. His brother was dating his girlfriend for seven years. I am not sticking around for seven years. So, I married my husband.

Q **What about your mother, which one do you think she would prefer? Haole? Or Japanese?**

A She preferred Haole, than a Japanese boy at that time. But my other sister, Daisy, the second daughter, married a Japanese boy. Our mother was ostracized for marring a Filipino. So, what can she say. It was bad enough that my mother married Filipino. Her first daughter was married to a Korean which was an arranged marriage, but it did not last. If the third daughter, me, married a Japanese, too, my mother would have been in hot water in the Korean community because she's letting her children marry again another Japanese. She would rather have me marry a Haole. My mother did tell my haole husband before she died that he was a very good man. She thought that he was very nice compared to my older sister's second husband who was Haole. He had a very different personality than my husband. She did compliment my husband that he was a very good son–in–law.

Q **So you left the islands in 1942. . .**

A Going back and forth, I think I made seven trips.

Q **And your mother, too, made quite a number of visits to Korea?**

A Yes, she made about three trips, I know definitely three...maybe four trips. The last trip that she made was as an American citizen. She said that the last trip was wonderful because she was able to go to the museums and to the different places where the Korean artifacts were, and visit palaces too, which she couldn't visit during her previous trips because she she was a Japanese citizen. Remember that the picture brides who came to Hawaii, came during the Japanese Occupation of Korea. They all had to have a Japanese citizen passport. This was changed many years after Korea was free, again.

My mother learned more about the Korean culture during these trips after the war because before she left Korea for the first time, she was a farmer's daughter in a small village. Her father, also, had a silver smith shop working with metals. He and other families in that area had some education, but not much. They were middle class families in Korea. I could show you pictures of my present cousins. I met my two cousins in Seoul after the war. One was an Assistant Director of the Korean CIA and the other was a vice president of the Samsung Company.

Yes. I was very pleased to meet my extended family. There was some concern about our background because a lot of Haole people married Oriental girls who came from the "bars" (night clubs) or from some poor background. The women wanted go to the United States. My cousin said that it wasn't that case with us. When he met my family, he realized that we came from a good background, too, as good or better than his own background. My husband's families...

his background is very good, too. We got banking officials, we got sheriffs, we got everything in the family. But, what surprised me the most was to find that a lot of our lost relatives in Korea, the men, they were in civil services. My family in Hawaii, the majority...nearly all of us are in some form of civil service jobs, also. So, how is it that you find two families thousands of miles apart who were not in contact for many years because of the wars have the same likes and dislikes and that we are all in civil service? We're both sides in business and in civil service work.

Q **Do you remember anything about involvement in the Independence Movement?**

A No. All I know is that my mother did send donation money, now and then. I would say that Church on Liliha Street, they were more active. Ours was more on the religious side. We didn't get involved in politics very much, but I know about some of the politics because being such a small Korean community, we knew each other. The children all knew each other even though we belong to different churches and different language schools.

Aki Kim, Dorothy Rudie's mother, visiting her parents' gravesite in Korea, circa 1960's.

My name is Rosie Kim Chang. I am a second generation Korean. My grandmother arrived here with my mother who was at that time, five years old. They arrived on one of the ships in 1904 from Korea.

Because my mother came with my grandmother at that time, my grandmother was not employed in the sugar fields. My grandmother did not come with her husband. What she did was, she went to do laundry for the Korean single men, while my mother was taken to the Susanna Wesley Home at that time. It was a school for the youngsters of the immigrants. So, my mother was brought up in Susanna Wesley Home. And she went to high school at McKinley High School, and graduated there. Later, my mother met my father, Chip Chong Kim.

My father, who came the same year as my grandmother and mother, arrived as a young man. Because he was too young to be sent to the fields, he was sent to Mills College which was the predecessor of the Mid-Pacific Institute. How they met, I am not familiar with. So, they got married after high school, and from what I understand, one of his early jobs was as a radio operator for CPC, the California Packing Company. While working there he, contracted tuberculosis and at that time he was sent to Leahi Hospital, where he died. He died when I was about 5 years old.

There were three siblings in our family at that time. My mother was not able to support herself. So, my grandmother did a match marriage for her. My grandmother was very thoughtful in getting a husband for my mother,

Susannah Wesley Home and Training School, circa 1906.

a man who had the same surname, Kim. So, my stepfather came in to the picture about 1924. He was, at that time, an officer in the Salvation Army. And from that marriage three additional children were born: Betty, Ruth, and Earl. A unique thing happened: my stepfather wanted a better paying job so, he was sent to California to learn a profession as a barber. When he came back, he was better able to support the family.

My siblings from the first father were Clara Kim Emerson, who became the first Korean to become a Public School Principal. My brother, Bill Kim, became a well-known sports editor for the local newspaper. Bill continued his activities with sports throughout his life and was featured in the newspapers often. He graduated from St. Louis High School. He became the Editor of the Catholic Newspaper. Years later, he studied law at Hastings University to become an attorney. He was about to become a judge, when he suddenly, he died in his early 40's.

Because my grandmother and mother were recruited from the Korean Methodist Church in Korea to go to Hawaii, they then, affiliated themselves with the Fort Street Korean Methodist Church. So, growing up, I remember that the Sundays were spent in church... in the morning, and in the afternoon and in the evening. As I grew up as a teenager, we added another day of the

Mary Ae Gee Kim and family, circa 1930. Left to right, front: Rosie, Betty, Ruth, Bill; standing: Clara, Kwan Yer (Mary Ae Gee's second husband), Mary Ae Gee Kim.

week for choir practice. Our whole social activity was immersed in the church. Thus, the church was our social foundation. The church also, was where we went to the Korean School for two reasons: one is to give support to the church, and secondly, to be able to keep up with the Korean language.

However, when World War II came into the picture, then, all foreign language schools were eliminated. Since then, we joined other social activities that were outside of the church and the children were able to to be affiliated with other young people when we grew older. The church became not as important to the Second or Third Generation, as it was with the new immigrants. There many new immigrants after World War II and the Korean War. They came to the islands in the late 1960's and the Church became their social foundation.

Now, about my own personal background...if you recall, Koreans were a small minority in the Hawaiian Islands, not as abundant as the Japanese or the Chinese. The Koreans were termed as "Others" in the census because we were less than one percent of the entire population in Hawaii. We were the first ethnic group that were dispersed in the Islands, widely, in urban Honolulu. And so, because the major Korean Methodist Church was on Fort Street, we lived in upper part of Fort Street, and later, we moved to the Punchbowl area. It was very close to the Korean Methodist Church on Fort Street. Before 1918, there was only one Korean Church in Honolulu.

Our home was amongst the Portuguese, also. And there, too, was the Catholic Church, which the Portuguese attended. We became so close to the Portuguese people that we were able to learn how to eat sweet bread. My brother, Bill, was sent to St. Louis College, a Catholic School, and since he was immersed in Catholicism, he became a Catholic and was baptized into that Church. That is at St. Louis College, where he first sold local newspapers and then, became the editor of the Catholic Herald. He was well-known when he grew-up.

My sister, Clara and I, were the only ones in the family that went to a public school. There was a prestigious public high school that would admit the non-Caucasian children who could speak English well. It was called Roosevelt High School, the English Standard School. When we were old enough, Clara and I took the exam for Roosevelt and was admitted, so we were both graduates of the English Standard School at Roosevelt High School. It was a prestigious school. Before that school, we were students at Royal School which is in the Punchbowl area. After high school, I went to the University for two years, then, was admitted to the Queen's Hospital, School of Nursing.

During my first position in the School of Nursing, I won the Director of Nursing Award for the Best Bedside Nurse. My first appointed position was as the Head Nurse. Then, in the late 40's, I went to the University of Pittsburgh, where I got my Master's Degree in Nursing Education. In fact, I followed my husband, Dr. John Chang, who was in Medical School at the University of Pittsburgh. While I was getting my Master's Degree in Pittsburgh, the Queen's Hospital Director in Honolulu wrote to me and said that they would like to appoint me as the Assistant Director of Nursing, which was unthought-of at that time... because all top positions up to that time were given to Caucasians recruited from the Mainland. No Honolulu local person was given such high position earlier. So, that was my job. Then, after that position, I was appointed to Head of the School of Nursing... not only as an Assistant, but the high position because my Master's was in Administration of the School of Nursing.

Then later, I became the Director the School of Nursing there. Later, I was promoted to Head the Hawaii State Hospital, since I did some testing for the Hawaii State for Personnel Services to reorganize nursing there. When the Regional Medical Program came up, a higher position, I was asked to join it. I did join that Program, and I remained there until 1987. Then, I went back to study to receive my Doctorate. After that, I was employed at the University, not in nursing, but in International Health, and I did some educational programs there, as well as research program. From there, I retired and continued my volunteer work for the Center of Asia Pacific Exchange. In this program, I coordinated the teaching programs for people from the Asia Pacific Region, and started to do seminars in Seoul and Pusan in South Korea. I enjoyed that very much. The Center of Asia Pacific Exchange was like a small East-west Center, which was the first large Asian study center in the USA. I enjoyed it very much and spent a lot of time with the Koreans.

Q **Did your mother speak with you sometimes in Korean?**

A No, my mother spoke English all the time. She spoke in front of the children in Korean, only, when she and my father did not wish us to understand what they are saying. And I think I adopt the spirit of nationalism about Korea from her because it was through immersion, not because she forced this to be a nationalist and so forth. We learned it through our desire...she didn't push it on us. We knew about the situation in Korea before they came over to Hawaii: the hardships that they had, the famine, the treatment that the Japanese had done, and it was, I think, just embedded in us. She didn't have to say, you have to hate the other ethnic groups. And, I think as a whole, the Koreans were more liberal than the Japanese or the Chinese. I think the Japanese and the Chinese, at least, among my friends, tell me that if they married outside of their race, they were kicked out of the household. But, I think the Korean families here were more tolerant, at least that was my understanding.

Q **Do you know anything about the split in the community?**

A Oh, yes, the thing is that, having gone through the Korean Methodist Church, I heard and saw a lot. Now, they didn't really, at that time, say bad things about the other church. But, we knew the fallout between the Korean Methodist Church, when Dr. Rhee took some of this fallout and set up the Korean Christina Church on Liliha Street. So,

271

we knew that, but other than that, we didn't really feel it. Because after all, Bill, my brother was named by Dr. Syngman Rhee. He named my brother Bill. But, I think it was before the fallout. We just had feelings about the fallout. We were too young to be involved. And we knew about Dongji Hoi and Kuk Min Hur, two separate organizations.

Q **How did it come about that Syngman Rhee named Bill?**

A That I don't know. Because I didn't ask my mother except, when she had said, "Well you know, it was Dr. Syngman Rhee who named him." It was before the fallout, I'm sure. You see, my parents stayed with the Korean Methodist Church.

Q **What year was it?**

A Bill was born in 1920. Long time ago, so I don't know when the fallout was.

Q **It began in 1916, but the final split was in 1918.**

A Yes. But my mother wasn't that active or had such intense feelings as some of the people had. Of course, she was partial because of her affiliation with the Korean Methodist church.

Q **Do you remember some of her friends?**

A No, I really don't, except that I know that Mary Hong Park...her family was very active with the Korean Methodist Church, and my mother was active in the same church work there. As I said, our whole life was immersed in church activities.

Q **What about Ha Soo Whang? Do you remember her?**

A Oh, absolutely. Ha Soo Whang was a leader, especially, for Korean girls. I was very active with the activities that she started; for example, at that time, I remember so clearly, that she setup so many activities at the Academy of Arts. I don't know who taught us Korean dances and so forth. But I remember performing there at that time, and there were other activities that she did, especially, for the Korean girls. I remember that when I was in high school, we went back to the

Honolulu Academy of Arts and at that time as a youngster, I thought the stage was so huge. But now, when I see the stage, it's so small. I had remembered it as being so large. And, I also remember Mr. Tai Sung Lee, Pearl Lee Kim's father. He was a very active leader among the Korean young people. He initiated some youth programs, too. He and Ha Soo Whang were both on the YWCA Staff, as well as active in the YMCA. They were very close to the Korean youngsters in Hawaii. I feel they never should be forgotten because they helped us through the teenage high school years.

My name is Esther Soon Yee Hong Kang. I was born June 10, 1917. My father was Hong, Young Soo, who was my mother's second husband. He was from Hwanghaedo, Korea. His family spent most of the time in Jejudo. He came to Hawaii to work in the sugar plantation in Kona which is on the "Big Island" (a name for the Island of Hawaii).

My father was very good with his hands in sewing. So, eventually, he worked on people's uniform and clothes. Then, he started a tailor shop in Kona on the Big Island (Island of Hawaii).

Esther Kang at the Korean Cultural & Food Festival, 1983, Korea Times.

My mother was Anna Lee. She never had a Korean name that I know of. She came from Seoul, Korea, as a picture bride at age 14 for her first husband who was not my father. When she saw her first husband who was 19 years old, she refused to marry him because she said he was, too, old. So, she stayed one month in the woman's compound. The wonen told her, "If you don't marry him, you will have to go back to Korea." So, she married him and they had six children. These children were my stepsisters and stepbrothers, that is, my mother's children from her first husband.

The first child was Paul Kae Hong. He was an unusually bright fellow. He didn't go to school. But he had an Electrical Engineering license from the Government at that time. My second brother, John, he was a carpenter. He did roofing, and he did all kinds of things to improve houses. My third brother was a contractor. He took jobs taking care of homes, fixed them up and sold for a profit.

When my older sister Dora, married a Chinese boy, my father didn't approve of her marrying a Chinese boy, she took my father to Court. She told the Court, "I want to know why my father won't allow me to marry Charlie Choo. My father told the Judge, "I don't want no 'Pake' (Chinese) for a son-in-law." The Judge scolded her father and allowed her to marry Charlie Choo, so she was married to Charlie Choo, again, this time, in front of the Judge in Court and in front of my father. When they left, it was all amicable. They had three children. They lived very, very happily.

Q   **Go on with your story about your mother meeting your father, your mother's second husband. Oh, tell us first what happened to the first husband?**

A   Oh, her first husband decided to go back to Korea. So, he told my mother he was going back to Korea and asked her if she wanted to go with him. She said, "No," she wanted to stay in Hawaii. So, he took their youngest son with him, leaving five children with her. He returned to Korea and was never heard from, again.

So, when my father, her second husband, saw my mother with her five children, he felt sorry for her, so he helped support them. When they got married, they had six children of their own. I was the oldest.

Q   **Name them.**

A   The six children are Soon Yee, Soon Ah, Soon Yea, Clara and Walter. I was the oldest of her second husband.

Q   **When did the family move to Honolulu?**

A   I think in a few years after he found out that he could sew. My mother

275

could sew, too. So, they started their own tailor shop when they came to Honolulu. They went to Fort Shafter (a military base outside of Honolulu). From there, they went to live near Schofield Barracks (near Wahiawa). And they did very well, there too.

Q **Did they both go to the Korean Christian Church? I know you go to the Christian Church. Did your father go, too?**

A Yes. Both went to the Korean Christian Church. My father was a great supporter of Dr. Rhee. So, my mother went along. And she worked hard for him, too. They went through a lot of heart aches. They went to the Korean Christian Church because they supported Dr. Rhee. Some of the other Koreans in the Korean Christian Church didn't support Dr. Rhee. So, they would have arguments right at Church (within the Korean Christian Church). But, in the end, it was ok.

Q **What year do you think your family moved to Honolulu? And where were you born?**

A According to my birth certificate, I was born in Honolulu in 1917. So, they must have married earlier than that. .

Q **Tell us about their activities in the church. Who was the stronger one in the family regarding church affiliation, your father or your mother?**

A My father was the stronger one.

Q **Was he the one who chose to follow Syngman Rhee?**

A Yes, right.

Q **What happened? How did he get to be a Syngman Rhee follower?**

A My father said he knew Syngman Rhee from Korea. So, when they came out here, they already were friends. The Methodist Church Congregation had frictions. So, Syngman Rhee said the Korean Methodist Church didn't have their own soul. They were led by the Methodist Church in the United States. They had to go according to that. So, Syngman Rhee got mad. And he said, "Why should we have to follow somebody on the Mainland?" So, he left. My father was one of the great followers of Rhee.

Q **So then, your father was a Methodist at one time.**

A Yes, they were all Methodists at one time. In fact, all Koreans were Methodists at that time, until Dr. Syngman Rhee walked off.

Q **Do you know anything more than that? What did your father do for Syngman Rhee?**

A Well, I know Syngman Rhee lived at our house for a while, and then, they started the KCI.

Q **When was this? What year was it that he lived at your house?**

A I can't remember. . . .

Q **How old were you?**

A I think four or five years old.

Q **Tell me more about what you remember, growing up in the Korean Christian Church.**

A When I went there, they accepted me. I just enjoyed myself there. My father was great; he was a great disciplinarian.

Q **What do you remember of KCI?**

A I remember it being a rambling building with lot of students in there. They were very very royal to Dr. Syngman Rhee. They studied real hard.

Q **Did you ever attend that school?**

A No, I didn't. Too young. But my older sisters and brothers went to that school.

Q **What do you remember them telling you about that school?**

A Well, they said that it was a good school. They learned a lot and they were given much opportunity to say what they wanted. They were disciplined.

Q   **What significant person do you remember during that time as the leaders of the Korean community? Such as Won Soon Lee? Do you remember Won Soon Lee?**

A   Yes, I remember him. He was a domineering member. I don't remember too much more about him, since I was so young. But, I do know that he used to come around and tell us what to do, and he'd tell all the people what to do. He was, financially, well-off, too. So, he was able to do much for the Korean community.

Q   **Tell me about your husband. Where did you meet him?**

  He was my brother's very good friend. My brother used to bring him around the house, and we used to go fishing together. Go riding, all this and that. I don't know how we became attached to each other.

Q   **What is his full name?**

A   David Taewui Kang. He was born in Kihei, Maui. And, his father died when he was ten years old. So, his mother was left with all his brothers and sisters. He had to quit school and work for the plantation companies, but he was very, very smart, and eventually, he became foreman of the sugar plantation. Because he was a foreman, there were certain privileges that other people didn't have. So, he said he could have a good life.

Q   **Where were his parents from?**

A   They were from Hwanghaedo. His mother? No, I don't know about his mother.

Q   **Do you know if his mother was a picture bride?**

A   Yes, his mother was a picture bride.

Q   **Do you know when they came to Honolulu?**

A   He was in school when they came to Honolulu. So, he must have been about six or seven years old.

Q **Have you ever met David's father?**
A No, I met his stepfather.

Q **His mother remarried?**
A Yes. His mother remarried to Mr. Kim. I lived with them many many years. He was very good man. Very punctual.

Q **What was his full name, do you remember?**
A I can't remember. Kim…

Q **Did they have children?**
A Yes, they have one son.

Q **Is he still alive?**
A Oh, Yes. Samuel Kim.

Q **Where does he live?**
A He lives in California.

Q **Where did you live when you were growing up?**
A I was growing up in the Liliha Street area. I remember the Filipino church there, very distinctly.

Q **What schools did you attend?**
A I went to Liliuokalani School and McKinley High School, and to the University of Hawaii. I lived on 19th Avenue at that time. Then, my father sold that place.
   Then, one day my mother packed all of her things in the truck and she left. I thought it was because of me. When she left, I ran after her and I said, "Omeomi, Omeomi" [mother: 어머니, 어머니]please come back. I will be good. She just left at that time.

Q **How old were you?**

A   I think about 12 years old.

Q   **What happened after that happened?**

A   And so my father had no choice but to ask welfare to back him up. And, the welfare told him that he would have to take his six children and put them in all different homes. My father said he didn't want that. He wanted the family to be together. So, they asked him "who is your oldest child?" He told them that I was the oldest and was that I was 12 years old. He assured them that I was capable of taking care of the younger children. So, the welfare worker said it was o.k. for me to assume the family care.

I remember washing clothes one o'clock in the morning. Everyday I had to go marketing, trying to make 25 cents dinners to be different every meal. It was very, very difficult. I never had a childhood. Never had dates. So busy taking care of my brothers and sisters.

Q   **Did your mother ever come back?**

A   No. Never came back to live with us.

Q   **Did she go back to Korea or was she still in Hawaii?**

A   She was still in the Islands. But once in a while she wanted to see us, but never lived with us. I remember when I got married, she came to the wedding. I told her, "Who told you you can come to this wedding?" She said, "You're my daughter so I came to the wedding."

Q   **Did she ever tell you why she left?**

A   Well, now when I think about it, I can see why she left. My father had six stepchildren and six of his own. When the children had an argument, my father would take our side, and so, my mother said, "Heck with this" (meaning that he sides only on his own children). So, she left.

Q   **Did she take some children with her?**

A   No, she didn't take any of the children with her. She left them all with my father.

Q **How about the children of the first husband?**

A The six above me were all grown up. They all had their own business working and one of my sisters was in college so . . .

Q **What happened to your mother?**

A She just lived with by herself on Wilder Avenue. She died of a heart attack.

Q **How many years did she live before she died?**

A Oh...many, many years, I think. Good ten years, I think. Today, I'm still sorry that I was not close to my mother. My father told us, "When you see your mother down the street, you cross the street."

Q **Tell us more about your youth...about anything.**

A Oh, when I was young, life was very, very hard because I have five younger brothers and sisters. My father would say I couldn't go out date on a date with any other nationality but Korean. But my first love was a Japanese boy. I remember this distinctly. One night, we came home, and we sat in the car. We just talked. When I came to the house, my father was sitting at the front door chair. As I came near, he just walked off and I knew he was mad. I told this to my Japanese boyfriend. We just quit dating. But, I still think about him. He was a nice guy. He became a dentist. I don't know if he passed away or not. He was really a nice guy.

Q **Tell us a little bit more about activities at the Korean Christian Church.**

A Oh, the Korean Christian Church was very, very active. We would get together and go down to the Korean Old Folks Care Home to sing for them and take food to them, like cookies and Dok [Korean rice cake]. We would make tea and serve them. We would go in and clean up the place. I had my name down there for entrance in the future. If there was a vacancy, I would go there. It was a nice little place. Now, the Korean Care Home takes in retirees of any nationality because they are under the State regulations about discrimination.

Q **What kind of activities did you do with Koreans? For instance, with the Wahiawa Korean Christian Church?**

A Well, I didn't do much with the Wahiawa Korean Christian Church. But we did go on home calls. If somebody was sick, the minister would call one of us to go with him. We would go visit them.

Q **There was a big raucous at the Korean Christian Church in the 1940's. Do you know anything about that?**

A Yes. I think that was terrible. I remember I was in church on a Sunday. I think it was a Rev. Park who came. Some ladies got angry and said "You get out of this church you don't belong to this Church." He responded that he belonged to this Church because he was a member of the Korean Christian Church because it was under God. They had big, big argument at church. I remember that distinctly.

Q **So what happened?**

A I don't know what happened after that.

Q **Could you name some outstanding personalities during 1940s and even 1930s? Have you ever heard of Tai Sung Lee? Tell me what you know about him.**

A Well, he was a soft spoken man. He was a nice guy. He was very, very disciplined. What he said sometimes was admirable. I have great admiration for that man. I think he was a mid-built man. I thought he was a good looking guy. Although he had a soft spoken voice, whenever, he was mad, you can hear the rafters ringing.

Q **You don't know what happened to your husband's father. Did you ever find out where David's mother came from?**

A She came from Seoul, Korea. She came from a well-to-do family where she had a private tutor and things of that sort. She wasn't used to all this hard work when she came to Hawaii.

Q **Did she tell you why she came?**

A She said she came to Hawaii as a picture bride. Anything to get away from Korea because Korea was very hard on women.

Q **Are there anything else you might to discuss?**

A In the very near end of their lives, my mother and my father supported each other. I remember my mother caring for my father when he was sick. And my father caring for my mother when she was sick.

Q **But didn't she leave him at one time?**

A Yes, she did. Even after she left him, she would come around and look after us and see how everything was.

Q **I thought you never saw her after she left.**

A After she left, no, we didn't see her for many many years. But then after that, she came back to family activities.

Q **About how old were you then? When she came back?**

A High school at that time.

Q **So younger kids are still young then.**

A Yes. They were all still young.

Q **You said you remember you were cruel to her?**

A Yes. I was cruel to her because I said all these nasty things to her. I said why you leave us and go by yourself, and leave us and let me do all the hard work. Afterwards, I realized that she had the reason to do what she did. Anybody would, after having six children for one husband and six children for another husband. And then, have one husband have sympathy only for his own children and nothing for the others. So, I could see my mother's view point at that time, although the step children were all grown up and married with businesses of their own.

Q **What about your father? Did he still work hard? Tailoring or did he change jobs?**

A He worked on this tailoring job. He was very, very good at his business of tailoring at Fort Ruger. He bought a lot of properties. He made money from rentals. He said that he made money from renting out rooms to the Koreans. He did alright.

Q **Where was that?**

A In Wahiawa. The building is still there. I still can see the building there.

Q **Did you ever meet Syngman Rhee, personally?**

A Oh, yes. Like I said, one time he stayed with us.

Q **Oh, that's right. Tell us about that a little bit more.**

A Well, we were all afraid of him because you know he was a Number 1 man. But he was very, very gentle. He talked to us when we got troubles with our parents. Syngman Rhee said you have to respect your parents. He was the man who taught me to have respect for my elders and respect for your teachers. And he was a really wonderful person. He didn't talk much. He didn't socialize much. He only read, read, and read. Even if his food wasn't good, he never complained about his food. He just ate his food. He was an exceptional man, Syngman Rhee.

Q **What about Mrs. Rhee.**

A She was nice, too...although she was haole. Because she was haole, we didn't consider her as one of us, but she was really nice. She tried to make us understand that even though she was haole and Dr. Syngman Rhee was a Korean, it didn't matter. They really proved something to us.

Q **Have you ever heard of Nodie Kimhaekim?**

A Yes. Nodie Kim. We thought Dr. Rhee would marry Nodie. But he had this haole girlfriend. We knew it was out of the question. Nodie understood and she was very tolerant. She accepted Mrs. Rhee. Nodie was very good. She started a Korean Women's group. And we went around singing at the Koreans centers and to all the old peoples' home not only Koreans. I sang there and we served out Korean Dodeok [떡]. We made tea and had a nice time.

Q **Do you remember Inez Kong Pai?**

A Inez Kong Pai was definitely for the Korean Christian Church. She claimed that her mother and her father helped start the Korean Christian Church. Her parents donated a quite bit of money to the Church. Anytime when there was a social gathering, she was always there. She was a great orator, too. She was a wonderful person.

Q **Who else do you remember in the second generation who were pretty strong Christian Church?**

A Robert Choi's family was very active. He always volunteered and donated time and money to the church. And whenever, there was a big occasion you would see Robert, right there.

Q **Do you think that the break between the Methodist Church and Korean Christian Church affected the second generation?**

A You mean, our age? No, I didn't think it affected us at all because we were loyal to Syngman Rhee. We knew that he left the Church not because of religion, but because of this mainland people telling us what to do in Hawaii, and that they don't know anything about Hawaii.

Q **Did second generation intermarry? Did they marry each other between the Methodist marrying Korean Christian Church members?**

A Oh, yes. They did. Sometimes, it was so difficult. I remember I was a Korean Christian Church member, and my husband was a Methodist. When we got married, I wanted to get married at the Korean Christian Church. And his mother wanted her son to get married in the Methodist Church. It was really, really difficult. So, what we did was we got married in the Korean Christian Church, but had the Moksa [Pastor, 목사] was from the Methodist Church to perform the ceremony with the help of the Korean Christian Church minister. I remember. It was really really nice.

Q **When did you marry?**

A I married in 1940 to David, who was a good friend of my brothers. How we ever got involved I don't know, but eventually we got married. We had three children and we lived very happily together. He was a very, very considerate person. After we got married we lived with his mother. His mother was very, very good to me. But my father-in-law was even nicer because, whenever my mother-in-law would show favoritism he would tell her, "You are not thinking of her, too." I remember those two arguing over that. My father-in-law wasn't a man of much words...he didn't say much. But he was a very, very thoughtful man. I loved that man. He did a lot for his children, too.

After I graduated from McKinley High School in 1935, I wanted to go to the University of Hawaii. The school recommended that I go to further my education. But because of our family financial situation, I just couldn't go to the University of Hawaii. I went to one of the smaller community college. David saw me study three, four clock in the morning and then, rush to school. So, he told me one day, "Why do you need that college degree except for your own ego?" I said that's why I need it. He said, he couldn't see me studying at three or four clock in the morning, rushing to school, coming home, doing my other work and, then, studying to go back to school. So, I just quit. Later, I was sorry that I quit because I could have continued, if I persisted.

Q **What kind of work did you do after that?**

A Oh, I went into the real estate business.

Q **Was your husband still working where?**

A Oh, my husband was a furniture manufacturer. And I helped him in his business sewing, getting him started. But once he was on his own, I thought maybe it would be better if I wasn't connected with it. So, when he hired two more girls who could do the sewing, I left the shop. And, he did very fine, too.

286

Interview with Howard Halm
regarding his paternal grandparents:
Sam Yo Halm and Mary Hong
son of: **Dr. Gilbert and Mary Kim Halm**

My name is Howard Halm. I was born in Honolulu, Hawaii in 1942, son of Dr. Gilbert Chi Num Halm and Mary Kim Halm.

My parents were born in Honolulu. You have already interviewed my mother about her lineage. I would like to say a few things about my paternal grandparents. My father's parents came to Honolulu in 1904 from the Port of Incheon. They came as a family with one son to work in the Hawaii sugar cane fields. My paternal grandmother's name was Mary Hong Halm. She was from Seoul. My grandfather's name was Sam Yo Halm. He was from Pyongyang.

When they came over from Korea, my grandfather was 47 years old and my grandmother was 35 years old. So, they were one of the few Korean families that came over as a family group. After living in Honolulu, they had 4 children. Richard, Jane, Henry and my father, Gilbert.

My father was born in 1912 and his brothers and sisters were born about two years apart. My grandfather came to Hawaii with several documents of which are still in my possession. One is a family genealogy which I think is called a "Kongbok". Recently, I was in Korea for the first time, and I met a lawyer there by the name of Halm. I sent him a copy of the Kongbok. He's going look to see if we were related somehow. My grandfather, also,

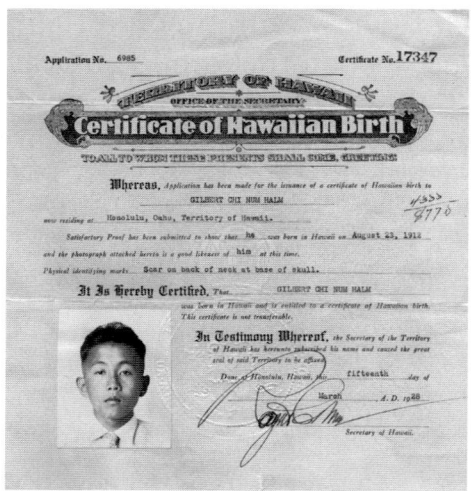

Gilbert Chi Num Halm was born in 1912, Birth Certificate in 1928.

had a map of Korea which showed the burial sites of his ancestors. The Kongbok goes back to the year of 1503, which is, obviously, within the Chosun Dynasty. He also, had his passport or his immigration document, which indicated that he had left Incheon on September 7, 1904. From what I understand, my grandfather being a sort of senior citizen even at that time, was very involved in the Korean Independence Movement, supporting and sending back a lot of money to some coalition. I was told by my friends that instead of sending back money and that if he invested in real estate here in Honolulu, especially, at that time, we'd be very well off today. But he instead supported the Korean Independence Movement. He never did go back to Korea, he died in Honolulu in 1925. My grandmother who died in Los Angeles in 1956 is buried next to him at the Oahu Cemetery in Honolulu.

I recall when I was 12 years that I sat down with my grandmother and asked about her life story. I could only communicate to her with stick figures because I didn't speak Korean, but we could communicate with stick figures, that is simple "pigeon English". That way she told me the stories that I told you in terms of her coming to California, and her coming to Los Angeles with her husband. She said when she came from Seoul to Honolulu, her first work was to wash the clothes for the sugar cane workers and she made money that way. She, also, was very good at making the Mook. She was obviously, a much older woman having been born in 1869. So, she was older than many of the men that came over as sugar cane field workers. Most of the men were born in the 1870s and the early 1880s. Her husband was born in 1857 so they were sort of the oldest couple in the community.

Q   **Did she have a Korean name?**

A   I'm sure she did. I'm not clear to why she used only the name, Mary.

I recall just a few months ago, when I was at Oahu Cemetery, I looked up the index card of everybody that has buried at the Oahu Cemetery. This goes back to 1850s. They have a Korean section up there. The Korean section is not categorized by denomination in the sense of religion or church affiliation. They do not have Korean Christians, Korean Methodists, Korean Episcopalians. They all are buried together there. So, I looked through the index cards. I was interested in the index cards of the Halm family. I saw for example 1925. The cards fold out by the name of my grandfather and my grandmother, when he died and her name was listed simply as Mary Hong. So, at least as, of 1925 she preferred to be called Mary Hong.

Q   **And no Korean name with it?**

A   I don't know any Korean name. There's no Korean name on her grave stone either which is interesting.

Q   **Is there any hint that they were Christians before they came?**

A   There is no hint. I am not clear exactly what they did, except that I understand my grandfather was a school teacher who traveled. That's what brought him from Pyongyang down to Seoul. He was traveling school teacher.

Q   **A number of Incheon people were Methodist who were recruited for the plantations in Hawaii, especially, if they were married couples.**

A   Well, you know, I am not that clear as to whether or not my grandparents were even Episcopalians. Do you know, mother, whether or not they were? (Mother replies) Yes, they went to our church.

O.K. I never really knew my grandmother was a really religious person. My mother remembers that they attended St. Luke's Church in the early days at least.

Q   **You mentioned something about a child who was born in Korea and came later to Hawaii.**

A   Yes. Uncle William was born in Korea. He was born probably in 1902 or 1901. But he came over around 1904 so, he was probably born in 1903.

Q Did you mention that it was your grandmother's child?

A My grandmother's child from another husband. What my grand-mother told me was that she had three children. William was her youngest. She met my grandfather. They fell in love and decided to leave Seoul and come to Hawaii.

Q Leaving the other two children?

A I believe so.

Q Anything else about your paternal grandmother's family?

A No, but I could probably learn a lot more if I could get somebody to translate the Kongbok. The Kongbok is written in old Korean so it's hard unless you're a scholar of the language back in the 1500s and 1600s. I'm working on this genealogy as I said through this attorney that I know, and once I am able to unravel that, then I could actually go back several centuries.

Q Tell us about your life in Hawaii.

A We moved from Honolulu, where I was born. I, as a youngster, lived near the corner of a McCully and Wilder. And then, we moved when I was about 5 or 6 years old to Nehoa Street near Roosevelt High School. And then, we moved from there to Kailua in 1949. Kailua, then, was a small town with about maybe 5,000 people. My father was the second dentist to move in that area. We lived in the outskirts of town where the cow pastures and swamps were in our neighborhood. I attended Kailua Elementary School, which was where my mother was on the staff of assistant teachers.

My father had his dental practice office in our large house, so when I came from school, my father would be there. My mother was at that time pursuing her college degree for her Education Degree. In 1952, I started attending Punahou School until 1957, which was when we moved to Los Angeles. And then, we moved to Los Angeles.

Q   **What happened to your maternal grandfather? Was he living with the family?**

A   My maternal grandfather died in 1942 before I was born. He died because of an industrial accident.

My paternal grandmother was very much like a lot of the Koreans that we see today. Very energetic, very much like an entrepreneur for many years. She must have bought and sold real property almost every year or maybe on the average of every other year. She was able to do that without any appreciable education, without being able to speak English, without having a car, without having a lawyer so to speak. She was able to buy and sell property, get the equity from one property to invest in the other property. She owned ten units by subletting in the Punchbowl area without problems. To me, that's a great story of perseverance. She died in 1971. I saw a lot of that kind of energy in the Korean people when I was in Korea, recently.

Q   **Who did she live with?**

A   She lived by herself. She was a very self-sufficient woman and she did not want to be dependent on any of her children even after she had a stroke in 1964. She preferred to live alone. Her son lived close by to care of her.

Q   **Which son?**

A   Noel. He is actually the only son.

Q   **What do you remember about the Korean community?**

A   Well, I don't remember anything about the Korean community at least not in Honolulu back then. I know a lot now about what the Korean community must have been back in the past because I do a lot of reading and I talked to a lot of people, and so, I know that at some point of the time and history of Koreans and that among Koreans in Hawaii, there was a split between the organization that they followed. What's his name? Youngman Park?

Q   **Youngman Park.**

A And Dr. Syngman Rhee. And Ahn, Chang Ho. I know that the divisiveness still persists today.

We had this conferences in 1996 and the topic was about the history of Koreans in Hawaii. We have a professor from Philadelphia who talked about 20 minutes about history, history of Koreans in the United States or at least in Hawaii. He did not once mention Syngman Rhee. That was my first realization that I had of how that conflict has persisted. I mean even until today people can have their debates about that. I don't know if you met Charles Kim yet, but Charles is the executive director of Korean American Coalition (KAC). Charles Kim is the President of the KAC right now, and he is here to talk at the Conference at the University of Hawaii.

Q **Tell us what's happening in Los Angeles, as well as KAC.**

A I'm the Chairman of the Board of Directors this year. And this is my last year. Bill is going to take it over as the Chairman of the Korean

Coalition Conference in Hawaii with representatives from several states, 1999. Left to right, front: Alvin Kang, Keith Kim, Howard Halm, Janis Koh, William Min; second row: Vice Consul Gerald Oh, Young Kim, Helen Kim, Nita Song, Joon Song, Byung Kwon Kim, Hyepin Kim, Julie Lee, Cathy Choi; third row: Mark Keam, Russell Park, unidentified, unidentified, Jimmy Lee, unidentified, unidentified.

American Coalition. Our President is Joseph Ahn who would be in Hawaii and our Executive Director is Charles Kim. What we are going to be doing in Hawaii is having a conference.

This is an annual conference. We call it a winter conference that we have each year. It is our hope that this conference will become a national conference, a meeting just like the JCL national meeting or the OCA national meeting. We've been having this conference that has been primarily a local Los Angeles conference. But this is going to be the first year when we have more from around the country. At the present time, the Korean American Coalition has about 7 or 8 chapters. We have affiliates in Washington D.C. and Seattle. We have a Chapter in Anchorage, Alaska, Sacramento, Soritos, Orange County and Torrents. We have a new member on the board, her name is Helen Be Kim, who came from New York. We are hoping to try to work out something with the people from New York. But our goal is to have a national organization that will do several things. First of all, it's to continue the programs we have for full time citizenship assistance for those who wish to become citizens. Next, once you become a citizen, we encourage our citizens to register voters so that we have voter registration drive at different times of the year.

Then, we have community education once a month. We have a general meeting where we have whatever the key issue is, whether it's some immigration reform or whether it's the mayoral election or some aspect of Los Angeles life that we have. The primary protagonist at the meeting is in support of Korean Medias to get the word out to the community and to educate the community about what's going on. We also, believe that it is very important to develop the leaders for the future. We have a very strong group, as you know there are over million Koreans in other countries. About 75% to 80% of them are first generation, the others are second and third generation. But the first generation, most of them have come over only recently, primarily, since the 1970s, even 1980s, as we speak. So, these are the people that we are focusing on. We will try to to develop leaders. And we have about 30 to 40 young college students that we bring in during the beginning of the summer. We send them to attend a leadership training camp. And then, about ten of them go out into different jobs and working as interns. We have a budget of about $600,000 a year and we have 22 full time and part-time staff people.

Q **When did KCE begin?**

A In 1983. We have an office in Washington D.C. We want to expand that our office because Korean American Alliance became an affiliate of KCE. They are the Korean American group in Washington D.C. We were hoping that they will become Chapter KCE next year to help us build that office so that we can have national voice.

One of the things I am sure you're familiar with about Korean history is that at the turn of the century, when Koreans and Korean-Americans went to Washington D.C., we couldn't get it because we had no voice and no power, we had nothing. So, I think a lot of how the first generation and second generation Koreans have felt — power-less — especially, following the riots of 1992. Typical example of the lack of power was when the riots were beginning. We called the Governor's office, asking them to immediately, calm down nationally. It took three days to calm down and by that time, hundreds and hun-

Judge Howard Halm, Superior Court of California
2009 to present, Grandson of Choo Chei Kim

dreds of businesses were destroyed...millions of dollars were lost. So, we want to avoid that situation in the future. That's why it's very important for the Korean-American community nationally, to organize and to become voters and to join into other coalitions and become a more powerful voice, so that Koreans will have been represented until the point of time where there is no first generation any more. It will be primarily, an American, Korean-American community.

Q **Tell us about yourself. What are you doing and your education, experiences.**

A I'm a lawyer. I practice civil instigations in downtown Los Angeles. I have my own law firm. We have about 25 lawyers. I have been very active in the bar community. I was the President of the Japanese and the Korean-American Bar Association. I helped to found the Asian-Pacific American Bar Association and was its first vice President last year. This year I am the President-elect for this year of the National Asian Pacific American Bar Association, which is the National Bar Association for all over the different Asian Pacific American Bar Associations about 35 chapters and about four thousands members.

INDEX

ABOUT AUTHORS

Roberta Whak Sil Chang, the principal writer and researcher for this book, is a second-generation Korean American born in Hawaii. Chang is a graduate of the University of Hawaii, with master's degrees in Social Work and Public Health Administration. As a Catholic missionary, Chang worked in Korea from 1960-1969 and witnessed the beginning of the second wave of Korean emigration to the USA. She has applied her research to a variety of projects, including documentaries profiling Koreans in Hawaii. Her short pictorial story on a new immigrant family coming to Hawaii in 1974, *We Want to be Americans*, was published by University of Hawaii Press. The national History Compilation Committee of the Korean Ministry of Education published her research on Korean organization leaders in Hawaii, *The Korean National Association and Syngman Rhee, 1915-1936*, Vol. 45. Her documentary *The Legacy of the Korean National Association*, was presented at the Hawaii International Film Festival in 1999. Over 900 photographs of Koreans in America were collected and over 100 Koreans above the age of sixty were interviewed for *The Koreans in Hawaii: A Pictorial History 1903-2003*.

로버타 장은 이 책의 중심저자이며 연구자로 하와이에서 태어난 2세대 한국계미국인이다. 로버타 장은 하와이대학에서 사회사업과 공중보건행정으로 석사학위를 받았다. 카톨릭수녀로 1960-1969년까지 한국에서 봉사했고 한국인들이 미국으로 대거 이민가는 두 번째 물결을 지켜보았다. 로버타 장은 하와이에 있는 한국인들의 기록을 남기는 작업을 비롯해서 다양한 프로젝트를 수행했다. 하와이에 온 새로운 이민가족에 대한 사진책인『우리는 미국인이기를 원한다』(1974)를 하와이대학교에서 출간했다. 한국교육부 산하 한국사편찬위원

회는 하와이의 한인단체 지도자들에 대한 그녀의 연구를『국민회와 이승만 1915-1936』(제 45권)으로 출간했다. 그녀의 다큐멘터리 〈국민회의 유산〉은 1999년 하와이국제영상 페스 티벌에서 상연되었다.『하와이의 한인들: 사진으로 보는 미주한인 100년사』를 출판하기 위 해 미국 한인들에 대한 사진 900점을 수집했고 60세 이상인 한인과의 인터뷰를 100건 이 상 수행했다.

Seonju Lee is a HK research professor of Ewha Institute for the Humanities at Ewha Womans University. She received her Ph.D. in English Literature at Ewha Womans University in 1997 and was a professor of Tourism English at Songho University. Lee authored *Dickens and Social Position and Capital* which was selected as an Excellent Academic Work by Ministry of Culture and Tourism. Her translation of I.A. Richards' Principles of Literary Criticism into Korean was also selected as an Excellent Academic Work by The National Academy of Sciences. Among her articles are "Korean-American's Diasporic Imagination" "Suki Kim and Chang-rae Lee as Performative Subjects in a Hybrid Culture" "Charles Dickens and Modernity" "Invisibility and Empowerment of Migrant Women's Labor".

이선주는 이화여자대학교 이화인문과학원 HK 연구교수이다. 1997년 이화여자대학교 영 문과에서 〈디킨즈 소설에 나타난 근대성연구〉로 박사학위를 받았다. 송호대학교 관광영 어과에서 근무했다. 저서로는『디킨즈와 신분과 자본』(2007 문화체육관광부 우수학술도 서), 번역서로는 I. A.『리처즈의 문학비평의 원리』(2007 대한민국학술원 우수학술도서)가 있다. 논문으로는 〈한국계미국인의 디아스포라적 상상력〉, 〈혼종문화 속의 수행적 주체로 서 수키 김과 창래 리〉, 〈이주여성노동의 비가시성과 임파워먼트〉 등이 있다.